CRITICAL RESEARCH AND CREATIVE PRACTICE WITH MIGRANT AND REFUGEE COMMUNITIES

Edited by
Brian Callan, Pearson Nkhoma
and Naomi Thompson

First published in Great Britain in 2025 by

Policy Press, an imprint of
Bristol University Press
University of Bristol
1–9 Old Park Hill
Bristol
BS2 8BB
UK
t: +44 (0)117 374 6645
e: bup-info@bristol.ac.uk

Details of international sales and distribution partners are available at policy.bristoluniversitypress.co.uk

Editorial selection and editorial matter © Brian Callan, Pearson Nkhoma and Naomi Thompson 2025

The digital PDF and ePub versions of this title are available open access and distributed under the terms of the Creative Commons Attribution-NonCommercial-NoDerivatives 4.0 International licence (https://creativecommons.org/licenses/by-nc-nd/4.0/) which permits reproduction and distribution for non-commercial use without further permission provided the original work is attributed.

British Library Cataloguing in Publication Data
A catalogue record for this book is available from the British Library

ISBN 978-1-4473-7279-0 paperback
ISBN 978-1-4473-7280-6 ePub
ISBN 978-1-4473-7281-3 ePdf

The right of Brian Callan, Pearson Nkhoma and Naomi Thompson to be identified as editors of this work has been asserted by them in accordance with the Copyright, Designs and Patents Act 1988.

All rights reserved: no part of this publication may be reproduced, stored in a retrieval system, or transmitted in any form or by any means, electronic, mechanical, photocopying, recording, or otherwise without the prior permission of Bristol University Press.

Every reasonable effort has been made to obtain permission to reproduce copyrighted material. If, however, anyone knows of an oversight, please contact the publisher.

The statements and opinions contained within this publication are solely those of the editors and contributors and not of the University of Bristol or Bristol University Press. The University of Bristol and Bristol University Press disclaim responsibility for any injury to persons or property resulting from any material published in this publication.

Bristol University Press and Policy Press work to counter discrimination on grounds of gender, race, disability, age and sexuality.

Cover design: Robin Hawes
Front cover image: Dreamstime/Natallia Khlapushyna

This book is dedicated to all the women, men and young people (and those who work with them in empowering ways) whose voices are central to the research and practice that underpin the chapters of this text. Thank you for sharing your stories and working together to find new ground in defiance of illiberal politics and policies of exclusion.

Contents

List of figures and tables	vii
Notes on contributors	viii
Acknowledgements	xi

1	Introduction: Critical research, crucial voices and creative practice *Brian Callan, Pearson Nkhoma and Naomi Thompson*	1

PART I   Critical research

2	Reflections on being 'outsider-insiders' and 'insider-outsiders': fluctuating positionalities in research with migrant and refugee women *Naomi Thompson and Rabia Nasimi*	15
3	From neoliberalism to neoexclusionism: how grassroots faith communities are resisting division and crossing borders *Naomi Thompson, Graham Bright and Peter Hart*	31
4	Agency and frustration: overcoming obstacles at the UNHCR *Brian Callan*	46
5	Exploring conceptions of 'home' with Afghan migrant and refugee women *Rabia Nasimi*	63

PART II   Crucial voices

6	Unaccompanied Afghan minors in the UK: integration dilemmas in retrospect *Rohina Sidiqi and Pearson Nkhoma*	81
7	Evolving paradigms: witnessing refugees' unstable passages to safety *Sarah Crawford-Browne*	94
8	In the refuge of the wake: intersectional considerations in therapeutic practice with African refugees *Eric Harper and Angela Rackstraw*	109
9	Kwapatakwapata! Young Malawian girls trapped in predatory odysseys *Pearson Nkhoma*	129

PART III   Creative practice

10	Social justice and professional values: exploring motivations and opportunities for values-led practice *Finbar Cullinan*	147

11	Finding new ground: a creative movement and art group with asylum-seeking women *Marina Rova, Claire Burrell and Marika Cohen*	159
12	New Town Culture: creative processes in social work with refugee and asylum-seeking young people *Rachel Hughes, Marijke Steedman and Brian Callan*	174
13	Conclusion: Challenging times and hopeful futures *Brian Callan, Pearson Nkhoma and Naomi Thompson*	189

Index   196

List of figures and tables

Figures
7.1	Intervention pyramid for mental health and psychosocial support in emergencies	98
8.1	Candle centrepiece	113
8.2	Assembling parts	115
8.3	Filling in	123
8.4	Stitch together	125
8.5	Remade	126
9.1	A drawing by Loni of an abducted child forced into prostitution	135
11.1	Mountains (therapist's image)	162
11.2	Staying afloat (therapist's image)	165
11.3	The moon (therapist's image)	171

Table
4.1	Respondents' roles and years' experience	52

Notes on contributors

Dr Graham Bright is Community Pastor at The Well Methodist Church, Darlington, a Church committed to working with a community of particular socioeconomic challenge, which includes significant migrant populations. He is also a counsellor in private practice and Associate Fellow at the Institute of Children, Youth and Mission.

Claire Burrell is a dance movement psychotherapist, clinical supervisor and artist, using dance improvisation, transdisciplinary and embodied practices. Her clinical work is located primarily in adult mental health and focuses on healing and recovery from trauma through body-oriented processes. Co-Director of ArtsMinded CIC, she has been Associate Lecturer in Dance Movement Psychotherapy (DMP) training courses at Roehampton and Goldsmiths Universities.

Dr Brian Callan is a study skills lecturer with the Global Banking School. He is an anthropologist whose work focuses on community, civil society, political engagement and the transnational flows of people and ideas. In this he attempts to understand the lived experience; the emotions, ideas, tensions and the subtle social interactions that carry us through life and how such experiences intersect with notions of the self, belonging, hope and failure.

Marika Cohen is an art psychotherapist who has extensive experience of working within the UK's National Health Service (NHS) mental health services. She is a clinical supervisor and Co-founder of ArtsMinded CIC, which primarily delivers arts therapeutic projects with refugees and asylum seekers.

Sarah Crawford-Browne, as a clinical social worker, has responded to humanitarian crises in South Africa, Sierra Leone, Pakistan, Afghanistan and South Sudan. She is always deeply concerned about the impact of living in violent neighbourhoods and the impact of contextual safety on trauma presentation. She is Lecturer in Medical and Health Humanities at the University of Cape Town, South Africa.

Finbar Cullinan is a social worker and clinician working with young offenders and has volunteered with Social Workers Without Borders (SWWB). SWWB offers a critical space for contemporary social work practice with migrants and as a vehicle for a collective professional voice, in an international profession, whose shared values have the potential to respond to the pressures of hostile immigration policies of national governments.

Dr Eric Harper is a political activist and works with homeless people who have mental health and alcohol and/or drug challenges. He has a background in working with refugees and asylum seekers in South Africa, the US and the UK, and ran a therapy service for the homeless. He is a psychotherapist, reflective practice practitioner, social worker, and Lecturer at Goldsmiths, University of London.

Dr Peter Hart is a youth worker and Lecturer in Inclusion, Childhood and Youth at the University of Leeds. His research interests are around young people's participation and professional ethics, and more recently the use of tabletop gaming for educational, social and therapeutic benefits. He is the founder of 'People's Meeples', a not-for-profit community interest company that uses gaming to reduce isolation and develop community-based mental health provision.

Rachel Hughes is a social worker specialising in adult safeguarding, dementia and ageing, and disability across the life course. Rachel conducted research on the New Town Culture collaboration between artists, curators and social workers in the London Borough of Barking and Dagenham. The research led to new forms of training and development, including an interdisciplinary form of reflective practice involving cultural and social care practitioners.

Rabia Nasimi is a civil servant and refugee rights activist who has been extensively involved with the Afghanistan and Central Asian Association (ACAA), supporting refugee integration in the UK. Her work at the ACAA oversaw and monitored grants and projects, as well as leading diaspora-led development programmes in Afghanistan. She also serves as a Trustee for the Separated Child Foundation.

Dr Pearson Nkhoma is Senior Lecturer in Community Studies at Goldsmiths, University of London. With a personal commitment to social justice and human rights, Pearson finds fulfilment in designing and undertaking participatory action research with children and young people who have experienced extreme forms of exploitation, aiming to inspire evidence-based interventions for them to lead just and dignified lives.

Angela Rackstraw is an art psychotherapist in South Africa, teaching at the University of Johannesburg. She has worked as an art therapist in marginalised and traumatised community settings for over 25 years, mostly with children and groups of women. Many of these women are refugees and have experienced gender-based violence and multiple losses and/or bereavements. She also offers support groups to mothers who are bereaved or experiencing anticipatory grief.

Dr Marina Rova is a dance movement psychotherapist, lecturer and researcher at Goldsmiths, University of London. Her professional background includes dance education, clinical practice in the NHS and community, as well as independent consultancy work. She continues to develop and publish inclusive and collaborative research that explores creative practice as a tool for growth and wellbeing.

Rohina Sidiqi has worked with the UN and numerous international NGOs focusing on humanitarian aid and women's rights. She has worked with the Refugee Council in the UK and volunteered with various other refugee organisations. Her own journey from Afghanistan to the UK fuels her commitment to support those forced to flee their countries due to war and various forms of exploitation, with a particular focus on girls and women.

Marijke Steedman is Senior Curator for Culture Programmes at Barking and Dagenham Council. She founded New Town Culture in Barking and Dagenham with a vision to embed creative approaches within social care services for children, young people and adults. Before this she was Curator and Head of Education at Whitechapel Gallery, Create and Tate, and edited the book *Gallery as Community: Art, Education and Politics*.

Dr Naomi Thompson is a qualified youth and community worker with experience of working in the local authority and voluntary sectors, working with marginalised groups in a variety of contexts. She is currently Reader in Youth and Community Work at Goldsmiths, University of London, with interests in issues of inclusion and exclusion for marginalised communities.

Acknowledgements

Many thanks to Rupert Spurrier, Sarah Green, the manuscript reviewers and all at Policy Press for their support to bring this book to fruition. A number of chapters in this volume have been previously published elsewhere. Acknowledgements are made, where necessary, at individual chapter level.

1

Introduction: Critical research, crucial voices and creative practice

Brian Callan, Pearson Nkhoma and Naomi Thompson

This edited volume presents a range of interdisciplinary voices, actively engaged with contemporary practices, policies and interventions with migrant and refugee communities in the UK and internationally. While one per cent of the world's population have fled their homes as a result of conflict or persecution, the UK and many of the world's wealthiest nations have sought to bypass international obligations on asylum, securitising the issue of migration and creating hostile environments for those seeking safety. Drawing directly on the voices and experiences of refugees, activists and professional practitioners, this collection examines the complexities of migration and the possibilities for innovative and compassionate interventions.

Given the extent of the forced migration problem, the complex and irregular motivations and needs of those involved, and the growth of populism and cultural contestations in the neoliberal Global North, the issue of how to effectively mitigate the suffering, anxiety and integration of refugees and migrant communities must be examined from multiple and innovative angles. In recent years, significant research has been carried out that has informed the development of new migration management policies. These are often grounded in the causes, drivers and consequences of migration, with subsequent national policies being based on underlying assumptions and vested interests. With a focus on the experiences of the myriad actors directly involved in the phenomenon of forced migration, from the voluntary sector, various professionals and, most importantly, the migrants themselves, this volume aims to augment this widely studied topic. It does this primarily from a UK perspective with some more international contributions (see Chapters 4, 7, 8 and 9). Rather than focusing on the issue of migration as a problem to be avoided, this interdisciplinary exposition aims to provide original insights on how practice may be better informed by the voices of those seeking a better way.

The applied and multidisciplinary nature of the text brings a new approach to other research texts about migration and the experiences of refugees and migrants. The text fills a gap for practice-based research on migration, and for a holistic perspective on interventions. There is a dearth of research that focuses on these broader experiences and interventions (beyond health, law and integration) and that draws on the self-defined priorities of migrants and refugees in talking about their lives and experiences. It complements the other work that exists on migration while drawing more practical than theoretical implications, to support applied researchers as well as trainees and professionals working with these groups.

The volume is divided into three main parts. The first, 'Critical research', offers insights from original research carried out with a range of organisations directly engaged with refugees and asylum seekers. From second-generation Afghans living in London, to faith-based community and voluntary sector workers, to professional staff at the UNHCR, this part aims to inform meaningful practice with refugee and migrant communities and provides clear implications for policy and practice, through the experiences of those involved.

The second part, 'Crucial voices', foregrounds the narratives and journeys of refugees and migrants. In economic, political and academic discourse, such voices are often overlooked and yet are crucial to understanding how policies and practices are experienced by those to whom they are ascribed. Intimate attention to these crucial voices must be central to research and in shaping meaningful practice interventions.

The final part, 'Creative practice', turns towards creative interventions being used in the social, community and therapeutic sectors. Highlighting the need for values-based practice, these chapters focus on the creative use of arts-based interventions which overlap social work, community engagement and therapeutic practices focused on wellbeing and trauma recovery. Though art-based interventions provide rich expressive avenues for migrants, particularly those with low level English and traumatic experiences, they are often overlooked and under-funded. Complementing the researchers and the voices and narratives of migrant communities, the closing chapters seek to raise the profile of such creative practices as effective and meaningful.

This introduction will outline how critical feminist and race theories, and particularly intersectionality, function as theoretical frames for migrant research, as well as how participatory and practice-based research offer a methodological thread; with a focus on research drawing on migrant voices to shape practice interventions. It explores ethics and notions of power in participatory research and practice with refugee and migrant communities. It distinguishes between refugees and migrants – unpacking the political definitions as well as the tensions and critiques. The chapter then unpicks some key concepts used in policy and practice with these communities and explores the tensions and debates around these terms. It then outlines the book's structure and its themed parts, and summarises chapters and how they come together to provide critical implications for research and practice with refugee and migrant communities.

Critical feminist and race theories

The book is framed in critical feminist and race theories and, specifically, intersectionality (Crenshaw, 1989; Cree, 2010; Erel and Acik, 2020). Critical feminist theories pay particular attention to the structures and divisions of gender in society, responding to the context in which women's voices and experiences were marginalised or missing from dominant sociological theories (Cree, 2010). Critical race theories are also relevant to our focus and justify an intersectional approach. The voices of migrant and refugee communities are still often marginalised today in theory, research, policy and practice – though scholars are seeking to address this, including those who have contributed to this text. For migrant communities, issues such as race, gender, religion, culture, poverty and displacement all contribute to their marginalisation. A framing in intersectionality allows us to recognise the range of factors that impact on their lives and experiences.

Critical and intersectional feminist and race theories present an appropriate frame because they emerged as a challenge to the marginalisation of people's voices and lived experiences – and encompass an understanding of the full range of factors that marginalise people. Intersectionality theory emerged from a critical feminist and race approach to recognise how gender and race are intersecting issues that cannot be viewed or responded to separately. In particular, it was developed to make more explicit that the experiences of oppression for Black women are unique and intertwined and cannot be simplistically divided along the lines of race and gender (Crenshaw, 1989). It explores how overlapping minoritised identities relate to systems and structures of oppression. Kimberlé Crenshaw's (1989) theory is today used widely to understand how people face multiple intersecting oppressions. An intersectional understanding allows us to recognise the multiple identities and oppressions experienced by refugee and migrant communities. This frame enables us to develop broader intersectional understandings of refugee and migrant lives, with potential to understand the complexly inter-related roles of factors such as class and poverty, religion and culture, race and ethnicity.

Previous research with refugee and migrant communities has emphasised these and other intersectional issues that impact on migrant lives and experiences of oppression. For example, Erel (2018) explores the dynamics of race and gender in outlining how racialised migrant families are presented as a threat by right-wing political discourses that suggest white European families lose out on support as a result of migration. They argue this, ultimately, leads to a lack of care for migrant families and a framing of them as undeserving. Thompson et al (2022) explore the experiences of migrant Muslim women in London, identifying how issues such as race, gender and religion intersect in their experiences of marginalisation, their ability to access support, as well as how community work that does engage them is precarious and under-funded.

Intersectional experiences and oppressions are themes that run throughout this text. They emerge in the research and analysis presented in Part I and the voices and experiences that are drawn out in Part II and throughout the book. It is also highly relevant to the creative practices explored in Part III, that represent a decolonising alternative to top-down interventions that disregard intersectionality and difference, through the holistic and humanising methods of expression and recovery through art, dance and music.

Power in participatory research and practice

The methodological focus of this text sits firmly within an interpretivist paradigm, recognising that people's feelings and experiences are highly relevant in qualitative research, and particularly practice-based research (Thompson et al, 2022). This approach draws on the methodological and ethical considerations for conducting practice-based research with refugees, as articulated by Temple and Moran (2011). Temple and Moran recognise the benefits to both refugees and researchers of engaging in participatory research. For refugee communities, for example, it allows a sense of ownership over the stories that are told about them as well as opportunities for skills development. For researchers, involving refugee communities as co-researchers enables them to more effectively reflect on their own interpretations and biases in such research. Temple and Moran also recognise the challenges such research brings, including the level of resources required to shape meaningful co-production and avoid exploitation or harm. They also identify that such research can fail to move beyond seeing refugee communities as a homogenous group (disregarding their intersectional differences) and that it also often fails to have meaningful or transformational impact.

We recognise the power dynamics that are present in such forms of participatory research and practice with refugees and migrants. These are also highlighted by Doná (2007) who argues, similarly to Temple and Moran, that reductionist or binarised representations of refugees and co-researchers should be carefully avoided. This should also impact on policy and practice interventions that are drawn from research and ensure these do not impose 'one size fits all' understandings and approaches onto refugee and migrant communities. Issues of power and positionality need a reflexive response, particularly where 'insiders' are involved in research or practice interventions. This includes developing a reflexive understanding of insiders and outsiders as non-binary positions that are affected by a person's status as researcher, practitioner and/or participant as well as the various components of their intersectional identities. Issues of power in participatory and action research (as well as practice) are unpacked by Thompson and Nasimi in Chapter 2, in their extended discussion of the implications of their fluctuating positionalities as insiders and outsiders in community research.

Our book draws throughout on the use of creative and narrative methods, both in research and practice, to ensure the voices of migrants and refugees as research participants and/or service users are brought to the fore, particularly in shaping interventions. This builds on a growing body of literature that explores the use of participatory and arts-based methods in research and practice with refugee and migrant groups (Kaptani and Yuval-Davis, 2008; Erel et al, 2017; Vachelli, 2018) – while recognising that, despite the growing body of research, such methods of work are yet to be widely funded in mainstream practice, often relying on voluntary, charitable and precarious support. Our focus on 'crucial voices' emerges from these practice and research methodologies, to sit alongside and very clearly overlap with our focus on critical research and creative practice. These crucial voices are central to all parts of the text, reinforcing the interdisciplinary, collaborative and creative nature of this book and its dual relevance for both practice and academic research.

Unpacking the terminology: migrants and refugees

There are various ways in which migrant individuals and communities are referred to, bound up in issues of power and politics. Categorisations are often constructed through policy definitions as well as used and abused in wider media rhetoric. Such categorising contributes to the 'othering' of migrant and refugee communities, and often reflects problematic discourses about them. The UN's 1951 Refugee Convention defines a *refugee* as 'someone who is unable or unwilling to return to their country of origin owing to a well-founded fear of being persecuted for reasons of race, religion, nationality, membership of a particular social group, or political opinion' (UNHCR, 2024a). In reality, whether someone is classed as a migrant or refugee is largely defined by host countries, with policies, governments and institutions reserving the right to decide whether someone's 'fear' is 'well-founded'. Right-wing governments and broader rhetoric focused on tackling the 'problem' of migration have influenced this.

Governments have developed processes to determine whether someone will be granted 'refugee status' after they seek asylum in a new country. Prior to such status being applied, they are defined by policy as an *asylum seeker* rather than a refugee (Refugee Action, no date). Whether someone can legitimately be considered for asylum is bound up in complex rules around when and where the individual first claims asylum – after displacement, during migration journeys or after arrival in a new country.

In the UK, someone with 'refugee' status is a person within the first four years of a successful asylum claim. Following this, they can apply for 'indefinite leave to remain' but rights to family reunion remain restricted until they are granted 'exceptional leave to remain'. Asylum seekers in the UK are not allowed to gain paid employment but are entitled to a very restricted level of welfare and healthcare which is lost if they are refused asylum (Taylor, 2009). Those whose claims are refused become undocumented migrants without recourse to public funds, unable to legally gain employment and under threat of deportation. The UNHCR (2024b) highlights that when a person is refused asylum, it does not mean that their claim was 'bogus'. Despite this, throughout the year ending in September 2022, 23,226 people were entered into UK immigration detention (UNHCR, 2024b).

The broader term of *migrants* is often used in political, media and populist discourse to refer to asylum seekers and refugees alongside those who migrate for economic or other reasons. This serves to diminish their reasons for migration and to frame an exaggeratedly large, homogenous group of migrants who are invading Western countries. These migrants are viewed as a burden on welfare and the taxpayer as well as over-burdening the employment market, despite their limited rights in this regard (Philo et al, 2013). Those risking their lives on journeys to seek safety and security are often referred to in derogatory ways such as 'terrorists' and 'cockroaches' by public media (United Nations Office of the High Commissioner on Human Rights, 2018). Such framings are racialised and serve to criminalise those fleeing harm.

Integration

Facilitating integration is a key priority of governments for settled migrant groups. However, Haverig (2013) argues that 21st-century integration policies have been driven by a *fear* of migrant communities. Such policies have increasingly shifted to a focus on acculturation and requiring migrants to assimilate to their host culture (Haverig, 2013; Kortmann, 2015). Kortmann (2015) argues that integration policies need to be developed that allow for migrants to both retain their religious, ethnic and cultural identities and make some individual adaptations to be included in the host culture. Viruell-Fuentes et al (2012) outline how a sole focus on the need for acculturation obscures the structural factors that compound difficulties faced by migrant communities. Through focusing solely on perceived cultural dissonance (and arguably cultural differences) of migrant groups, policy can effectively obscure how society reinforces the intersectional discrimination and marginalisation faced by these groups.

In line with Kortmann (2015), some alternative definitions frame integration as more than merely acculturation, suggesting it is a two-way process. Valtonen (2004) also recognises the need for those who are required by their new countries to integrate, to maintain their own identities that reflect their lives and cultures to date. She defines integration as 'The ability to participate fully in economic, social, cultural and political activities without having to relinquish one's own distinct ethnocultural identity and culture' (Valtonen, 2004: 74). This definition recognises the intersectional experiences of migrants and how these will continue to shape their identities post-migration. This more nuanced understanding of integration as a two-way process has been embraced, at least in theory, by policy in Scotland. The 'New Scots: Refugee Integration Strategy 2018 to 2022' defines integration as 'A long-term, two-way process, involving positive change in both individuals and host communities, which lead to cohesive, diverse communities' (Scottish Government, 2018: 10). This conception of integration as a mutual process places accountability for successful integration not just on the individual but on the society they are joining. However, such a definition is not popular among (particularly right-wing) governments and the dominant approaches to integration remain persistently focused on acculturation and the individual's responsibility to conform, ignoring the systemic and structural issues that make this challenging.

Arguably, conceptions of integration have been dominantly framed in 'othering' discourses. Narrow policy definitions of integration emphasise the outsider status of those whose intersectional religious, racial, cultural and other identities do not reflect the norm. This is reflected in research, where first and later generations of migrant communities have reported that they feel under pressure to choose between national, religious and other identities (Rostami-Povey, 2007; Mandaville, 2009; Ahmed, 2015; Casey, 2016).

Empowerment

Empowerment is recognised as a key value of social, therapeutic and community practice. It is arguably more helpful and person-centred than a focus on integration and recognises the power dynamics that work against marginalised groups. Definitions of empowerment frame people's increased participation in their communities and society as leading to greater social justice: 'Empowerment is a social-action process that promotes participation of people, organizations, and communities towards the goals of increased individual and community control, political efficacy, improved quality of community life, and social justice' (Wallerstein, 1992: 1).

However, it is also a contested concept, with critiques bound up in questions around who has (or should have) the power to give, thus disputing how far it can be viewed as a means to pursue social justice. It is problematised by those who argue that the notion of professionals *giving power* to others is top-down, paternalistic and colonial in nature (Belton, 2009; 2017). This reminds us to be wary of how such concepts can be exploited and to remain reflexive about the dynamics of power between professionals and the groups they work with, particularly in relation to the intersectional oppressions these groups face, ensuring that interventions support rather than obstruct social justice.

Other scholars argue that skilled community-based professionals support marginalised groups to draw out their own power, rather than them being empowered (or given power) by those working with them (Fitzsimons et al, 2011). Sadan (2004) draws on Kieffer's notion that the process of empowerment is usually borne out of a sense of disempowerment: 'The empowerment process in most cases begins from a sense of frustration: people's sense that there exists an unbridgeable gap between their aspirations and their possibilities of realizing them' (Kieffer, 1984, cited in Sadan, 2004: 151). As such, it is widely viewed as a process of rebalancing power, particularly for marginalised groups.

For marginalised groups, such as refugee and migrant communities, empowerment may be a transformational process. Such a process needs to be couched in practices that recognise inequalities and intersectional oppressions, as well as how institutions such as governments and statutory services are central to marginalising such groups in the first place. As such, empowerment should not only be concerned with an individual or community empowering themselves but with challenging the structures that reinforce the disempowerment of certain groups. This links back to the need to view integration as a mutual process, where responsibility for successful inclusion lies with society and not just individuals.

Overview of the book

Part I of the book focuses on drawing out critical research that can inform meaningful practice with refugee and migrant communities. It covers research exploring migrant experiences and narratives of home, implications of the current political context (particularly neoliberalism and populism) for community practice, barriers and frustrations in international human rights work, and issues of power and positionality in research with refugee and migrant communities. In Chapter 2, issues of power and positionality in research with refugee and migrant communities are explored by Naomi Thompson and Rabia Nasimi, drawing on their own intersectional identities and insider/outsider status in research with migrant women. Following this, in Chapter 3, Naomi Thompson, Graham Bright and Peter Hart critique the neoliberal and exclusionist political context. They draw on their research with faith-based community workers to argue for more grassroots and bottom-up approaches to practice with marginalised groups, which challenge rather than collude with problematic political discourses. Brian Callan presents his research exploring the challenges experienced by UNHCR staff in Chapter 4 and their work for social justice and transformation in the global context. Rabia Nasimi draws on the individual narratives of second-generation migrants living in London, whose parents fled Afghanistan for the UK in Chapter 5, which explores the complex interrelationships between home and migration within this particular urban location.

Part II brings together chapters that draw on the narratives and journeys of refugees and migrants, presenting the voices and experiences of practitioners and activists working on the ground with these communities internationally. Rohina Sidiqi and Pearson Nkhoma explore the experiences of unaccompanied minors from Afghanistan in Chapter 6. In Chapter 7, Sarah Crawford-Browne considers trauma-informed responses to migrant journeys, highlighting the need for such interventions to reflect the intersectional and complex experiences of those in her case examples from South Africa, Sierra Leone and Pakistan. Eric Harper and Angela Rackstraw, in Chapter 8, reflect on the narratives of refugees from different African countries, based on three decades of work with these communities, framing their discussion in a consideration of issues of relationships, power and intersectionality. In Chapter 9, Pearson Nkhoma draws on his participatory research with child migrants in Malawi, moving within and across borders, and with lived experience of trafficking for prostitution.

Part III draws on creative practice from the social, community and therapeutic sectors. It starts with a consideration of the need for values-based practice from Finbar Cullinan in Chapter 10, drawing on his research with volunteers engaged with Social Work Without Borders (SWWB). In Chapters 11 and 12, community arts work emerges as a particular focus of creative interventions that overlaps social work, community work and practices focused on wellbeing and trauma recovery. Marina Rova, Claire Burrell and Marika Cohen outline arts-based therapeutic interventions with migrant women in temporary accommodation. Rachel Hughes, Marijke Steedman and Brian Callan explore social work practice through arts work with refugee and asylum-seeking young people. These chapters outline the creative practice examples and explore what they offered to communities in expressing and understanding their experiences and working towards recovery. We bring these creative practices to light to raise their profile as effective and meaningful interventions for refugee and migrant communities, supported by the research and engagement with the voices and narratives of these communities in the preceding parts of the book.

In the concluding chapter, we reassert the critiques of problematic political contexts in the UK and beyond that marginalise refugee and migrant communities. We also highlight the potential for hopeful futures through more creative approaches to policy and practice that recognise the complex and intersectional experiences of these communities. Such hopeful interventions would resist viewing refugees and migrants as a homogenous group or 'problem' to be dealt with. The critical research, crucial voices and creative practices that emerge through the book build a case for such hopeful futures and the transformation of the global stigmatising discourses that surround migration.

References

Ahmed, S. (2015) 'The voices of young British Muslims: Identity, belonging and citizenship' in M.K. Smith, N. Stanton and T. Wylie (eds) *Youth Work and Faith: Debates, Delights and Dilemmas*, Lyme Regis: Russell House, pp 37–51.

Belton, B. (2009) *Developing Critical Youth Work Theory*, Rotterdam: Sense.

Belton, B. (2017) 'Colonised youth', *Youth & Policy*, 19 September, Available from: www.youthandpolicy.org/articles/colonised-youth/

Casey, L. (2016) *The Casey Review: A Review into Opportunity and Integration*, London: Department for Communities and Local Government.

Cree, V.E. (2010) *Sociology for Social Workers and Probation Officers*, London: Routledge.

Crenshaw, K. (1989) 'Demarginalizing the intersection of race and sex: A Black feminist critique of antidiscrimination doctrine, feminist theory and antiracist politics', *University of Chicago Legal Forum*, 1989(1), Available from: https://chicagounbound.uchicago.edu/uclf/vol1989/iss1/8

Doná, G. (2007) 'The *microphysics* of participation in refugee research', *Journal of Refugee Studies*, 20(2): 210–29. https://doi.org/10.1093/jrs/fem013

Erel, U. (2018) 'Saving and reproducing the nation: Struggles around right-wing politics of social reproduction, gender and race in austerity Europe', *Women's Studies International Forum*, 68: 173–82. https://doi.org/10.1016/j.wsif.2017.11.003

Erel, U. and Acik, N. (2020) 'Enacting intersectional multilayered citizenship: Kurdish women's politics', *Gender, Place & Culture*, 27(4): 479–501. https://doi.org/10.1080/0966369X.2019.1596883

Erel, U., Reynolds, T. and Kaptani, E. (2017) 'Participatory theatre for transformative social research', *Qualitative Research*, 17(3): 302–12. https://doi.org/10.1177/1468794117696029

Fitzsimons, A., Hope, M., Cooper, C. and Russell, K. (2011) *Empowerment and Participation in Youth Work*, Exeter: Learning Matters.

Haverig, A. (2013) 'Managing integration: German and British policy responses to the 'threat from within' post-2001', *Journal of International Migration and Integration*, 14(2): 345–62. https://doi:10.1007/s12134-012-0245-5

Kaptani, E. and Yuval-Davis, N. (2008) 'Participatory theatre as a research methodology: Identity, performance and social action among refugees', *Sociological Research Online*, 13(5): 1–12. https://doi.org/10.5153/sro.1789

Kortmann, M. (2015) 'Asking those concerned: How Muslim Migrant organisations define integration. A German-Dutch comparison', *Journal of International Migration and Integration*, 16(4): 1057–80. https://doi:10.1007/s12134-014-0387-8

Mandaville, P. (2009) 'Muslim transnational identity and state responses in Europe and the UK after 9/11: Political community, ideology and authority', *Journal of Ethnic and Migration Studies*, 35(3): 491–506. https://doi:10.1080/13691830802704681

Philo, G., Briant, E. and Donald, P. (2013) *Bad News for Refugees*, London: Pluto Press.

Refugee Action (no date) 'Facts about refugees: claiming asylum is a human right', Available from: www.refugee-action.org.uk/about/facts-about-refugees/

Rostami-Povey, E. (2007) 'Afghan refugees in Iran, Pakistan, the U.K., and the U.S. and life after return: A comparative gender analysis', *Iranian Studies*, 40(2): 241–61. https://doi: doi.org/10.1080/00210860701269576

Sadan, E. (2004) *Empowerment and Community Practice*, Available from: www.mpow.org/

Scottish Government (2018) 'New Scots: Refugee Integration Strategy 2018 to 2022', Available from: www.gov.scot/publications/new-scots-refugee-integration-strategy-2018-2022/

Taylor, K. (2009) 'Asylum seekers, refugees, and the politics of access to health care: a UK perspective', *British Journal of General Practice*, 59(567): 765–72. https://doi:10.3399/bjgp09X472539

Temple, B. and Moran, R. (2011) *Doing Research with Refugees*, Bristol: Policy Press.

Thompson, N., Nasimi, R., Rova, M. and Turner, A. (2022) *Community Work with Migrant and Refugee Women*, Bingley: Emerald.

UNHCR (2024a) *Convention and Protocol Relating to the Status of Refugees: Text of the 1951 Convention Relating to the Status of Refugees*, Available from: www.unhcr.org/3b66c2aa10.html

UNHCR (2024b) 'Asylum in the UK', Available from: www.unhcr.org/uk/asylum-in-the-uk.html

United Nations Office of the High Commissioner on Human Rights (2018) 'Refugees and other migrants do not lose their rights by crossing borders', 20 June, Available from: www.ohchr.org/EN/NewsEvents/Pages/RefugeesMigrantsDoNotLoseTheirRights.aspx

Vacchelli, E. (2018) 'Embodiment in qualitative research: Collage making with migrant, refugee and asylum seeking women', *Qualitative Research*, 18(2): 171–90. https://doi.org/10.1177/1468794117708008

Valtonen, K. (2004) 'From the margin to the mainstream: Conceptualizing refugee settlement processes', *Journal of Refugee Studies*, 17(1): 70–96. https://doi:10.1093/jrs/17.1.70

Viruell-Fuentes, E.A., Miranda, P.Y. and Abdulrahim, S. (2012) 'More than culture: Structural racism, intersectionality theory and immigrant health', *Social Science and Medicine*, 75(12): 2099–106. https://doi:10.1016/j.socscimed.2011.12.037

Wallerstein, N. (1992) 'Powerlessness, empowerment and health. Implications for health promotion programs', *American Journal of Health Promotion*, 6(3): 197–205. https://doi:10.4278/0890-1171-6.3.197

PART I

Critical research

This first part of the book, 'Critical research', offers insights from original research carried out with migrant communities – and a range of social and community practitioners and organisations, directly engaged with refugees and asylum seekers. It focuses on drawing out critical research that can inform practice interventions. From second-generation Afghans living in London, to faith-based community and voluntary sector workers, to professional staff at the UNHCR, the section aims to inform meaningful practice with refugee and migrant communities and challenge problematic assumptions about them.

The part connects key themes and threads, as outlined in the introduction to this book. It draws on participatory methods through research exploring migrant experiences and narratives of home. It recognises the implications of the current political context that stigmatises migrant communities through research with grassroots practitioners seeking to challenge these problematic discourses. At an international policy level, it engages with research exploring the barriers and frustrations for professionals in international human rights work. Additionally, it engages with the issues of power and positionality in research with refugee and migrant communities and recognises the importance of an awareness of intersectional identities.

In Chapter 2, issues of power and positionality in research with refugee and migrant communities are explored by Naomi Thompson and Rabia Nasimi, drawing on their own intersectional identities and insider/outsider status in research with migrant women. Following this, in Chapter 3, Naomi Thompson, Graham Bright and Peter Hart critique the neoliberal and exclusionist political context. They draw on their research with faith-based community workers to argue for more grassroots and bottom-up approaches to practice with marginalised groups, that challenge rather than collude with problematic political discourses. Brian Callan presents his research exploring the challenges experienced by UNHCR staff in Chapter 4 and their work for social justice and transformation in the global context. Finally, in Chapter 5, Rabia Nasimi draws on the individual narratives of second-generation Afghans living in London, whose parents fled Afghanistan for the UK – and explores the complex interrelationships between home and migration within this particular urban location.

2

Reflections on being 'outsider-insiders' and 'insider-outsiders': fluctuating positionalities in research with migrant and refugee women

Naomi Thompson and Rabia Nasimi

This chapter reflects on the process of using insider research with a community-based organisation working with Muslim women from refugee and other migrant backgrounds in London. We explore the use of reflexivity and participatory action research and examine the dynamics of power in such research. Through our exploration of how the organisation has used insider research with marginalised groups of women, we argue that without the involvement of both 'insiders' and 'outsiders' in the research, key findings that draw on the women's personal experiences would not have emerged. As such, there are methodological implications for wider research and practice with refugees and migrants, as well as other marginalised groups.

The chapter begins with an outline of the project and its methods before we present an overview of relevant literature on longitudinal and insider research, reflexivity and community-based participatory action research. Within this, we consider the power dynamics of involving insiders in research with marginalised groups. We then present a sample of our research data; exploring how the theme of 'feeling safe' reflects insiders creating safe spaces for both practice and research, as well as considering if there are limitations to integration if services only expose marginalised groups to those they share characteristics with. Our main discussion considers our positionalities as researchers and the impact of our levels of insider status on the research. The chapter was written collaboratively by one of the insider researchers (Nasimi), a practitioner at the women's project under study, and the project's external academic researcher (Thompson). Through our discussion, we demonstrate how our fluctuating statuses as insiders and outsiders were both helpful, and at times inhibiting, to the research. Our consideration of our fluid status as insiders and outsiders in the project recognises that these are not fixed or absolute positions. We argue that some level of 'insider' status is needed in effective research and practice with marginalised groups, while the involvement of partial outsiders alongside can also be helpful.

The project

This chapter reflects on the process of conducting research in a women's project based in a small London-based grassroots charity over three years. The charity works primarily with refugees and migrants from Afghanistan and other central Asian countries living in London, providing services that include English language classes, employment workshops, a women's support group, a Saturday school and homework club, youth and family support services, drop-in and telephone advice, volunteer placements, and cultural and social events.

The project employed an external academic researcher who worked with the charity's staff and volunteers to undertake the research. The academic researcher began by immersing herself in the project by observing sessions and meeting with staff and beneficiaries before working with them to develop and refine bespoke tools for the research. The methods used over the three-year study included observational research by the academic researcher who spent substantial time at the project, as well as registration data from participants, workshop evaluation forms, other sessional paperwork and interviews. The women who attended the project were supported by staff and volunteers to complete evaluation forms after ten workshops each year. This bespoke evaluation form was developed, tested and refined with the women. Interviews took place with approximately ten women and five staff members or volunteers each year.

The research obtained ethical approval via Goldsmiths, University of London. Consent to participate in the research activities was embedded into registration forms as an opt-in question for the women who participated in the project. This covered use of their registration data, workshop evaluations, case studies and beneficiary interviews. Interviews were conducted by the academic researcher with the help of an interpreter from the organisation's staff or volunteer team. These were not audio-recorded but notes were taken and consent re-confirmed verbally before the start of each interview. Separate consent forms were used for interviews with staff and volunteers where these were audio-recorded.

Longitudinal research

The research employed Qualitative Longitudinal Research (QLR), exploring women's experiences of the project over three years. Wenham (2015: 45) argues that QLR 'enhances our understanding of the dynamics of … people's lives, and crucially, the processes attached to social inclusion or marginalisation'. She explains how the longitudinal nature of the approach allows for an understanding of people's feelings, experiences and capacity over time that goes beyond an isolated snapshot at a moment of crisis.

Wenham draws on Neale and Flowerdew (2003) to demonstrate how QLR also allows for a consideration of how structure and agency interplay in these experiences: 'it is only through time that we can gain a better appreciation of how the personal and the social, agency and structure, the micro and macro are interconnected and how they come to be transformed' (Neale and Flowerdew, 2003: 190).

This is highly relevant for exploring the experiences of marginalised groups such as refugee and migrant women, as well as for considering the kinds of community practices that support them to navigate their lives, including overcoming both individual and structural challenges.

Insider research

As participants with refugee backgrounds may have experienced events and situations where their voices were not respected, it is important to avoid causing harm through doing this in research (Masten and Narayan, 2012). Zulfacar (1998: 48) states that diaspora communities often give significant importance to family privacy and therefore an outsider interfering with this privacy is encountered with distrust. Lipson and Meleis (1989: 106) also note, in their widely cited methodological paper, that suspicion of strangers is common among people from war-torn countries.

Refugees and migrants are often treated as 'outsider' groups and encountered with distrust by society. This distrust becomes mutual as they are marginalised from services and systems. Insider researchers are important in this context. Such insiders bring a lived understanding of the participants' experiences. Additionally, they may have a more equal and trusted status with participants and are thus more able to effectively communicate about issues of power such as the rights and limits of confidentiality, as well as ensuring informed consent and respecting non-consent. Researching *with* rather than *on* marginalised groups has been highlighted by researchers as an important ethical principle that ensures such groups are empowered rather than exploited (Greenfields and Ryder, 2012).

Post-positivist approaches have been influential in understanding research as partial and subjective and influenced by both the participants and the researcher (Cloke et al, 2005; Rose, 1997). The need to redress some of the power imbalances between researcher and researched led to calls for more 'insider' research, which was based on shared attributes (such as language, ethnicity, gender and class) (Merton, 1972; cited in Botterill, 2015).

According to Horváth et al (2018: 7) 'Insider-research means research done by members of the organisational system and communities in their own organisations' and a person can be defined as an insider researcher where they 'possess knowledge, insights and experience before engaging in the actual research'. However, it has also been recognised by Narayan (1993) that insider researchers are necessarily set apart to an extent from other insiders of an organisation or community group through them assuming the status of researcher. This raises questions of power in relationships with other insiders and how fully someone's insider status can remain once they assume the role of researcher. It suggests it is not possible for someone to become a researcher and to also fully remain as an insider.

Following the development of insider research as a distinct methodology, it faced critique from feminist scholars who argued the insider/outsider distinction relies too heavily on binary opposites, or absolute notions of sameness and difference (Rose, 1997). Such scholars argue that the insider/outsider binary is a myth, because a researcher's role, position and status is neither impervious nor absolute (Merton, 1972; Mercer, 2007). Intersectional approaches similarly critique the insider/outsider binary, as researchers and participants both engage with and move between multiple positionalities and therefore both may inhabit 'insider' and 'outsider' status at different times (Anthias, 2012; Botterill, 2015; Ryan, 2015). This fluidity was, to some extent, recognised as early as the 1950s in Pike's (1954) description of the 'etic' and the 'emic' researcher. The etic researcher is the outsider, approaching groups with a largely objective perspective, and usually aiming to generate generalisations and conclusions that transcend a specific group. The emic researcher is the insider, with a subjective position in relation to a particular cultural group they wish to study. However, Pike argued that the two perspectives work in a complementary way in research studies – as well as that even the etic researcher brings an emic (or personal/subjective) position when entering a group they are largely an outsider to. We recognise the nuance and complexity in defining ourselves as 'insiders' or 'outsiders' and later in this chapter, we explore further the fluidity between the levels of 'insider' and 'outsider' status that we inhabited in our research.

Reflexivity

There is clearly a need for insider researchers to reflect on and manage the dynamics of power produced by their status. Finefter-Rosenbluh (2017) suggests that insider researchers need to engage in reflexivity in order to ensure they reflect on their own perspectives and biases, draw on more than their own perspective on issues, and move beyond commonly shared understandings to draw out the full range of experiences, meanings and interpretations from others inside the organisation under study. There is a risk of blurring boundaries of roles and positions which comes with being an insider, and of imposing your own values, beliefs and perceptions onto research participants (Drake, 2010).

Arguably, researcher reflexivity is needed whether approaching qualitative research with marginalised communities as 'insider' or 'outsider', as neither position is neutral to power and bias. Reflexivity is the 'active acknowledgement by the researcher that their own actions and decisions will inevitably impact upon the meaning and context of the experience under investigation' (Horsburgh, 2003: 309). When researchers and participants occupy different positions within social structures, there is a need to be reflexive about the power dynamics at play. Bourdieu (1996) suggests that researchers may inflict 'symbolic violence' through misunderstanding or misrepresenting research participants, and therefore advocates for reflexive practice in research. For 'insider' and 'outsider' researchers, there is a need to 'focus on self-knowledge and sensitivity' and to carefully 'self-monitor' the impact of biases, beliefs, and personal experiences on the research (Berger, 2015: 2).

Participatory action research

Veroff and DiStefano (2002: 1192) argue that in action research epistemological questions need to be addressed such as: 'what is the relationship between the knower and the known?' and 'how are the researcher and the participants affected by the research?'. Partnerships between academic and community organisations support participation of marginalised groups, as such partnerships can mitigate important concerns around power, social relations, participation, learning and community benefit, within research. Community-based participatory research (CBPR) is an approach that encourages partnerships between researchers, practitioners and participants in order to develop a clearer understanding of problems and work collectively in order to address them (Israel et al, 2005: 3). CBPR contains three main elements – participation, research and action (Minkler, 2005) – and involves a systematic investigation of community issues with the aim of education, action or social change (Green et al, 1995, cited in Minkler, 2005). As a form of action research, CBPR involves using partnerships to develop meaningful interpretations of data and test them in the field of action in order to improve a given situation. As such, problem-solving and making change are ontological commitments of participatory action research that support active participation of all partners in the process. There is little doubt that research that involves people from different sectors can enhance knowledge about social life (Griffith, 1998). This is reflected in a range of disciplinary areas that have used CBPR as a useful strategy to answer complicated questions such as in health (Israel et al, 2005; Minkler, 2005) and psychology (Kloos et al, 2012; Jason and Glenwick, 2016), among other disciplines. Goodson and Phillimore's (2010) capacity building research aimed to empower leaders of refugee community organisations. Their methodology centred around providing systematic training for community leaders to act as researchers and to collect robust and reliable evidence. They argued that this process benefited the community researchers through providing opportunities to learn new skills and work with other groups to deliver a project.

Our own research with refugee and migrant women was participatory to the extent that staff and volunteers helped to shape the research and to collate the data. Many of these volunteers were also project beneficiaries that had taken on volunteering roles within the project over time. These staff and volunteers were also research participants. As such, the roles of researcher and participant overlapped substantially. In addition, we developed and changed the research methods and tools over time in response to how they were received by participants and volunteers, including rewriting interview schedules.

The longitudinal nature of the research allowed for a process of reflexive adaptation in response to each stage of the process. The interpersonal relations built through such longitudinal engagement can help to overcome power hierarchies, a legitimate concern in any ethnographic study. Here, we argue that a longitudinal and participatory research process helped researchers build trust with community members and to be sensitive to avoiding any misunderstandings or damaging encounters for the already marginalised groups involved. The safety of participants, many of whom had already experienced multiple traumas in their lives, was paramount.

Feeling safe

The presence of insider researchers was significant to participants feeling safe. It was also significant to the women's feeling of safety that the community project itself was a grassroots community organisation founded by a refugee family. In the second year of the women's project, 'feeling safe' emerged as a theme from interviews. This theme would arguably not have emerged if the practice itself was not provided by insider practitioners – the participants cited in interviews that they had felt able to access and engage with the project because of cultural sensitivity, language-speaking and meeting others with similar backgrounds to themselves. Similarly, nor would the personal examples shared in the research have been shared with a research team of complete outsiders – see our discussion of the nuances of this in the positionality section later in this chapter. We outline here how this research theme emerged from the practice of the project before we go on to examine how our positionalities as researchers impacted on our engagement with participants.

The women reported a general feeling of safety at the women's project that was reflected in them feeling they had grown in courage or confidence through their involvement over time. This manifested in practice in their confidence to engage with each other, to learn English and to set goals for their lives – with some women even facilitating workshops for their peers. Many of the women had not perceived mainstream services to be a safe space they could access and they reported that because the women's project was different to these more formal providers that they had built the confidence and courage to sustain their engagement and deepen their participation.

> After coming here I have built courage and I feel more confident. Before coming here, I tried to go to college but I couldn't keep going. I find this more helpful. (Darya)

> I like coming here. I am more confident now. I feel comfortable here. (Sadeen)

Feeling safe, comfortable and having the confidence to keep participating was a significant impact on the women's lives and their integration with society because many of them were not accessing any services at all prior to attending the women's project. Many reflected how 'outsider' services had not been easy to access.

After relationships had been built with the insider practitioners over time, the women took part in workshops that engaged with topics relating to safety and protection. This was done in a culturally sensitive way by female facilitators with relatable cultural backgrounds, creating a safe space in which to address these issues. Workshops on hate crime, domestic violence and female genital mutilation are particular examples where difficult topics were facilitated in a non-threatening way that enabled the women to engage in discussion.

The women's project coordinator reflected that some of the women did express discomfort discussing these topics, particularly domestic violence. However, other women expressed how grateful they were to have a space to discuss and gain a greater knowledge of these issues in a women-only space. One of the women, who was a domestic violence survivor, stated how she wished she had the information sooner.

> There is a restrictive order placed on my husband. I really liked the domestic violence workshop. When they talked about forms of control, I realised if I had come here sooner I wouldn't have taken the abuse for so long. He didn't let me take part in activities and being outside the home. He stopped me having money and told me who I could talk to. (Gulzar)

Another woman who had experienced a hate incident in public that had made her afraid to leave her home outlined the impact the hate crime workshop had on her feeling safe enough to go out again.

> One day I was walking with three friends and a man spat on us and told us to go home and that we were all immigrants. I didn't do anything

because I thought the police would want evidence. But now I know what to do. Someone came from the Council and told us how to deal with situations like that and that I should go to the police. I didn't go out for a long time after it happened and I didn't want my daughter to see it but she was there. The workshop was so helpful to know how to deal with it. After the workshop I had more courage and wasn't scared anymore because I had the information about what to do and who to call. I felt confident leaving the house again, I felt like I knew I would be safe. (Soraya)

This feeling of safety within and beyond the project was key to the women becoming more integrated and less isolated. Their willingness to engage in research activities was arguably impacted by them feeling safe within the project more broadly. Had they not felt safe, they would have resisted sharing such personal experiences as those quoted above with the researchers.

From isolation to integration

A key aim of the charity's work with women was to facilitate their integration in community and society. This arguably requires some level of engagement with outsiders, external services or those who are not the same. We have previously argued that there may be some limits to integration where marginalised groups access specialist services where everyone shares similar characteristics and experiences (Thompson and Nasimi, 2022). Arguably, such engagement has potential to reinforce isolation rather than facilitate integration. However, Bright et al (2018) found that safe spaces need to be created for 'inclusion within', particularly for groups that are isolated and excluded by society, in order to support their inclusion more broadly. This was reflected in the women's project in them forming new friendships with those they could relate to as well as those who were different. The women reported particularly the impact of making friends with women from other countries.

> I have met people from Pakistan, Bangladesh, Somalia, people who are Arabic, from different countries. I can say 'hello' to them! (Bahar)

> I have so many new friends from different places with different languages … I'm friends with everyone. I see some of them outside of here now. (Razia)

This reflects the argument that insider and outsider status are not binary. Some of the women made friends with people from outside their own community for the first time through their engagement with the project. This allowed for a process of staged integration – where the women were able to feel safe because they shared some characteristics with women from similar backgrounds before making further steps towards their integration. This is reflected in practice through women reporting that over time they were able to engage more with their children's schools, feel more confident and independent in a range of public places, and even seek voluntary and paid employment roles.

> I feel very strongly about education – it's very important to have … I have had the help here to understand about my child's study and what they learn in school … And it's helped me in terms of going to meetings at my child's school. Before I couldn't, now I can. (Darya)

> They've helped me a lot with learning to drive and how to deal with situations like talking to police … It's helped me with finding my way around and getting the right buses … It's also helped when I go to the doctor's and filling out forms and things like that. (Soraya)

A key step towards these outcomes was having a space to learn English that was accessible and culturally sensitive.

> It's women only and I can bring my children – it's different to other classes. (Sadeen)

> This place means freedom to me because my husband didn't let me go to college but I explained there are no men here. (Mariam)

The outcomes achieved by the women had not been achieved through external services that the women had previously struggled to access. Several research studies and reports have identified the barriers marginalised migrant and refugee women face in accessing mainstream services (Guista and Kambhampati, 2006; Change Institute, 2009; Social Policy Research Centre, 2014).

Through the women's project, the women both experienced the safety of having peer mentors they could relate to as interpreters, workshop leaders and volunteers, as well as having the opportunity over time to take on such roles themselves. This reflects why participatory research was an appropriate method for the project, as it shares similar principles with this form of practice, to provide opportunities for learning, skills development and empowerment (Goodson and Phillimore, 2010).

The impacts of our researcher positionalities

On first glance at our status as the authors of this chapter and researchers on the project, it appears that one of us is clearly an outsider researcher

(Thompson) as the external academic and the other of us is a clear insider researcher and practitioner (Nasimi), sharing a similar background with the project participants and working for the charity since before the research took place. However, as we examine in more depth our insider-outsider status, some complexities emerge. For example, despite not sharing racial or cultural identities with the participants and having no experience of migration journeys, Thompson was a partial insider simply because she is a woman. It would not have been appropriate or possible for a man to conduct the research because it required entering and inhabiting a women-only space. Through the research, it emerged from some women that they were only able to attend the women's project with the permission of their husbands and this had only been allowed because the women's project was facilitated and attended only by women.

While Thompson was initially perceived by participants as an outsider despite being a woman, she became more of an insider over time as she visited the project over three years and became familiar to those women who attended long-term. This process of becoming more of an insider was supported by her delivering a workshop in the second year of the project where she shared more about herself which included her connecting with the women about aspects of her life, identity and goals, including becoming a mother at a young age, engaging in study after becoming a parent, and her experience of travel. Her insider status was enhanced in moments she participated with the group but often reverted when she more formally inhabited the role of researcher, when writing notes or conducting interviews, or when longer gaps occurred between her visits. Her outsider status was sometimes a barrier and, at other times, helpful in gathering research data. Over time, as her presence was accepted, her formal status as 'the researcher' made women willing to engage in in-depth conversations with her about their lives and experiences, in order to support and advocate for their project to an outsider who was scrutinising it. They were, for example, willing to leave their language classes or workshops temporarily, despite these being cherished events to them, in order to have such conversations.

The presence of insiders (staff and volunteers) to act as interpreters in interviews may have at times limited what women reflected back about the women's project. A desire to please those offering the service led, in year one of the evaluation, to women struggling or refusing to answer a particular question in interview: 'what would you change about the women's project?' Despite this reluctance to respond to this question, women would often approach Thompson later more informally with suggestions for improvement, such as more structure to the childcare or consistency in the English teachers. It appeared that they were uncomfortable making these suggestions when directly asked what they would like to change, and this may have been partially due to the presence of a project 'insider' in the interviews. However, it was only through reflexive conversations with such insiders that the question was adapted to 'what would make the project even better?' A question phrased in this way would typically be avoided in research due to its leading nature. In this context, however, it allowed the women to overcome a cultural barrier to being seen to criticise those who are helping you, something Thompson was naïve to before such insider conversations.

Reflexivity in research design was important from the start so that as Thompson engaged with project insiders (staff, volunteers and beneficiaries) she was able to adapt the methods and tools as necessary, such as in the case of the change to the question outlined above. Another example that occurred in year one of the project was that after evaluation forms for workshops were designed and then checked by staff and volunteers, more adaptations were needed after trialling with the women in larger groups where one-to-one and translation support proved necessary for the women to respond to the questions. The questions had included some 'before and after' number scale questions designed to measure changes to knowledge, confidence, thinking and behaviours. These questions proved confusing for women with a range of first languages to complete and were adapted to 'yes/no' questions about whether changes to knowledge, confidence, thinking and behaviour around particular issues had taken place as a result of the workshops.

Nasimi's positionality as a former child refugee from Afghanistan, with parents that migrated to the UK with her and her siblings when she was a young child, as well as being a UK-educated woman in her mid-twenties and a staff member at the charity, will undoubtedly have impacted how she approached the research as well as the knowledge produced from her encounters. Her shared characteristics with the group under consideration allowed her to relate to participants and build a rapport. This insider status also gave her an understanding of both the nuances and complex emotions of migrant identity formation. Being part of the group under study means 'simultaneously being an onlooker in the stalls and a member of the cast' (Shaw, 1996: 10).

The involvement of staff and volunteers allowed insiders a level of ownership over the research but may have meant that participants assumed the practitioner-researchers were already knowledgeable about their lived experiences and potentially that they held back elements of their stories when they were present. Botterill (2015) draws on her research with Polish migrants in the UK, describing how her participants 'took ownership' of the construction of particular narratives. Their enthusiasm in sharing these narratives were intertwined with the assumption that, as someone who was not Polish or a migrant, the researcher lacked knowledge that an 'insider' would have taken for granted (Botterill, 2015: 3). Therefore, sharing a similar background with the participants could mean that they might position you as already an 'expert' on their experiences and not share everything it was important to know. Nasimi's status as insider did present a barrier at times; for example, when the participants did not want to be seen criticise the project and censored some of what they might have said in interviews. Nasimi knowing some of the people that the participants might reference in their discussion might also expose their feelings of vulnerability to the information being disclosed. To an extent this was mitigated in this research, as the external researcher led the interviews and as such they might have felt more open to going into detail about their experiences. However, the presence of an interpreter in the room may have perpetuated a feeling of vulnerability/exposure at times. Despite this risk of exposure, the presence of an insider in interviews appeared to increase the comfort to speak overall, with the exception of when the participants had potential critiques to share about the project. This discomfort in these moments potentially exposes the limits of Nasimi's insider status, in her role as a senior member of staff in an organisation providing a service to the women taking part in the research, and the power imbalance this brings. This power dynamic was more equalised when the insiders present at interviews were volunteers who had been project beneficiaries themselves in the recent past.

This raises questions as to what extent Nasimi could claim insider status and again highlights the problematic binary in defining oneself as either insider or outsider. Her position in the organisation gave her a level of authority as did her status as a co-researcher, setting her apart from the research participants (Narayan, 1993). The imbalance of power that such authority in the organisation brings means that participants' desire to please or to 'say the right thing' may have impacted on interviews where she was present, as in the example of the question about what participants would change about the project. When such questions are being asked, not having an insider present may enable participants to respond more effectively to issues of power. There are also ways that Nasimi and Thompson were insiders in different ways, at different times and with different women. For example, Thompson had the shared experience of being a mother with many of the women and informal conversations about this enhanced her insider status at times. Nasimi, by contrast, was younger in age and shared many characteristics in common with the women who were not married or who did not have children. Overall, however, Nasimi's experience of arriving in the UK with her family at a very young age to seek asylum gave her trusted status and shared understandings with participants, and allowed her to have insider status as both a practitioner and researcher on the project, which was crucial to the effectiveness of both. As at least a partial insider at all times, she could be an effective mediator between the women and outsiders, enabling them to trust Thompson, for example, when she was first introduced to the project as the external researcher.

Despite the benefits of being part of the community the researcher wishes to explore, there is also a risk of blurring boundaries by imposing the researcher's own values, beliefs and perceptions as well as the projection of biases (Drake, 2010). This may have been what participants feared in the moments they chose to hold back. Nevertheless, it is important to acknowledge that 'no research is free of the biases, assumptions, and personality of the researcher and we cannot separate self from those activities in which we are intimately involved' (Sword, 1999: 277). The question is then, how Nasimi used her experience to offer deeper understandings of the phenomenon, without imposing her experience on the participants (Pillow, 2003). This required a level of reflexivity in considering how interviews might best take place and how analysis of data was conducted. As such, she purposely engaged in activities such as listening more than talking, and acting as interpreter rather than interviewer. This arrangement meant that participants could feel comfortable talking with someone they knew well as an insider while understanding that they needed to tell their whole story for the external researcher to understand. While insider researchers were involved in data collection as well as being research participants themselves, the data analysis was conducted by the external researcher. The collaborative adaptations we made to research tools and interview schedules from the start of the project as we engaged with insiders demonstrates how reflexivity was crucial to all phases of the research process from the formulation of research questions, to collection and analysis of data, and the drawing of conclusions (Guillemin and Gillam, 2004; Bradbury-Jones, 2007).

Conclusion

While we had previously identified ourselves as either insiders or outsiders in relation to the research, through reflexivity over time, we came to understand that we were insiders and outsiders to different extents at different times. While we are both women, our authority as project leaders and researchers meant we were at all times, to some extent, apart (Narayen, 1993). This was important to recognise in order to reflect on the power dynamics at play in the practice and research of the project.

Understanding that there was fluidity between our positionalities as insider and outsider enabled us to utilise moments of shared understanding, while remaining reflexive about our role and influence on the research, as well as to understand when our insider and outsider status was helping or hindering the research. Factors such as our gender, race, age, language, marital and parental status, as well as our role in and relationship to the organisation, all impacted on the research. The use of participatory research methods allowed us to draw on the insider status of project volunteers and beneficiaries to play a role in refining the research methods and as interpreters in interviews.

We argue that understanding the nuances in our status as insiders and outsiders was crucial to the research – rather than these being viewed as absolutes. We suggest that some level of 'insider' status is needed in effective research and practice with marginalised groups, while the involvement of partial outsiders alongside can also be helpful. Careful thought is needed as to what would not work along this insider-outsider spectrum – with the poles being necessarily avoided. For example, in the case of this research, a researcher who was not a woman would have not been able to penetrate the safe women-only space, nor would it have been appropriate to do so. However, claiming full insider status between the project and research participants and their insider practitioners and researchers would also downplay that power dynamics are still at play in such relationships of status that require consistent acknowledgement and reflexivity. Researching others necessarily brings power into play regardless of the researcher's status beforehand.

Acknowledgements

The three-year women's project and its evaluation was funded by The Pilgrim Trust.

This chapter draws on methodological discussion and research data that was originally published as part of our co-authored book, published by Emerald: Thompson, N., Nasimi, R., Rova, M. and Turner, A. (2022) *Community Work with Migrant and Refugee Women: 'Insiders' and 'Outsiders' in Research and Practice.*

References

Anthias, F. (2012) 'Transnational mobilities, migration research and intersectionality: Towards a translocational frame', *Nordic Journal of Migration Research*, 2(2): 102–10.

Berger, R. (2015) 'Now I see it, now I don't: Researcher's position and reflexivity in qualitative research', *Qualitative Research*, 15(2): 219–34.

Bourdieu, P. (1996) 'Understanding', *Theory, Culture & Society*, 13(2): 17–37.

Botterill, K. (2015) 'We don't see things as they are, we see things as we are: Questioning the "outsider" in Polish migration research', *Qualitative Sozialforschung / Forum: Qualitative Social Research*, 16(2): Article 4, Available from: https://core.ac.uk/download/pdf/132221458.pdf

Bradbury-Jones, C. (2007) 'Enhancing rigor in qualitative health research: Exploring subjectivity through Peshkin's I's', *Journal of Advanced Nursing*, 59: 290–98.

Bright, G., Thompson, N., Hart, P. and Hayden, B. (2018) 'Faith-based youth work: Education, engagement and ethics' in P. Alldred, F. Cullen, K. Edwards and D. Fusco (eds) *The SAGE Handbook of Youth Work Practice*, London: Sage, pp 197–212.

Change Institute (2009) *The Afghan Muslim Community in England Understanding Muslim Ethnic Communities*, London: Change Institute.

Cloke, P., Crang, P. and Goodwin, M. (2005) *Introducing Human Geographies*, London: Hodder Arnold.

Drake, P. (2010) 'Grasping at methodological understanding: A cautionary tale from insider research', *International Journal of Research and Method in Education*, 33(1): 85–99.

Finefter-Rosenbluh, I. (2017) 'Incorporating perspective taking in reflexivity', *International Journal of Qualitative Methods*, 16: 1–11.

Goodson, L. and Phillimore, J. (2010) 'A community research methodology: Working with new migrants to develop a policy related evidence base', *Social Policy and Society*, 9(4): 489–501.

Greenfields, M. and Ryder, A. (2012) 'Research with and for Gypsies, Roma and Travellers: Combining policy, practice and community in action research' in J. Richardson and A. Ryder (eds) *Gypsies and Travellers: Empowerment and Inclusion in British Society*, Bristol: Policy Press, pp 151–68.

Giusta, M.D. and Kambhampati, U. (2006) 'Women migrant workers in the UK: Social capital, well-being and integration', *Journal of International Development*, 18(6): 819–33.

Griffith, A.I. (1998) 'Insider / Outsider: Epistemological privilege and mothering work', *Human Studies*, 21: 361–76.

Guillemin, M. and Gillam, L. (2004) 'Ethics, reflexivity and "ethically important moments" in research', *Qualitative Inquiry*, 10: 261–80.

Horsburgh, D. (2003) 'Evaluation of qualitative research', *Journal of Clinical Nursing*, 12(2): 307–12.

Horváth, Z.E., Szakács, A. and Szakács, Z. (2018) 'Insider research on diversity and inclusion: Methodological considerations', *Mednarodno Inovativno Poslovanje*, 10(1): 1–11.

Israel, B.A., Eng, E., Schulz, A.J. and Parker, E.A. (eds) (2005) *Methods in Community-Based Participatory Research for Health*, San Francisco: Jossey-Bass.

Jason, L. and Glenwick, D. (eds) (2016) *Approaches to Community-Based Research: Qualitative, Quantitative and Mixed Methods*, Oxford: Oxford University Press.

Kloos, B., Hill, J., Thomas, E., Wandersman, A., Elias, M.J. and Dalton, J.H. (2012) *Community Psychology*, Belmont, CA: Cengage Learning.

Lipson, J.G. and Meleis, A.I. (1989) 'Methodological issues in research with immigrants', *Medical Anthropology*, 12: 103–15.

Masten, A.S. and Narayan, A.J. (2012) 'Child development in the context of disaster, war, and terrorism: Pathways of risk and resilience', *Annual Review of Psychology*, 63: 227–57.

Mercer, J. (2007) 'The challenges of insider research in educational institutions: Wielding a double-edged sword and resolving delicate dilemmas', *Oxford Review of Education*, 33(1): 1–17.

Merton, R.K. (1972) 'Insiders and outsiders: A chapter in the sociology of knowledge', *American Journal of Sociology*, 78(1): 9–47.

Minkler, M. (2005) 'Community-based research partnerships: Challenges and opportunities', *Journal of Urban Health*, 82: ii3–ii12.

Narayan, K. (1993) 'How native is a "native" anthropologist?', *American Anthropologist*, 95(3): 671–86.

Neale, B. and Flowerdew, J. (2003) 'Time texture and childhood: The contours of qualitative longitudinal research', *International Journal of Social Research Methodology: Theory and Practice*, 6(3): 189–99.

Pike, K.L. (1954) *Language in Relation to a Unified Theory of the Structure of Human Behavior*, Glendale, CA: Summer Institute of Linguistics.

Pillow, W.S. (2003) 'Confession, catharsis, or cure? Rethinking the uses of reflexivity as methodological power in qualitative research', *International Journal of Qualitative Studies in Education*, 16: 175–96.

Rose, G. (1997) 'Situating knowledges: Positionality, reflexivities and other tactics', *Progress in Human Geography*, 21(3): 305–20.

Ryan, L. (2015) '"Inside" and "outside" of what or where? Researching migration through multi-positionalities', *Forum Qualitative Sozialforschung / Forum: Qualitative Social Research*, 16(2): Article 17.

Social Policy Research Centre (2014) *New and Emerging Communities in Hounslow – Mapping and Needs Assessment*, London: Social Policy Research Centre.

Shaw, I. (1996) *Evaluating in Practice*, Bodmin: Arena.

Sword, W. (1999) 'Accounting for presence of self: Reflections on doing qualitative research', *Qualitative Health Research*, 9: 270–78. https://doi.org/10.1177/104973299129121839

Thompson, N. and Nasimi, R. (2022) '"This place means freedom to me": Needs-based engagement with marginalized migrant Muslim women in London', *Community Development Journal*, 57(2): 339–59. https://doi-org.gold.idm.oclc.org/10.1093/cdj/bsaa029

Thompson, N., Nasimi, R., Rova, M. and Turner, A. (2022) *Community Work with Migrant and Refugee Women: 'Insiders' and 'Outsiders' in Research and Practice*, Bingley: Emerald.

Veroff, J. and DiStefano, A. (2002) 'Special issue: Researching across difference', *American Behavioral Scientist*, 45: 1185–307.

Wenham, A. (2015) 'Innovations in the measurement of youth work: the contribution of qualitative longitudinal methods' in N. Stanton (ed) *Innovation in Youth Work: Thinking in Practice*, London: YMCA George Williams College, pp 44–9.

Zulfacar, M. (1998) *Afghan Immigrants in the USA and Germany: A Comparative Analysis of the Use of Ethnic Social Capital*, Munster: Lit Verlag.

3

From neoliberalism to neoexclusionism: how grassroots faith communities are resisting division and crossing borders

Naomi Thompson, Graham Bright and Peter Hart

Over centuries, since long before state services existed, faith-based groups have engaged with their communities to respond to social need and have been key to the development of varying expressions of community work. Such practice has often had an antagonistic relationship with states and institutions due to it operating from the 'grassroots' rather than 'top-down', and through its facilitation of empowerment and critical consciousness, rather than compliance. For example, the Sunday Schools of the late 1700s, that taught young people to read and write, were criticised for giving working class young people such power, lest they challenge the social order (Thompson, 2018). In this chapter, we draw on empirical research with faith-based community workers in England and Scotland and explore how they are resisting neoliberalism and right-wing populism. Our research did not focus specifically on migrant and refugee groups, but the arguments of this chapter have clear resonance for understanding the current context, local and global, within which grassroots community work with these groups takes place. While our research is located in the UK, debates around neoliberalism, populism, resistance and social justice have international relevance, with the detrimental impacts of capitalism and division felt globally, compounding the exclusion of the most marginalised groups, such as migrant and refugee communities.

Neoliberalism since the 1980s has seen youth and community work distorted to focus on people's deficits rather than their potential, to promote individualism over collectivism, and to conform with a measurable 'return on investment' agenda that ignores the softer, long-term outcomes of the work in favour of the values of the market (Duffy, 2017; Davies, 2019; Taylor et al, 2018). We argue that, more recently, neoliberalism has morphed into something more sinister that we term neoexclusionism, where those most in need of community services support have become increasingly maligned. A key shift in context between the ideologies of neoliberalism and neoexclusionism has been the move away from any claim towards liberal values. Instead, discourses of division and fear have been politicised with marginalised groups further stigmatised. Migrants and refugees are groups where stigmatisation can be argued to be a political practice used by states to coerce people's thinking (Tyler, 2020). Our conceptualising of neoexclusionism is related to, but distinct from, Featherstone's (2008) work on populism. He argues resistance to the globalising and homogenising agenda of neoliberalism can be manifest as exclusionary nationalist practices seeking to prevent transnational alliances. We argue, however, that neoexclusionism is not disconnected from capitalism and neoliberalism, rather it has emerged from the predictable failure of these forces to meet their espoused egalitarian and distributive aims. Our research demonstrates how faith-based youth and community workers seek to resist this oppressive culture by bringing people together to resist division and fear.

Successive post-2010 UK governments have implemented years of austerity and a focus on 'localism' rather than state-led interventions. These austerity and localism agendas have perhaps rendered visible the work of grassroots faith communities. For example, the Trussell Trust, which operates from Christian foundations and principles, increased its services and campaigns significantly after the 2008 recession and continues as the largest provider of UK foodbanks today (Trussell Trust, 2024). Similarly, Sikh communities have actively welcomed homeless people into their Gurdwaras to share Langar, as well as, in some cases, taking Langar outside the Gurdwara to feed people who need it in their local communities (Singh, 2015). In 2017, faith communities responded to the London Grenfell Tower fire by opening churches and mosques to provide food and shelter and to act as distribution centres for donations to those affected. Alongside this, faith groups were part of the movement of local activists and groups coming together to hold government and austerity policies to account for this tragedy. Since then, faith groups have worked in partnership with secular and state agencies to provide food, resources and care to communities affected by the COVID-19 pandemic and subsequent cost of living crisis (Baker, 2023). We argue that faith-based community work does not only work to meet need, but also to name and challenge injustices (Pimlott, 2015). The faith-based community workers in our research are resisting neoliberalism and neoexclusionism through their work to bring people together, challenge the stigmatisation of communities, and resist the asset-stripping that governments have imposed on communities.

Our research with faith-based youth and community workers

This chapter draws on research conducted with nine faith-based youth and community workers in the UK. Our participants represented a range of faith backgrounds (Muslim, Sikh, Buddhist, Jewish and Christian). Some were volunteers while others were paid professionals working for faith-based organisations. The research aimed to draw out rich qualitative description. We used Interpretative Phenomenological Analysis (IPA), which involves in-depth qualitative analysis within and across cases in small samples of data (Smith et al, 2009). The initial write-up of our study appears as a chapter in the *Sage Handbook of Youth Work Practice* (Bright et al, 2018).

For the purposes of this chapter, we have revisited our analysis to explore what it tells us about how grassroots faith-based community work is responding to and resisting both neoliberalism and neoexclusionism. It should be noted that, while our participants were working across generations, the focus of the original study was on work with young people; thus, the data contains more about their work with young people than other age groups.

The main themes that emerged from our original analysis were as follows:

1. Engagement: the forms of practice used in faith-based youth and community work
2. Education: the pedagogical approaches that underpin these methods of engagement
3. Ethics: the values and purposes of the work including a strong focus on facilitating inclusion

In this chapter, we re-dialogue with our findings to consider how faith-based community workers respond to neoliberal and neoexclusionist discourses. Within this, we identify new sub-themes that illustrate how the engagement practices of the faith-based community workers challenge neoexclusionism, using an educational approach that centres on 'border pedagogies' where groups learn together across differences (Giroux 2005; Coburn, 2010), and that draws on an ethical framework encompassing values that resist division and fear.

Morphology: neoliberalism to neoexclusionism

Tania de St Croix (2016: 27) sums up neoliberalism as 'an almost religious ideology in which the private and the market are necessarily good, and the public is seen as bad'. Under this rubric, the rule of the market is hegemonised while public services, and those who use them, are framed as problematic. Arguably, capitalism and its espoused claims of meritocracy merely attempt to obscure growing structural inequities through thinly-veiled discourses of blame. Neoliberalism was always destined to fail large groups of people, who now, more than ever, must be stigmatised in order to justify the rubric of capitalist logic.

The neoliberal project is characterised by its emphasis on marketisation, shrinking the state, a shift towards localism of services, and commissioning public services that can demonstrate return on investment. One of the clear challenges of this context for voluntary and community services is that it promotes competition over collaboration as organisations are forced to compete for limited funding. However, this undermining of collaboration is by no means an unfortunate by-product of financial stringency. Solidarity has been systematically undermined, as seen in the UK through anti-lobbying restrictions on charities, increasingly punitive responses to protest, and the undermining of trade-unions (de St Croix, 2016; Mayo, 2017; Bell, 2022). As such, individualisation has been purposefully unleashed as a mechanism of neoliberal rationality. This individualisation has permeated public discourse over the last 40 years. The values of the meritocracy necessitate that we view those in need of welfare or intervention as at fault; as lazy, greedy, morally corrupt and, ultimately, responsible for their own failure. The neoliberal era and the illusion of the meritocracy have precipitated and obscured widening inequalities.

Top-down, deficit-focused policies that have emerged in this period have fed global populist discourses; the UK's counter-terrorism strategy, Prevent, is a pertinent example. Such policies create division and intolerance in which people fear and blame each other for societal problems, rather than seeing them as symptoms of structural inequalities cemented by neoliberal governments. Mayo (2017) explains how blame for the housing crisis in London, created through disinvestment in social housing, has been diverted onto migrants, and feeds wider discourses about immigration as problematic. Recent UK policy on immigration has continued to emphasise the exclusion of migrants – for example, focused on stopping boats from crossing the English Channel from mainland Europe and the controversial (now abandoned) strategy to send asylum seekers to Rwanda. Mayo argues that as neoliberal austerity policies have increased inequality, people have sought more radical alternatives leading to a polarisation in politics. Globally, the 'radical right' has gained significant traction in this context, resulting in the growth of right-wing populism. While the recent UK general election has seen the Labour Party take power, their success was supported by the swathes of Conservative votes lost to Reform UK, Nigel Farage's extreme-right party.

Neoexclusionism is both related to neoliberalism and distinct from it. It is a context that has emerged as the neoliberal promise of prosperity has remained unfulfilled for many. As neoliberalism has failed, instead of something more social democratic emerging, something more sinister has birthed. This is no accident. It has been achieved through undermining solidarity, stigmatising groups who hold little power to resist, and the political mobilisation of fear and division.

Analyses of neoliberalism in relation to community and youth work recognise it has shifted to something more than financial efficacy and stringency. de St Croix states that while there has been an ongoing focus on supposedly inevitable cuts and cost-saving, it also the case that 'social inequalities and traditionalist values became more deeply embedded' (2016: 14). This indicates that the liberal values purported to underpin the neoliberal project have shifted to a more 'traditionalist' set of values. Similarly, Mayo (2017) recognises increasing populism in the neoliberal era, framing it as a symptom of the failure of market forces. However, we argue that a continuing focus on critiquing neoliberalism in many such analyses has distracted from the shift in ideology and values underpinning neoliberalism as it gave way to creeping neoexclusionism. Within this shift, there has been a move from any attempt to claim adherence to liberal values, to an embracing of deeply conservative ones (Zizek, 2018). The levels of mistrust, suspicion and control that have emerged through neoexclusionism go beyond the neoliberal project. For example, right-wing nationalist movements driven by hate and division have been politically mobilised in global election campaigns, such as those of Donald Trump and Boris Johnson, as well as in the 2016 referendum of the UK's membership of the EU. Elements of these campaigns have been explicitly racist. The UK Independence Party (UKIP), for example, unveiled a poster portraying a long line of refugees from racially minoritised groups with the words 'breaking point' during the Brexit referendum campaigns. This misleading image served to mobilise hostility towards refugees and asylum seekers. Following the referendum, UKIP re-emerged as The Brexit Party and, more recently, has gained significant traction as Reform UK.

We argue that neoexclusionism emerged in the neoliberal era following global events like 9/11 but is now a powerful force more dominant and sinister than neoliberalism. Politicians, media and public discourse have mobilised against the groups most pertinently failed by neoliberalism. These most failed groups have become both the objects of blame for their own failure and for the hardships experienced by other groups who have also been failed by the neoliberal project. This politically-driven narrative supports the continuation of the current system of economics. As such, neoexclusionism is a global force that mobilises right-wing, nationalist movements to obscure the failures of neoliberal capitalism by stigmatising the most vulnerable groups – and perhaps, most often, those who have been displaced.

In this context, fear of 'the religious other' has grown, particularly in relation to minoritised racial and religious communities. The 'othering' of such groups is seen particularly pertinently in expressions of Islamophobia and the fear of migrants across the Western world. The hostility that stems from this fear extends to refugees and asylum seekers, who have been reframed from being viewed as displaced, to groups whose motivations for migration are not to be trusted. References to refugees as 'terrorists' and 'cockroaches' have been deployed by public media (United Nations Office of the High Commissioner on Human Rights, 2018). The growth of exclusion and 'othering' of religious groups in this context led the faith-based community workers in our study to seek both safe spaces for their communities, and opportunities for dialogue between their communities and others, as well as campaigning against the societal discourses that exclude them (Bright et al, 2018).

Community development and resistance

A key debate in the community development field over recent decades has centred on tensions around whether practice should focus on the assets or deficits of individuals and communities. This debate sits within wider tensions between 'top-down' and 'bottom-up' practices, and between radical and consensus forms of community development. State-funded and mainstream services have most often imposed a top-down assessment of problems that can increase stigmatisation and fail to adequately address the needs of particular communities. The UK's counter-terrorism strategy (Prevent), for example, presents a particularly problematic top-down strategy that frames Muslim communities as dangerous. While counter-extremism policy does also increasingly nod towards right-wing radicalism (Home Office, 2015), this has not often been a key focus of media and political discourse around it. Policy has been criticised for increasing stigmatisation and isolation of Muslim communities (Abbas and Awan, 2015). While 'community cohesion' had a focus in policy discussions in the early 21st century, it has been undermined by an ideological commitment to austerity and through deficit-focused policy interventions such as Prevent (Mayo, 2017).

Asset-focused forms of community development emerged in Western contexts over the last few decades as a form of community self-help, becoming popular in the UK in the early 21st century. Asset-based community development (ABCD) has often been celebrated as the solution to problematic policy making (IDeA, 2010). It is based on the idea that by focusing on 'capacity, skills, knowledge, connections and potential in a community', practitioners and services are able to see beyond 'problems that need fixing' (IDeA, 2010: 7). It critiques practices that focus on people's deficits and argues that people need to be part of shaping their own solutions and services. However, while ABCD has a clear role to play in reducing top-down stigmatising of communities, it has been suggested it may overlook inequalities, or even reinforce them, by over-emphasising self-empowerment (MacLeod and Emejulu, 2014). The focus on assets rather than problems may mean the needs of marginalised groups are ignored, as well as the structural barriers to meeting such needs. As such, MacLeod and Emejulu (2014) argue that the turn towards a focus on assets rather than needs in community development has further legitimated neoliberalism, funding cuts and inequalities. Arguably, while there is a clear rationale for focusing on community assets rather than defining communities by their problems, for interventions to be progressive, they also need to actively resist neoliberal discourses of self-help and austerity.

Featherstone et al (2011) introduced the concept of 'progressive localism'. They critique the 'austerity localism' that is part of the politically-driven neoliberal agenda to reduce welfare provision, arguing that more progressive forms of localism are needed that actively resist neoliberalism. Such forms of localism recognise that as inequalities continue to grow, excluded groups need community development responses that resist neoliberal ideas of 'self-help', and that campaign for their needs to be met through state investment. Beyond this, there is a further need to challenge the division and inequality created by the neoexclusionist discourses of division and fear. According to Featherstone et al (2011), progressive localism involves local organisations working together to resist, rather than collude with, problematic policy discourses. Such progressive local partnerships could play a role in resisting neoexclusionism. This goes beyond plugging gaps left by state cuts to challenging inequality and individualism, thus resisting both neoliberalism and neoexclusionism.

In our research, we found that faith-based community workers were developing progressive partnerships based on 'border crossings' (Giroux, 2005; Coburn, 2010) that bring people and groups together to build community, and challenge division and mistrust. In the previous analysis of our data, we found these community workers were facilitating 'inclusion within' by providing safe spaces for excluded groups, and 'inclusion without' by developing collaborative work with and between their own faith community, other faith groups, and the wider community (Bright et al, 2018). While resistance, protest and solidarity have been systematically undermined during the neoliberal era (Pimlott, 2015; de St Croix, 2016), we argue that faith-based community workers are generating resistance through such progressive local partnerships.

Faith beyond walls

A spectrum of practice emerged from our research interviews with faith-based community workers. This ranged from provision that was open to all to more specific sessions for those from within the faith community. Another realm of engagement was inter-faith work which brought young people of different faiths together. Other forms of dialogical work included engaging with the local communities in which faith organisations were located. These practices included enacting commitments to meet social and community needs, and to break down intolerance and misunderstandings about the faith group. These approaches, in particular, can be viewed as a bulwark against neoexclusionist discourses. They demonstrate a deep commitment to breaking down divisions and enabling community 'border crossings'.

Responding to austerity

Research participants were keenly aware of how their work with young people and communities contributed to civil society. Given the climate of neoliberalism and austerity, they appeared acutely aware of gaps in service provision, and how the work they did was able to respond. Their work spanned small social action projects to taking over local authority provision that was no longer funded:

> So what we've done in the past is we've got a group of kids, Muslim kids, Christian kids, gone down to the local supermarkets who support what we do, and then the foodbank collection so we hand people leaflets if they want to donate for us, and then the food that people give us within that hour, our trolleys full of food and we'll walk it round to the local foodbank and give it to them there. (Steven, a Revert Muslim youth worker with an inter-faith organisation)

> So we have, well we have a centre ... a council property ... that was going redundant because of the lack of youth work that there was in the city. So we took on that and picked up an existing, sort of existing project that they ran as a youth, open access youth project provision there. And we had previously ran one here, which we'd closed down due to residents' complaints, we had a very high volume of young people, roughly about, well between 120 and 140 on a Friday night, and of that about 90% of those were Traveller young people. So that caused significant issues in a quite affluent area so we had to shut down before, before we were shut down, but the council approached us and asked us to re-open that at this new youth centre which is nearer the Traveller sites and also it's a real area of need where it is. (Beth, a Christian youth worker)

While Beth was the only example of someone who had taken over a local authority provision, all of the participants were responding to local need. Warsan, a Muslim youth worker, framed the purpose of setting up a Muslim Scouts group as a diversion from anti-social activities for young people, who weren't accessing (and/or felt excluded from) other provisions on offer. Even Jim, a Christian youth worker, who was explicit about the ultimate purpose of his work being to share the Christian faith, was running a youth club to serve local young people that he described as having 'no agenda'.

The community workers were also keen to frame how their work went beyond meeting local need to challenging negative perceptions of their faith communities. Steven explained how through social action projects such as litter picking, Muslim young people were challenging perceptions of their community as 'problematic citizens'. Balraj, a Sikh youth worker, explained how socio-political engagement was a key element of his practice, with his young people engaging in protests and campaigns, actively resisting austerity and right-wing populism. These practices, as well as responding to neoliberal austerity, were challenging neoexclusionist discourses that stigmatise religious and minoritised groups.

Resisting individualisation

Our participants appeared to be resisting the neoliberal focus on individualism in their work with young people. Their practice was built on recognising the need for reciprocal relationships between people and on fostering interdependence and intergenerational support through, for example, mentoring and mediation. As well as challenging neoliberal values of individualism, this bringing generations together challenges the division and fear between generations that is present in neoexclusionist discourses, where the young are demonised, rather than the impacts of austerity and asset-stripping being recognised. Forging relationships with young people, between young people, and between young people and the wider faith community were key aspects of the community workers' practice. The commitment to intergenerational mentoring was most central for the Buddhist participants, both of whom were volunteers in their faith community.

> I mean the main, we refer to him as the President Ukedu, if you like the teacher, almost like a mentor, in terms of practising his Buddhism his main focus, one of the main focuses he has is encouraging the youth. Yeah, I mean guidance and encouragement is quite significant in terms of, a lot of energy's put into thinking about the young people in terms of their futures in a way, yeah'. (Kana)

> I have got my mentor in life who is a Buddhist leader and he really encourages us to nurture the future, to nurture the youth because, you know, obviously you have to have someone to do young people, they are the [unclear] of the future, and it's not just this life but it continues eternally. (Saori)

Similarly, Jim explained how building relationships, family and community in his church was a significant part of his role:

> So what we try and do is say 'well, we've got, we've got a community here that young people can be part of and feel valued in, that's brilliant' ... And so, like I've been really, I have been really pro-active in the church, trying to integrate young people with the life of the church, recognising that they need that community ... I think it's quite rare for like a young person to drop out of their wider family, as in their

blood family. So you kind of think well, that, you know, some would, for various reasons, but actually on the whole, and so you think well why do they drop out of church, they obviously don't see it as family or a community that they can connect with, or belong to or be part of, or are valued by. So it's easy to walk away.

This fostering of generational connections challenges the mistrust between generations and asset-stripping of the young that is prevalent in the neoliberal and neoexclusionist era.

Working together

Working between different faiths and groups was a key theme across the interviews. By collaborating, participants in the study engaged in resisting market values of neoliberalism and the divisions created by neoexclusionism. This was most apparent in the work of the inter-faith organisation for which both Mark and Steven worked. Each outlined how creating a sense of community between young people of different faiths was central to their work. Such inter-faith work was also explicit in other participants' narratives. Warsan, for example, outlined how her Muslim Scouts group has engaged with the local Christian and Sikh Scouts groups:

> Recently we organised a faith show, so like the Mosque, the Gurdwara and the Church which was really good, like they got to speak to like, like I think there was for the Church there was a priest and for the Mosque it was just like one of the boy trustees and I think the same for the Gurdwara.

Daniel, a Jewish youth worker, was also engaging in inter-faith work: 'We go outside the community and talk to other faith groups and particularly, I think, politically it's very important for Jews and Muslims to be talking as much as possible.'

Other youth workers who weren't engaging in explicit inter-faith work emphasised how young people of other faiths were welcome and had attended their activities. Within these collaborative practices, a pedagogical approach of facilitating dialogue and crossing borders between communities and groups was apparent. These approaches represent grassroots attempts to foster inclusion and understanding, which challenge neoexclusionist discourses of division and mistrust.

Safe spaces

Research participants described the importance of creating safe spaces for young people in their faith communities. This facet of practice predominantly took the shape of sessions run primarily for young people subscribing to a particular faith tradition. For example, Warsan's Muslim Scout group was created as a safe space for the young people in her community to gather and engage with each other. While this could be seen as an exclusive or exclusionary space, Warsan described this work as being concerned with developing a safe, inclusive space for a group that often experiences stigma and exclusion in other contexts. This is particularly pertinent for those groups most heavily stigmatised under neoexclusionism, such as young Muslims.

Similarly, Balraj demonstrated an innovative approach to creating a safe space for Sikh young people to discuss issues they were facing, through an online strategy to support young people who were facing negative experiences at school due to their Sikh faith. Daniel explained that his youth group was a safe space for young people to openly discuss their interpretations of what it means to be Jewish and LGBTQ+. The need to foster safe, inclusive spaces for young people of faith (and other intersecting identities) was, at least in part, a response to the stigma created by neoexclusionism.

Challenging division and fear

Neoexclusionist discourses of division, fear and mistrust have been reinforced by problematic policy making and practice as well as through media reporting of particular groups as problematic. Recent policies focused on preventing the arrival of asylum seekers and on monitoring migrants on visas (such as the pressures on universities to monitor attendance at classes for international students) exacerbate exclusionist discourse. The community workers were keenly aware of the impact of such discourses on their faith communities and a key aspect of their practice was providing a positive representation of the faith community to the wider public. Mark explained how he had worked with the Muslim community in his area to open up the mosque to people of other faiths to help break down misunderstandings. He also described how he and his organisation refused to do any inter-faith work where there was any inference that they should address radicalisation. Indeed, his and Steven's organisation was deeply committed to resisting a deficit focus:

> I think it was only last month we got offered a large amount of money and I can't remember who, it was like an anti-extremism unit, and that's now changed, oh it was anti-terrorism and it's now changed to extremism, but it's kind of the same group of people running a different department with a slightly bigger pot of money and they're offering it and we're like, no we can't, as nice as the money would be, we're not going to be used as your inter-faith gurus to help you with that kind of thing. (Mark, a Christian youth worker with an inter-faith organisation)

Similarly, Balraj described how he opened up his local Gurdwara for public events including charity events, tours and visits, with the explicit aim of enabling connection with, and learning about the local Sikh community.

> The Gurdwara's always open like last year we did, I remember, we did count that had 50,000 visitors that came to Gurdwara last year … One of the first things we did back in 2012 was we did like a charity event, and we raised funds for a local children's hospital that needed to raise funds for a new wing that they were making of this hospital. So, we did a fundraising event and we fundraised almost £8000 for that because we managed to get all of the community together.

At times, the community workers needed to challenge discriminatory practices more formally. For example, Balraj highlighted how his Sikh community were able to influence a large high-street chain to change their policy across Scotland, after the experience of one local woman:

> Two years ago we had a woman who was refused a job at [a high-street shop]; she went through the interview process, she was given a full offer of employment in writing, and on the day that she arrived at work they said that she would have to take off her Sikh articles of faith like the bangle, because she was in breach of the health and safety policy, and if she would not do that then she would have to leave the premises and she would no longer be able to work there. So, like that in itself presents a problem. You know we obviously fought that case and it was fine, she got the job back and [the company] changed their policy.

This theme also overlaps with the 'working together' theme discussed above. However, the distinction lies in the difference in intent, one being to represent minoritised and misunderstood faith communities to the wider public, the other being to facilitate relationships between people of different faiths for their own sake. This positive representation and building of community relationships was the most pertinent way the community workers were resisting the fear and division created by neoexclusionism rather than simply the individualism that comes with neoliberalism.

Conclusion

The faith-based community and youth work we encountered in our research appears to represent a form of ABCD, with the community workers working with communities in positive and empowering ways. They were doing this in a context where funding for community work was scarce or misplaced. There is a question to be raised about whether these practices collude with the state, rather than offering an active resistance to neoliberalism, by simply plugging gaps in provision and reinforcing the ideologies of austerity and community-led self-help. For example, Beth's work to replace local authority provision could be seen as either a challenge to neoliberalism and austerity or a collusion with it, potentially reinforcing that such work should be delivered by communities rather than the state (Featherstone et al, 2011; MacLeod and Emejulu, 2014).

However, there are indications in our findings of faith-based community workers seeking to actively challenge the discourses of division and fear promoted by neoexclusionism. For example, and perhaps most explicitly, in the work of Steven and Mark to bring young people of different faiths together while resisting problematic funding offers, and the activism and protests engaged in by Balraj and his Sikh youth group, some of which focused specifically on issues facing migrants and refugee communities. While our research was not focused on migrants and refugees, the findings have resonance for community work with these groups where the need for resistance of division and fear, positive representation, and community 'border crossings' are arguably most pertinent. Further research is needed to understand how far grassroots community work with these groups is effectively supporting them to resist and counter neoexclusionism.

Overall, we argue that faith-based community work is going some way to resist the forces of neoliberalism and neoexclusionism, and the values of individualism, deficit and fear that underpin these forces – through bringing different communities and groups together. However, there is a need for a clearer understanding and further exploration of the concept of neoexclusionism and its impact on communities – as well as how far community development practitioners, both faith-based and not, are explicitly challenging, resisting and speaking out against neoexclusionist discourses within their practice.

Acknowledgement

A version of this chapter was originally published as an article in *Radical Community Work* journal in 2021: 'From neoliberalism to neopopulism: How grassroots faith communities are resisting division and crossing borders', *Radical Community Work*, 4(2).

References

Abbas, T. and Awan, I. (2015) 'Limits of UK counterterrorism policy and its implications for Islamophobia', *International Journal for Crime, Justice & Social Democracy*, 4(3): 16–29.

Baker, C. (2023) 'Faith/Secular partnerships in a post COVID-19 policy landscape: A critical case study of deepening postsecularity in the Temple tradition', *Journal of Church and State*, 65(4): 396–407.

Bell, K. (2022) 'Defending the right to strike', London: Trades Union Congress, Available from: https://www.tuc.org.uk/blogs/defending-right-strike

Bright, G., Thompson, N., Hart, P. and Hayden, B. (2018) 'Faith-based youth work: Education, engagement and ethics' in P. Alldred, F. Cullen, K. Edwards and D. Fusco (eds) *Sage Handbook of Youth Work Practice*, London: Sage, pp 197–212.

Coburn, A. (2010) 'Youth work as border pedagogy' in J. Batsleer and B. Davies (eds) *What is Youth Work?* Exeter: Learning Matters, pp 33–46.

Davies, B. (2019) *Austerity, Youth Policy and the Deconstruction of the Youth service in England*, London: Palgrave Macmillan.

de St Croix, T. (2016) *Grassroots Youth Work: Policy, Passion and Resistance in Practice*, Bristol: Policy Press.

Duffy, D. (2017) *Evaluation and Governing in the 21st Century: Disciplinary Measures, Transformative Possibilities*, London: Palgrave Macmillan.

Featherstone, D. (2008) *Resistance, Space and Political Identities: The Making of Counter-Global Networks*, Oxford: Wiley-Blackwell.

Featherstone, D., Ince, A., MacKinnon, D., Strauss, K. and Cumbers, A. (2011) 'Progressive localism and the construction of political alternatives', *Transactions of the Institute of British Geographers*, 37: 177–82.

Giroux, H.A. (2005) *Border Crossings: Cultural Workers and the Politics of Education* (2nd edition), Abingdon: Routledge.

Home Office (2015) *Counter-Extremism Strategy*, London: Home Office.

IDeA (2010) *A Glass Half Full: How an Asset Approach can Improve Community Health and Wellbeing*, London: Improvement and Development Agency/Local Government Association.

MacLeod, M.A. and Emejulu, A. (2014) 'Neoliberalism with a community face? A critical analysis of asset-based community development in Scotland', *Journal of Community Practice*, 22(4): 430–50.

Mayo, M. (2017) *Changing Communities: Stories of Migration, Displacement and Solidarities*, Bristol: Policy Press.

United Nations Office of the High Commissioner on Human Rights (OHCHR) (2018) 'Refugees and other migrants do not lose their rights by crossing borders', Available from: https://www.ohchr.org/EN/NewsEvents/Pages/RefugeesMigrantsDoNotLoseTheirRights.asp

Pimlott, N. (2015) *Embracing the Passion: Christian Youth Work and Politics*, London: SCM.

Singh, J. (2015) 'From the temple to the street: How Sikh kitchens are becoming the new foodbanks', The Conversation, 22 July, Available from: https://theconversation.com/from-the-temple-to-the-street-how-sikh-kitchens-are-becoming-the-new-food-banks-44611

Smith, J.A., Flowers, P. and Larkin, M. (2009) *Interpretative Phenomenological Analysis*, London: Sage.

Taylor, T., Connaughton, P., de St Croix, T., Davies, B. and Grace, P. (2018) 'The impact of neoliberalism upon the character and purpose of English youth work and beyond' in P. Alldred, F. Cullen, K. Edwards and D. Fusco (eds) *The SAGE Handbook of Youth Work Practice*, London: Sage, pp 84–9.

Thompson, N. (2018) *Young People and Church Since 1900: Engagement and Exclusion*, London: Routledge.

Trussell Trust (2024) 'Latest stats', Available from: https://www.trusselltrust.org/news-and-blog/latest-stats/

Tyler. I. (2020) *Stigma: The Machinery of Inequality*, London: Zed Books.

Zizek, S. (2018) *First as Tragedy, Then as Farce*, London: Verso.

4

Agency and frustration: overcoming obstacles at the UNHCR

Brian Callan

International Protection is a core concept in International Refugee Law which aims at protecting the fundamental rights of a specific category of persons outside their countries of origin, who lack the national protection of their own countries. The Office of the United Nations High Commissioner for Refugees (UNHCR) is the international organisation mandated with 'providing international protection, under the auspices of the United Nations, to refugees who fall within the scope of the present Statute and of seeking permanent solutions for the problem of refugees' (UN, 1950, para. 1). This chapter explores how that mandate is carried out in practice. It begins by outlining the development of the international conventions which provide the framework for 'international protection', by which refugees are afforded civil, political, economic and social rights normally provided by nation-states. The history, scale and structure of the 'Refugee Agency' also demonstrates the complexity required to provide the protection mandate, which itself operates within a global network of national and international institutions, non-governmental organisations (NGOs), private companies, donors and other 'stakeholders' in what Betts (2010) has called the 'refugee regime complex'. Since 2010 in countries across the Global North, notably in Europe and the US, there has been a marked increase in political narratives where the fear of 'floods of migrants' or 'migration crisis' have fuelled discourse to 'take back control' of our borders and laws or to 'build that wall' (Callan, 2016). This has led to a reconsideration of obligations under international law in the wealthy Global North around the treatment of refugees and asylum seekers, with notions of 'burden sharing' or outright 'offshoring' policies where *both* money and refugees are to be 'processed' in poorer states in the Global South, such as the UK government's attempts to send asylum seekers to Rwanda. To understand how such an environment affects the ability of the UNHCR to enact its mandate to provide protection and other services to displaced people, this study surveyed ten professional staff at the agency on what frustrates them and how they keep motivated under such conditions. The findings highlight the continued centrality of people, both *to* and *within* the organisation. However, there is also a sense of a 'global protection drought' in which the content of protection is at risk of being lost.

Conventional wisdom

Ostensibly, the management of forced migration is coordinated by two institutions which came into being in the aftermath of the Second World War. The first is the 1951 Convention Relating to the Status of Refugees which defines the status of refugee and sets out the rights to which they are entitled. The second is the Office of the United Nations High Commissioner for Refugees (UNHCR), the organisation responsible for overseeing United Nations (UN) member states' implementation of that 1951 Convention. The original Convention was drawn up at a conference of international representatives in Geneva, to deal with the refugee crisis caused by the land war in Europe. It was signed by 26, mostly European, states with Cuba and Iran represented by observers. A large number of NGOs were also present as consultants at the conference, including the International Council of Women (ICW) and the International Labour Organisation (ILO). Taking the UN's 1948 Universal Declaration of Human Rights principle that 'human beings shall enjoy fundamental rights and freedoms without discrimination' (UNHCR, 1951: 12) as its starting point, the final Convention built upon a number of previous international treaty instruments and formed a legal document of definitions and rights in 46 Articles. The Convention was adopted on 25 July.

Article 1, which covers almost three pages of the Convention, concerns the definition of the term 'refugee'. Over a series of sub-clauses A–F regarding to whom the Convention does (and does not) apply, a key passage appears in paragraph (2):

> As a result of events occurring before 1 January 1951 and owing to wellfounded fear of being persecuted for reasons of race, religion, nationality, membership of a particular social group or political opinion, is outside the country of his nationality and is unable or, owing to such fear, is unwilling to avail himself of the protection of that country; or who, not having a nationality and being outside the country of his former habitual residence as a result of such events, is unable or, owing to such fear, is unwilling to return to it.

Gendered language notwithstanding, the phrases 'fear of being persecuted' and 'outside the country' have long caused considerable contention over various conceptualisations of the term and status of 'refugee' (Adelman, 1983; Barnett, 2004; Pinson, 2010) and precludes Internally Displaced Persons (IDPs), an issue that came to prominence in the 1980s (Weiss and Korn, 2006).

Article 35 of the Convention gave the UNHCR an explicit mandate to monitor its implementation. In this, signatory states must 'undertake to co-operate' with the UNHCR 'in the exercise of its functions' and 'its duty of supervising the application of the provisions' of the Convention. That original Convention was augmented by the 1967 Protocol Relating to the Status of Refugees (OHCHR, 1967) which removed time limits and geographical constraints in the original wording and to date 149 states are parties to one or both legal texts. Those who do find themselves stateless or forced beyond their national boundaries are, by law, afforded 'international protection' in line with the articles of the Convention. This protection regime, in the first instance, gives refugees certain civil, political, economic, and social rights and, in the longer term, reintegration assistance through a number of formal processes, the so-called 'durable solutions' of local integration, resettlement or repatriation.

The Refugee Agency

The UNHCR, headquartered in Geneva, is a truly international organisation. As of late 2023 it has a global workforce of over 20,000 operating in 134 countries. Around 90 per cent of the workforce is based in the field, and many are drawn from the local populations and the refugees themselves. In the agency's latest Global Appeal (UNHCR, 2024) it acknowledges 130.8 million 'people of concern' across the world. comprising 32 million refugees, 10.8 million 'returnees', 62.9 million IDPs, 6.9 million asylum seekers, 4 million 'stateless persons', 6 million 'others of concern' and over 6 million 'in need of international protection'. In order to fulfil its 'mandated responsibilities' to these people, the agency operates through four core pillars: the Refugee Programme, the Stateless Programme, Reintegration Projects and IDP Projects. Its projected budgetary requirements for 2024 (at the time of writing) stand at US$10.6 billion, most which is sourced from voluntary donations. This donor base includes 69 donor governments, private contributors, foundations, corporations and individuals. The fund is highly dependent on governmental donors for the majority of its income, with the top three in 2023 being the US, Germany and the EU. The US$10 billion budgetary projections in the 2024 Global Appeal also project a more than US$6 billion funding gap.

The UNHCR's mandate and work have changed at various stages in its history. In 1967, the geographical scope of its work expanded from Europe to the rest of the world. In the 1980s, it took on a growing role in providing material assistance to refugees. Since the 1990s, it has taken on a growing role in humanitarian relief, expanding on a role of providing relief to refugees and, increasingly, IDPs, through its framework of *Guiding Principles on International Displacement* (UNHCR, 1998). From the early

2000s, it has become increasingly active in the broader area of migration and the issue of 'mixed movements' in particular. Mixed movements (sometimes called mixed migration) refer to situations where a number of people are travelling together, generally in an irregular manner, using the same routes and means of transport, but for different reasons. This issue led to *The 10-Point Plan in Action*, designed to address the increasing complexity of migration paths and patterns, acting as a 'source of guidance for UNHCR, other UN agencies, governments and civil society' (UNHCR, 2007). Most recently, in 2018, the UN General Assembly affirmed the *Global Compact on Refugees*, as 'a framework for more predictable and equitable responsibility-sharing, recognizing that a sustainable solution to refugee situations cannot be achieved without international cooperation' (UNHCR, 2020). The four key objectives identified in this compact are: to ease the pressures on host countries; enhance refugee self-reliance; expand access to third-country solutions; and support conditions in countries of origin for return in safety and dignity.

A complex world

In terms of the scale of displacement, the geographical spread of the phenomenon, the historical accumulation of articles and frameworks (which reflect emergent issues, and expand upon the remit of the agency and the international network of its workforce and donors), fulfilling the mandate of the 1951 Convention is a complex undertaking. However, the UNHCR and its affiliates are not alone 'with actors other than states and migrants – from NGOs to private security companies and labour brokers – playing an ever more central role' (Pascucci, 2017: 250). Increased mobility, globalisation, civil unrest and changing national sentiments since the start of the 21st century have seen a range of new international institutions engaging with the issue of human mobility. International, regional and local rules and regimes relating to travel, labour migration, human rights, humanitarianism, development and security have created overlaps, aporias and contestations of authority and responsibilities that constitute what Betts (2010) calls a 'refugee regime complex'.

Within this complex, Betts identifies a number of benefits and challenges for the UNHCR. On the one hand there are regional consultative processes aimed at managing migration. These include, for example, the Intergovernmental Consultations on Asylum, Refugees and Migration (IGC, 2024) which coordinates governments largely of the Global North, or the Bali Process on People Smuggling, Trafficking in Persons and Related Transnational Crime (TBP, 2024) chaired by Indonesia and Australia. These can enable states to address their concerns with 'spontaneous arrival asylum' through control of travel, security and the practice of 'intercepting' migrants, thus bypassing 'without overtly violating their explicit obligations' (Betts, 2010: 16) to refugees who arrive on their territory. Such considerations are often driven by the political climate of the potential host nations, and the European 'migrant crisis' which began in 2014 is a case in point in the complex interplay of international organisations, sovereign states and local NGOs. While Turkey and Germany became two of the top five hosting countries, a number of states in the Western Balkans built hundreds of kilometres of razor-wire fences along their borders. While media and political narratives of 'fears', 'floods' and 'crisis' fuelled xenophobic civil society movements, such as PEGIDA in Germany (Paukstat and Ellwanger, 2016), the image of Alan Kurdi's young lifeless body on the beach in 2015 became the global emblem of the humanitarian plight of the migrants and mobilised local volunteers throughout Europe and beyond, despite state opposition (Callan, 2016; Křeček, 2016; Molnar, 2016).

On the other hand, attempts to intercept the refugee 'problem' since the start of the 21st century have led to the redistribution of costs and benefits, or 'burden sharing', within the refugee regime and created greater interdependence between Northern and Southern states (Betts and Milner, 2006; Betts, 2010). The vast majority of forcibly displaced people worldwide, some 76 per cent, are hosted in low- and middle-income countries (UNHCR, 2023a), mostly internally displaced or hosted in neighbouring states. The concept of burden and responsibility sharing looks to enhance the quality of refugee protection in these nations. With that in mind, the channelling of monies and other resources from the relatively wealthy North in order to better facilitate protection mandates is often welcomed by the hosting nations. However, this formulation of control over compassion can have a knock-on illiberal effect, as when Tanzania explicitly cited EU asylum control practices as a justification for its own restrictive approach towards Burundian refugees (Betts and Milner, 2006). Similarly, a number of states in the Global North, including Australia, Denmark and the UK, have attempted or deployed 'offshoring' policies by sending *both* money and asylum seekers themselves to have their applications processed in poorer states in the Global South (Gammeltoft-Hansen, 2011; Fleay and Hoffman, 2014; Collyer and Shahani, 2023).

Such is the extraordinary socio-political and economic complexity in which the UNHCR struggles to fulfil its mandate to protect, return, reintegrate and resettle 1.6 per cent of the world's population. These are men, women and children who have been divested of home and shelter, personal safety, friends, family and the esteem of recognition. The UNHCR has the massive task of implementing guidelines and frameworks, acknowledging donor requirements and regional consultations, while negotiating political manoeuvres and national sentiments on a daily basis across the globe. In this the agency has adapted and migrated beyond its original boundaries, in order to negotiate such alternative arrangements and to continue to interpret that mandate 'in a liberal and humanitarian spirit, in accordance with their ordinary meaning, and in light of the object and purpose of the 1951 Convention' (UNHCR, 2003: 2). Nonetheless, internally techno-bureaucratic practices and results-based management (RBM) (Jacobsen and Sandvik, 2018) and the widening gap between asylum laws and actual asylum practices of member states (Trauner, 2016) present tangible obstacles to this humanitarian mandate, while the exclusionary rhetorics of resurgent right-wing populist and nativist agendas have sought to delegitimise the very humanity of the people themselves (Crawley and Skleparis, 2018; Krzyżanowski et al, 2018).

Methodology

Ongoing external critique and adaptation are, of course, essential for the proper functioning of any large organisation and, as we have seen, the UNHCR has been subject to and had to adapt to changing political vagaries and evolving needs over the decades. However, the professional staff in the Refugee Agency, from fieldworkers and regional staff, specialists in child protection or law, or analysts and officers in international protection have rarely been polled for their views on the challenges *they* face in implementing their mandate. Inspired by Graeber's (2019) methodology of anonymously canvasing employees about their jobs, this project devised a simple survey with two open-ended questions:

- What frustrates you when you are trying to do your job?
- What keeps you motivated?

The first question sought to understand how staff themselves navigate the 'refugee regime complex' (Betts, 2010) from the multiple field sites to the agency's headquarters in Geneva. Further guidance was given, encouraging respondents to reflect on their role and whether existing structures, policies, politics and practices make this more difficult. With an understanding that such frustrations can be stressful, alongside the psychological impact of bearing witness to suffering (Cody, 2007), the second question prompted the respondents to reflect on 'where you find support and strength, to keep going under challenging circumstances'.

Though anonymity was key a small number of demographic questions were added, including years of experience in the agency and service area (Policy and Law, Field Protection, Resettlement and Complementary Pathways).

Given the sensitivity of critiquing an inherently political workplace, a small-scale snowball sampling method was employed for recruitment, in which initial contact was made with individuals, through my personal

Table 4.1: Respondents' roles and years' experience

Role	Years' experience
Policy and Law	29
Regional Rep	12
Head of Office	36
Field Protection	10
Parliamentary Diplomacy	11
Principles to Realities	10
Protection in East	20
Displacement	28
Oversee Protection	12
Coordinator	22

network, who have previously worked in the agency. These contacts then distributed the survey through their own personal networks of colleagues. In all ten responses were collected and, while this is a small sample, the project is qualitative in nature and, together, the respondents have over 190 years of experience with the agency, in various service areas, and have worked on field sites across the globe, with several of them moving into senior roles in the organisation.

Table 4.1 shows the current roles of participants and their years of experience with the Refugee Agency.

Findings and discussion

The two questions used to survey the participants could be considered quite distinct, in purpose and quality. Clearly, any large transnational organisation operating within budgetary constraints and hierarchal management, planning and communication structures will regularly be a source of frustration for employees when dealing with so many stakeholders, while also attempting to provide ever expanding services on the ground. As such, responses could tend towards pithiness and manifest obstacles. Conversely, asking about motivation can often be more of a psychological inquiry, provoking affective reflection. The analysis here thus considers the two questions separately, in the hope that both sets of results provide useful insight. The first set of findings fall under the rubric 'Frustrations', and consist of the largely, though not exclusively, manifest themes of 'Lack of resources', 'Structural fog' and 'Protection drought'. The second set proved to be much more personal, moral and human centred in the themes of responses recorded under 'Motivations': 'The people we work with', 'Positive outcomes' and 'It matters'. Although the following findings are presented separately, ultimately the discussion will attempt to synthesise the inherent relationship between the inevitability of obstacles and the motivations that enable or demand that we must continue to cope.

Frustrations

Lack of resources

The first and most obvious issue emerging from the analysis is a lack of resources. However, while 'budgetary constraints' were mentioned, more often it was insufficient human resources that was seen as a problem.

> [T]here is insufficient human resources for the work we have to do and therefore things do not get finished/drag on. (Head of Office, HO)

The HO also singled out 'inconsistent human capacity on child protection' and an unwillingness or inability to develop a workforce strategy to address such shortcomings. The Parliamentary Diplomat (PD) was also particularly concerned with a similar overarching problem in the 'limited institutional support for career management for colleagues interested in shaping our organization'. This affected the organisation's ability to 'retain talent', 'develop the next generation of leaders' and 'fulfil our roles'. More specifically, in terms of skills, the PD lamented:

> In the not-so-distant past, UNHCR used to be a leader on analysis, reflection and research on refugee issues – all topics directly related to knowledge creation and dissemination and feeding into the exercise of our mandate. The elimination of our research series pointed to a direction of far less interest in this topic.

Structural fog

Alongside limited resources, organisational problems such as bureaucracy, administrative rules, repetition and duplication were frequently cited by respondents. In something of an overlap with skills shortage, a sub-theme of 'ill communication' emerged that points to structural issues in the organisation.

> The planning of our collective work is not done collectively so we don't have a clear way to identify synergies and effectively plan together – and then during implementation of our plan our management complains we are not working effectively together when the problem stems from the way in which planning is done in silos. (Child Protection, CP)

Instances of '[l]ast minute requests becoming the norm', unwillingness to 'share information' or 'requesting more than one person to complete the same task' seemed to lead to frustration and a sense of competition rather than cooperation. At its worst such ill communication led to 'trust issues', turning discussions into a 'personal thing' or ultimately 'leading to confusion over common objectives and undermining outcomes'. This structural fog also affected the capacity for clear analysis and reflection, as outlined by Policy and Law (PL):

> Less reflection leads to poorer long-term thinking and planning which is in turn reflected into multiple initiatives to move into topics where we don't have a clear mandate or a competitive advantage, making us have to dedicate time to initiatives whose value is not really clear in detriment of those closer to our mandate at a time where it faces many challenges.

On a more personal level, of course, this can also lead to internal disaffection: 'Working in a small office, information is important and not being in the information loop is frustrating and can lead to feelings of a hierarchy in the office, not just of a fear of missing out.' (Coordinator)

Protection drought

While any large organisation will have internal issues around resources and organisational structures, the particular global political complexities within which the UNHCR is expected to provide its mandated provisions led to some of the most concerning responses.

> The organization has progressively shifted from a mandate-oriented approach to a donor-oriented approach. The need to survive is understood, but along the way we have lost focus of our mandate in favor of pursuing donors' priorities. Therefore, we are often left to wonder how donor-driven interests are compatible (or not) with the exercise of our mandate. (PD)

The shift towards satisfying the desires of donors, who are largely member nation-states of the UN, also troubled the Regional Rep (RR), who was particularly candid in their replies:

> Increasing and unabashed member state politicking has frustrated me and questions the faith in the so-called 'protection systems' evolved for forced displacement in the last 7 decades. Those who pretend to protect push the limits when it politically suits them, while genuine needs may be allowed to fall by the wayside.

The RR's loss of faith was not only limited to donor related concerns:

> Refugee hosting states and those with IDPs have learnt to 'play the game' with developed western states and leverage other aspects such as trade and regional politics to divert attention/questioning of their record for protecting the forcibly displaced … As expected, affected states play their own increasingly blatant politics by forcing returns/blocking borders/shipping off asylum responsibilities and so on.

Within the internationalist framework of the UN, the sovereign self-interest of member states, in both the Global South and Global North, stands in uneasy – if not dysfunctional – opposition with the universalist principles of accords such as the Universal Declaration of Human Rights and The Convention Relating to the Status of Refugees. This has led to what the RR called a 'global drought of protection' in which few are faithful to the accords they signed up to.

> [T]he environment for international protection today has shrunk to low ebbs and tragically there is no shame left in doing so. The fact that most member states are unclean in this mess - does not allow any of them to hold a moral high ground and assert respect for protection principles. We are in a sea of diminishing returns. (RR)

Such honest reflections are sobering. While additional resources can theoretically be acquired, procedures streamlined and information transparently disseminated, transforming the international protection environment is not a task that the UNHCR alone can undertake. Indeed, this is not within their remit but falls rather to wider, global reappraisal of relationships between nation-states, international humanitarian law, and associated conventions and accords. With the shadows falling over such universal humanitarian principles we turn now to what keeps the professional staff going through such darkness.

Motivations

The people we work with

When asked to reflect on what keeps them motivated, *people* featured prominently in the minds of all respondents, in the form of 'similarly committed colleagues and partners' (PL), 'who are passionate for what we do' (PD). There was near unanimity in the sense that support came in the form of other colleagues. Oversees Protection (OP) expresses the level of coordination and commitment needed:

> For example, timelines and understanding deadlines are a very real concern for reporting – and there are many parts to the whole – the

drafters of the report in one region, the headquarters folks in another that will approve the report, my office liaising with another part of the system for final clearance and final submission for translations. I find support and strength when working with these colleagues and we can talk to each other about what is needed and understand further what obstacles they might be facing and what help is needed, then we can all better meet the deadlines, as well as have greater collegiality, esprit de corps.

RR echoes that 'Real protection, needs hands on sites to make it happen – it is a 360 degree voice and perspective' but most respondents agreed that 'The people we work with' includes 'the local people, forcibly displaced people, local and national authorities and vested motives of regional/global powers' (RR). The sense that complex cooperation is required 'whether internal or external partners/stakeholders' is always guided by the 'vision to achieve protection/solution outcomes' or 'the fact that innocent people suffer for no fault of theirs'. Field Protection (FP) sums up the centrality of people in their mission: 'Direct contact with the people we work for. Listening to their needs and goals, working with them to find solutions, and remembering they deserve our best provides a lot of motivation to work hard and push through the frustrations.'

Positive outcomes

This focus on the ultimate humanitarian purpose of the UNHCR was also apparent from testimonies where, despite the challenges outlined above, the respondents somehow succeeded in moving the dial. However, achieving 'outcomes that benefit displaced and stateless persons' or the 'daily lives of refugees, IDPs and statelessness persons' (PL) is not necessarily solely something that happens in the field. Structure and policy aimed at long-term efficacy were also cited: 'In such a large organization, there aren't really avenues for most of us to have an impact on the organization as a whole, but I see these colleagues as the most substantial contribution I can provide to UNHCR when I am no longer here.' (FP)

Here we see again the importance of recruiting and empowering capable and motivated people in organisational structures, an issue of importance given the relative seniority of the sample. However, it is what such people have been able to achieve in the wider provision of protection such as 'orientations and trainings on programming for child protection which was initially questioned by DSPR [Division of Strategic Planning and Results] and DIP [Division of International Protection] colleagues but which is now seen as a good practice' (CP). This relationship between individuals and organisational structures in achieving positive outcomes was neatly expressed by one participant who described their job as 'Turning protection principles into realities on the ground'.

> Being in a position where I have the right title and portfolio to actually make an impact on the way we work to promote critical thinking, proper planning, strong protection principles and strong relationships with and *accountability to the people we work for*. (Emphasis added)

More succinctly this impact was described as, 'Clear strategic objectives with the intention to achieve them. Changes in people's lives' (OP).

It matters

Ultimately, the motivations of this admittedly small but relatively senior selection of global civil servants fall back on notions of compassion and common humanity based on the liberal and universalist principles that underpinned the foundations of the UN in the post war period. These motivations were described as:

> Commitment to the core mandate of the organization. (PL)

> My work, the mandate, the vision, the continuously increased need for political solutions to displacement [in] the face of growing contemporary challenges. (PD)

Mentions of the mandate refer to the underlying purpose of the UNHCR, and thus the professional staff who are employed there, to monitor the implementation of the 1951 Convention Relating to the Status of Refugees. However, it is not purely principles that matter, and both passion and compassion are part and parcel of the job. Indeed, staff suggested it would be hard to endure the challenges the agency faces were it not for the humanitarian impetus they held at heart. They described this as:

> A belief that it all matters and we can make a difference regardless of challenge. (RR)

> I am drawn to this work as a matter of passion, commitment and because it isn't easy. (HO)

> [T]he fact that the situation globally is worsening, rather than improving is distressing and hardens my resolve. (PL)

Conclusion

The world has seen significant change since the end of the Second World War when universalist, Western liberalist philosophies were drawn upon to create a series of policy documents and associated organisations which, it was hoped, would prevent a repeat of the global carnage that defined the first half of the 20th century. When the Universal Declaration of Human Rights was accepted by the General Assembly of the United Nations on 10 December 1948, the assembly had only 58 member nations. The Soviet Union and certain allies of the Eastern Bloc, such as Poland and Yugoslavia, abstained from voting, as did Saudi Arabia and South Africa. Honduras and Yemen did not vote, and Resolution 217 was passed by 48 countries, from Afghanistan to Venezuela. Liberation struggles across Africa in the 1960s and 1970s, the rise of political Islam in the Iranian Revolution and the collapse of the Soviet Union at the end of the 1980s have all contributed to a proliferation of independent nation-states and today there are 193 members of the UN.

Questions of scale seem important to address here. This survey is simply too small to serve as a guide for policy changes and the findings are informative rather than definitive. Politically and philosophically, many more people are citizens of many more independent states, with competing conceptualisations of rights and duties. The dominance of Western, secular modes of understanding the human condition has been subject to substantial postcolonial critique (Binder, 1999; Mutua, 2002; Cistelecan, 2011; Akoth, 2014) and we live in what Habermas (2008) has called a 'post-secular' world. In many of the 'Western' states that saw, or see, themselves as beacons of universalist liberal principles, a turn towards 'nativist' exclusionary politics is evident (Callan, 2016; Mishra, 2017). The global financial crisis of 2007–2008 – centred particularly in the US, the UK and Europe – hastened a long decade of austerity in these regions, decimating fundamental state services, while the 'rescue' of the banking industry (arguably orchestrated by central banks) channelled a massive wealth transfer from the bottom to the top of the socioeconomic ladder, increasing inequality (Piketty and Goldhammer, 2014; Engler and Klein, 2017; Sherman, 2019). Finally, in terms of scale, in 1951 the UNCHR was responsible for approximately 2 million refugees; in 2023, it estimated there were more than 110 million individuals forcibly displaced worldwide (UNHCR, 2023b; O'Neill, 2024).

This is the context in which discussions around 'offshoring' or 'burden sharing' occur in the Global North. The study here presents a counter-point to such abstract considerations which seek ways to subvert international law and conventions. The testaments presented here do not sit easily with such 'donor-driven' discussions, where 'people' and humanitarian principles were clearly central in the voices of the participants in both their frustrations and motivations. Within the UNHCR, an inability to retain and nurture human resources, and a perceived lack of analysis and reflection, aggravates the structural fog leading to 'poorer long-term thinking and planning'. It might seem that the people tasked with providing protection need some protection themselves. Most troubling is the sense of an overall global protection drought, with 'unabashed politicking' in both rich donor countries and lower income hosting nations both learning to 'play the game'. Yet at the same time the sense of mission and purpose is striking in the motivations of the staff at UNHCR. A spirit that extends across the globe and involves millions of people, from local populations, those displaced and protected, local and national authorities, international organisations and the compassion of countless civil society contributors large and small, creating a global protection regime which does dramatically change people's lives. There is a tension between a global civil society who see shared humanity in the faces of others and the uncivil times in which we seem to live, where the 'other' is demonised and scapegoated for political ends. This contention is, at its core, a philosophical one which extends well beyond issues of forced migration but the mandate and work of the UNHCR act as an exemplar and an attempt to embody and realise our common humanity in a complex and unequal world. Because it matters.

References

Adelman, H. (1983) 'Defining refugees', *Refuge*, 2(4): 1, 3. https://doi.org/10.25071/1920-7336.21445

Akoth, S.O. (2014) 'Human rights critique in post-colonial Africa: Practices among Luo in Western Kenya', *Anthropology Southern Africa*, 37(1–2): 94–106. https://doi.org/10.1080/23323256.2014.969530

Barnett, M.N. (2004) *Rules for the World: International Organizations in Global Politics*, Ithaca, NY; London: Cornell University Press.

Betts, A. (2010) 'The refugee regime complex', *Refugee Survey Quarterly*, 29(1): 12–37. https://doi.org/10.1093/rsq/hdq009

Betts, A. and Milner, J. (2006) *The Externalisation of EU Asylum Policy: The Position of African States*. Working Paper 36. Oxford: Compas, Available from: https://www.compas.ox.ac.uk/2006/wp-2006-036-betts-milner_eu_asylum_policy_africa/

Binder, G. (1999) 'Cultural relativism and cultural imperialism in human rights law comment', *Buffalo Human Rights Law Review*, 5: 211–22.

Callan, B. (2016) 'Civil societies and uncivil times: The rubber band ball of transnational tensions', *Contention*, 4(1–2): 1–14. https://doi.org/10.3167/cont.2016.040101

Cistelecan, A. (2011) 'Which critique of human rights? Evaluating the postcolonial and the post-Althusserian alternatives' in A.S. Rathore and A. Cistelecan (eds) *Wronging Rights?: Philosophical Challenges for Human Rights*, London: Routledge India. https://www.taylorfrancis.com/books/edit/10.4324/9780203814031/wronging-rights-aakash-singh-rathore-alex-cistelecan?refId=be894827-c2b1-4a1b-a875-9992e853e48c&context=ubx

Cody, W.K. (2007) 'Bearing witness to suffering: Participating in cotranscendence', *International Journal of Human Caring*, 11(2): 17–21. https://doi.org/10.20467/1091-5710.11.2.17

Collyer, M. and Shahani, U. (2023) 'Offshoring refugees: Colonial echoes of the UK-Rwanda migration and economic development partnership', *Social Sciences*, 12(8): 451. https://doi.org/10.3390/socsci12080451

Crawley, H. and Skleparis, D. (2018) 'Refugees, migrants, neither, both: Categorical fetishism and the politics of bounding in Europe's "migration crisis"', *Journal of Ethnic and Migration Studies*, 44(1): 48–64. https://doi.org/10.1080/1369183X.2017.1348224

Engler, P. and Klein, M. (2017) 'Austerity measures amplified crisis in Spain, Portugal, and Italy', *DIW Economic Bulletin*, 7(8): 89–93.

Fleay, C. and Hoffman, S. (2014) 'Despair as a governing strategy: Australia and the offshore processing of asylum-seekers on Nauru', *Refugee Survey Quarterly*, 33(2): 1–19. https://doi.org/10.1093/rsq/hdu004

Gammeltoft-Hansen, T. (2011) *Access to Asylum: International Refugee Law and the Globalisation of Migration Control*, Cambridge: Cambridge University Press.

Graeber, D. (2019) *Bullshit Jobs: A Theory*, London: Penguin.

Habermas, J. (2008) 'Notes on a post-secular society', sightandsound, Available from: http://www.signandsight.com/features/1714.html

IGC (2024) *Inter-Governmental Consultations on Migration, Asylum and Refugees (IGC), International Organization for Migration*, Available from: https://www.iom.int/inter-governmental-consultations-migration-asylum-and-refugees-igc

Jacobsen, K.L. and Sandvik, K.B. (2018) 'UNHCR and the pursuit of international protection: accountability through technology?', *Third World Quarterly*, 39(8): 1508–24. https://doi.org/10.1080/01436597.2018.1432346

Křeček, J. (2016) 'Volunteering as protest: Against state failure or the state itself?', *Contention*, 4(1–2): 77–92. https://doi.org/10.3167/cont.2016.040107

Krzyżanowski, M., Triandafyllidou, A. and Wodak, R. (2018) 'The mediatization and the politicization of the "refugee crisis" in Europe', *Journal of Immigrant & Refugee Studies*, 16(1–2): 1–14. https://doi.org/10.1080/15562948.2017.1353189

Mishra, P. (2017) *Age of Anger: A History of the Present*, New York: Macmillan USA.

Molnar, P. (2016) 'The boy on the beach: The fragility of Canada's discourses on the Syrian refugee "crisis"', *Contention*, 4(1–2): 67–76. https://doi.org/10.3167/cont.2016.040106

Mutua, M. (2002) *Human Rights: A Political and Cultural Critique*, Philadelphia: University of Pennsylvania Press.

OHCHR (1967) 'Protocol relating to the Status of Refugees', Available from: https://www.ohchr.org/en/instruments-mechanisms/instruments/protocol-relating-status-refugees

O'Neill, A. (2024) 'Refugees and displaced persons worldwide 1951–2023', Statista, Available from: https://www.statista.com/statistics/1309846/refugees-displaced-worldwide/

Pascucci, E. (2017) 'The humanitarian infrastructure and the question of over-research: Reflections on fieldwork in the refugee crises in the Middle East and North Africa', *Area*, 49(2): 249–55. https://doi.org/10.1111/area.12312

Paukstat, A. and Ellwanger, C. (2016) '"Wir Sind Das Volk": Narrative identity and the other in the discourse of the PEGIDA movement', *Contention*, 4(1–2): 93–108. https://doi.org/10.3167/cont.2016.040108

Piketty, T. and Goldhammer, A. (2014) *Capital in the Twenty-First Century* (Illustrated edition), Cambridge, MA; London: Harvard University Press.

Pinson, H. (2010) *Education, Asylum and the Non-Citizen Child: The Politics of Compassion and Belonging*, Basingstoke: Palgrave Macmillan.

Sherman, E. (2019) 'How great recession bank rescue profited the wealthy and hurt lower income people', Forbes, Available from: https://www.forbes.com/sites/eriksherman/2019/08/30/how-great-recession-bank-rescue-profited-the-wealthy-and-hurt-lower-income-people/

TBP (2024) 'The Bali Process on people smuggling, trafficking in persons and related transnational crime', Available from: https://www.baliprocess.net/

Trauner, F. (2016) 'Asylum policy: the EU's "crises" and the looming policy regime failure', *Journal of European Integration*, 38(3): 311–25. https://doi.org/10.1080/07036337.2016.1140756

UN (1950) *Statute of the Office of the United Nations High Commissioner for Refugees*, Available from: https://www.unhcr.org/sites/default/files/legacy-pdf/4d944e589.pdf

UNHCR (1951) *Convention & Protocol Relating to the Status of Refugees*, Available from: https://www.unhcr.org/media/convention-and-protocol-relating-status-refugees

UNHCR (1998) *Guiding Principles on Internal Displacement*, ADM 1.1,PRL 12.1, PR00/98/109, Geneva: UNHCR, Available from: https://www.refworld.org/docid/3c3da07f7.html

UNHCR (2003) *Internal Flight or Relocation Alternative within the context of Article 1A(2) of the 1951 Convention and/or 1967 Protocol relating to the Status of Refugees (HCR/GIP/03/04)*, Geneva: UNHCR, Available from: https://www.unhcr.org/publications/legal/3f28d5cd4/guidelines-international-protection-4-internal-flight-relocation-alternative.html

UNHCR (2007) *The 10-Point Plan in Action*, Geneva: UNHCR, Available from: https://www.unhcr.org/the-10-point-plan-in-action.html

UNHCR (2020) 'The Global Compact on Refugees', Available from: https://www.unhcr.org/the-global-compact-on-refugees.html

UNHCR (2023a) 'Figures at a glance', Available from: https://www.unhcr.org/figures-at-a-glance.html

UNHCR (2023b) 'Refugee data finder', Available from: https://www.unhcr.org/refugee-statistics/download

UNHCR (2024) 'Global appeal 2024', Available from: https://reporting.unhcr.org/global-appeal-2024-6383

Weiss, T.G. and Korn, D.A. (2006) *Internal Displacement: Conceptualization and its Consequences* (1st edition), London, New York: Routledge.

5

Exploring conceptions of 'home' with Afghan migrant and refugee women

Rabia Nasimi

Migration to the UK from Afghanistan is a relatively recent phenomenon, and it was not until the mid-1990s that people from Afghanistan came to the UK in greater numbers (Fischer, 2018: 21). However, successive episodes of conflict and violence in Afghanistan have led to increased displacement and migration, the most recent following the fall of Kabul to the Taliban in 2021. Thirty years of migration and resettlement have resulted in a significant and vibrant community of first and now 'second-generation' Afghans, born or largely raised in the UK. The latter exist in an almost liminal state, shared by many other migrant communities, where spatial, affective and spiritual tensions on the meaning of 'home' are continuously negotiated. This chapter draws on individual narratives of second-generation Afghans living in London, whose parents fled from Afghanistan. As an activist, scholar and an Afghan raised in the UK, my work with these participants also exists within the fluctuating research positionality of being 'insider-outsider'. Such ordinary complexity of identity is also evident from the voices in this chapter, with some identifying as both British and Afghan while others feeling a need to adjust to a Western way of life. In this we find that 'home' is a multiplicity of spirituality, affect and conflict shaped by wider power relations, but we shall begin with a review of the particular experiences of second-generation migrants in the literature and meanings of home.

Home, migration and the second generation

The concept of home is a spatial, embodied, imagined and symbolic site, as well as a process that is experienced on multiple scales: a dwelling, a neighbourhood, cities and nations and across transnational space (Blunt and Dowling, 2006). While there is a considerable body of research in the field of immigration and ethnic minorities, few studies have focused on the second generation (Timmerman et al, 2003: 1063). The experiences of second-generation refugees are usually subsumed within a wider analysis of ethnic minority people

(Crul et al, 2012). It is important to address this gap because, in comparison to the first generation, those belonging to the second generation do not choose to emigrate and live in another country and, for this reason, their frame of reference is inevitably different (Timmerman et al, 2003: 1068).

In migration research, there is a common expectation that the second generation will be better adapted to the receiving host society than the first generation (Sürig and Wilmes, 2015: 9). There is a need to compare each generation's experience with forced migration because some aspect of the original trauma will be passed down to the next generation (Loizos, 2007). Although the second generation did not actually witness the trauma, Hirsch (2008) argues that they experience 'post memory', a concept that conveys the impact of the transmission on the recipient, which can be so powerful that it can 'constitute memories in their own right' (107). Expanding on Bloch's (1999) work, this research also holds that the refugee cycle does not end with the refugee's generation but extends to the second generation.

Braakman and Schlenkhoff (2007) highlight the considerable pressure experienced by the second generation either to consider themselves to be living in exile with their parents or to make their country of birth the centre of their lives. This contrast highlights the complex experiences faced by refugees, suggesting that we should not homogenise them as a community (Taylor, 2015). A study by Fischer (2018) also confirmed that young people from Afghanistan had difficulties relating to the events and experiences that shaped their parents' perceptions of life in the diaspora. This research, therefore, provides an opportunity to focus on the second-generation Afghans in London 'who are often forgotten in policy arenas and in research' as, inevitably, their experiences may also be shaped by their parents' histories through to migration and resettlement (Bloch, 1999: 16).

In focusing on second-generation migrants in London, the research does not seek to prioritise or reify the significance of ethnicity, but also does not assume that people from Afghanistan constitute a 'community' in an unproblematic sense. Glick Schiller and Çağlar (2009: 184) are critical of 'the persistence of the ethnic lens' whereby 'migrants from a particular nation-state or region are assumed to constitute an ethnic group before their identity, actions, social relations and beliefs are studied' and which overlooks the complex networks of which migrants are a part (Vertovec, 2007). In particular, this research highlights the specific experience of migrants within particular groups while acknowledging the complex and diverse contexts within which their identities are situated.

Home and homeland

Home is therefore both a spatial location and an emotional experience, existing on multiple levels (Blunt and Dowling, 2006). The experiences of refugees demonstrate that home is not necessarily a place of nurture or a private refuge from the external world. For some, home is associated with insecurity, violence, isolation, displacement or oppression, and is potentially a site of conflict (Blunt and Dowling, 2006; Brickell, 2012). Moreover, home often exists within experiences of mobility and an individual may feel a sense of home in multiple contexts (Al-Ali and Koser, 2002; Blunt and Dowling, 2006), a degree of complexity reflected in my own findings.

Several studies also emphasise the importance of the concept of home for people who migrate, and how the process of migration also leads to a new understanding of home (Al-Ali and Koser, 2002; Blunt and Dowling, 2006; Martinez, 2014). Gilao (2008) writes, on being 'home' following her first trip to Somalia from Canada, having been displaced at a very young age, that she found herself in a 'constant mental state of compare and contrast' (Gilao, 2008: 117). Kibria (2002) observed that emotional aspects of home are less explored, such as an ambivalence between different homes, guilt towards family left behind or the difficult return of migrant children who may not conceive their first home to be the home of their parents.

For the second generation, the trip to their parents' home of origin might not be a return 'home' for themselves. Despite this state of uncertainty, Erdal and Oeppen's (2013) participants used the word 'home' to refer both to the Bay Area of San Francisco and to Afghanistan. Hence, the idea of multiple homes, each serving a different purpose, remains possible for the second generation, furthering the potential for conflict and uncertainty in being and belonging.

Migration and transnational studies

The concept of transnationalism has been widely acknowledged as a useful framework for analysing the processes associated with migration since its emergence in the 1990s (Conradson and Latham, 2005). While research on transnationalism originally focused on migration flows to the US, its use has broadened to explore how economic, social and cultural practices and communities are formed and transformed across transnational spaces (Portes 1996; Smith, 2001; Glick Schiller, 2004; Ley, 2004). Faist (2000) proposes the concept of 'transnational social spaces' when focusing on the social meaning of the spaces that transnational communities inhabit and move between, and how space becomes meaningful for members of transnational communities. While Faist adopted a broad focus, Blunt and Bonnerjee (2013) developed the concept of 'diaspora cities' to explore the significance of the city as a site for home, attachment and belonging for those in the diaspora.

The association between the diaspora and the homeland has also been criticised by Brah (1996), who provides an alternative description of the links between the diaspora and the 'homeland', arguing that a 'homing desire' is not the same as a desire for a territorial 'homeland', which can instead be seen as 'the lived experience of a locality' (1996: 192). Braakman and Schlenkhoff (2007) used this concept to argue that, among people from Afghanistan, the sense of belonging to British society is incomplete and, therefore, they experience an unfulfilled 'homing desire'. However, this focused on first-generation migrants and we are left to wonder whether the second generation experience the same tensions.

The immigration experience not only includes crossing national boundaries but also leaving behind family members. Brah (1996) developed the concept of 'diaspora space', which includes both those who have migrated and also those who have not, a perspective that emphasises the contested nature of diasporic spaces. Braakman and Schlenkhoff (2007) found that some young people with few memories of Afghanistan 'yearn to feel they belong somewhere, and they project their desire for a true home' in Afghanistan (11).

Finally, research on 'Afghans in the diaspora' (Chopan, 2000; Nawa, 2001; Braakman, 2005) highlights gendered ideas that dictate what is allowed or restricted for young men and women from Afghanistan. Nawa (2001: 9) states that drinking, smoking and dating, although considered 'un-Afghan' behaviour, are usually tolerated by the community for males. In contrast, restrictions on females are more strictly defined and monitored, with responsibilities placed upon a woman in the belief that 'her reputation is likely to affect the reputation of her entire family' (Braakman, 2005: 85). Girls raised in families from Afghanistan are especially frightened of *ghaybat* (gossip) as this can ruin their family name and honour, which is 'as breakable as porcelain' (Chopan, 2000: 97). In light of this, this chapter focuses primarily on female migrants, exploring how they negotiate the challenges of living as a young woman in London and considering alternatives to gendered ideas of home and identity.

Methodology: Researching home and migration in London

Building on established approaches that have been used to study home and mobility, the project combined qualitative semi-structured interviews and visual perspectives of home to understand the participants' everyday experience of the city. This approach drew on the perspective that people's understandings of the social world emerge from their everyday practices (de Certeau, 1984; Simonsen, 2007; Hitchings, 2012).

The decision to focus on London was based on official statistics for the settlement of people from Afghanistan. According to the Office for National Statistics (2009), the majority of immigrants from Afghanistan settled and remained in London and other research reaffirms that, in contrast to other centres of population, such as Birmingham and Bradford, London is where the largest migrant group from Afghanistan live in the UK (Change Institute, 2009). As participants with refugee backgrounds might have experienced events and situations where their voices were not respected, it was important to make an effort to avoid causing harm in this way (Masten and Narayan, 2012); thus, anonymity and confidentiality were crucial and pseudonyms were used throughout (Seale, 2004: 120). My positionality as an 'insider-outsider' researcher was also important to this research (see Chapter 2, this volume).

The research involved 21 in-depth semi-structured interviews with representatives selected from different 'socio-economic, ethnic and political backgrounds' (Fischer, 2018: 405) to reflect the diversity of the migrant population from Afghanistan. Fourteen females and one male were invited to interview from the following ethnic groups: Tajik, Pashtun, Uzbek and Hazara. English and on occasion Farsi/Dari were used to undertake the interviews.

Discussion: Home as multiplicity

Home, as a concept, becomes more complex when combined with migration, a process which itself involves physical and social movements. Another layer of complexity is then added when focusing on the second generation, given that they face a choice between seeing themselves as living in exile or considering their country of birth as the centre of their life (Braakman and Schlenkhoff, 2007). Roshan illustrates the indefinite nature of home: 'Many things remind me of home, for example, receiving packages from my aunts, such as traditional clothes, dried nuts and fruits, going back to Bedford and eating my mum's traditional food, celebrating Nowruz and many more.'

This section focuses on home as spirituality and religion; a site of emotions and identity crisis.

Home as spirituality and religion

One of the many ways in which home was understood was spiritually, through religious practices. Constructing a sense of religious identity can be seen as a form of belonging which can be mobilised and taken on the migration journey and may also alleviate difficulties with resettlement. Religion can signify a moveable home, a practice or sense of inner belonging and security that is not tied to physical, social or environmental factors but can be transported and practised at any location. It can make the unfamiliar familiar and provide a sense of inner stability that remains unshaken so long as faith remains. Mahtab talks about not feeling at home either in the UK or in Afghanistan: 'Home is a spiritual state of mind for me. I don't feel at home in either place as it has not and does not accept me due to my distinctly dual identity.'

For Mahtab, spirituality was not simply a religious act, but a way to feel that she belonged to something, when she did not feel accepted in society or at 'home'. In this case, the home that has been lost could be Afghanistan but, living in the UK, Mahtab has not been able to create a sense of home. Mahtab's experience confirms Den Boer's (2015) argument that religious practices create a 'spiritual home' which transcend the home that has been lost or left behind. For Alia and Safa, religion was also a means to connect with people with a similar lifestyle and cultural heritage, while in London:

> I remember Eid, we also went to the mosque without fail. At the beginning it was at any mosque, but now there is an Afghan mosque in Hounslow which we all go to. This was because my dad wanted us to keep ties to our roots, and didn't want us to live apart from the Afghan community. When it's Eid we know we have to go, it's a must. (Alia)

> It's compulsory for us to go to the mosque, as it's a Friday and we are off on that day. So, my father says we have to go for our culture. It's good to be mixed with the Afghanistan culture. So, he takes us, he will call each of us down by the name as we get ready to leave home. (Safia)

These experiences confirm Tolia-Kelly's (2004) argument that lived realities of religious practices and beliefs are used by migrants in their everyday lives, including in the domestic space. As highlighted above by Alia's experience, cities have been re-shaped by diasporic communities as they establish places of worship in their new environments, which sometimes shape a shared imagination of the homeland (Anderson, 1991). Although not directly mentioned in the above quotations by Alia and Safa, an undertone of control and coercion exists: visits to the mosque were either 'compulsory' or what a parent wanted. The idea of religion as a home can place increased importance on adherence to religious practices, especially by first-generation migrants towards the second generation. It could be argued that attending mosque was important for Alia and Safa's parents, as an institutional vehicle for the cultural reproduction and socialisation of the second generation (Chong, 1998). Another possible inference is that, when home is defined by religion, a disagreement about religious ideology, or a failure to follow religious restrictions, is no longer simply a matter of disagreement about faith but instead becomes a fracture in the shared home.

Roxanna, who lived in the Netherlands prior to coming to the UK, describes her experience of practising religion as being a unique and valuable experience related to the city of London. The possibility of being united by a common difference from wider society is what makes London special.

She praises the inclusive nature of London, by comparison to her previous village in the Netherlands:

> My younger brother started Quran classes in a mosque. We couldn't do that in Holland. We had to learn it online. So here it's so much easier. We can just go. We were in a village in Holland. We were the only Afghan or Muslim family.

What Roxanna is depicting could be characterised through the urban cosmopolitanism of London as an inclusive space. It could also imply that home as a site of spirituality and religion is not an experience that can be developed anywhere. Cosmopolitanism can be seen as 'a particular stance towards differentness in the world, one that involves an openness to, and tolerance of, diversity' (Young et al, 2006: 1687). Sandercock (2003: 2) argues that cosmopolitan cities are places characterised by 'genuine acceptance of, connection with, and respect and space for, the cultural other', and 'the possibility of a togetherness in difference'. The specific mention of London also confirms the importance of the 'city-scale' in migrant experience, an aspect which is often ignored in research (Glick Schiller and Caglar, 2009). Not all spiritual experiences are positive, however, and Omid recalls his negative experience in a religious setting: 'If you spoke during the Imam's lessons, he put pencils between your fingers. They didn't have positive views on the Jewish community.'

This Imam's punitive behaviour and intolerance of other faiths had an impact on Omid and his own relationship with Islam. This example suggests that the urban cosmopolitanism of London and everyday contact with different social groups do not necessarily translate into values of mutual respect and dialogue (Valentine, 2008). Binnie and Skeggs (2004) note that constructions of cosmopolitanism as being open and tolerant overlook the politics of class, race, gender and sexuality with which cosmopolitanism is intertwined. For Omid, this lack of respect and tolerance discouraged him from religious education and, despite his parents' belief that attending the mosque was good for him and his siblings, he eventually left the classes. Today, Omid and his siblings consider themselves atheists, as his sister, Farida, explains:

> I don't like to be something I am not; I don't want to call myself Muslim and be an advocate for something I'm clueless about. When I went to university, it was full of atheists, full of people who weren't religious, a lot of them did science, and there was always talks of religion and anti-religious views. That's when I started to question my beliefs. I was never a very strong Muslim, perhaps the strongest was when I was forced to go to the mosque. Now, I think there could be something out there, but I don't know what; I don't want to say

whether its God or not, whether I am Muslim or not. I want to go to mosques, churches and see what's out there.

The majority (71 per cent) of Afghans in England do identify as Muslim; 15 per cent identified as Sikh and 4 per cent as Hindu (Change Institute, 2009). Identifying as non-religious and considering oneself atheist is not common among people from Afghanistan and, even when individuals do not hold strong religious beliefs, they prefer to identify as Muslim in public because of social and cultural norms. It would be interesting to explore further how experiences within the home (including the 'religious home') may lead to the second generation distancing itself from religion, as indicated above.

Others, however, felt that there was hostility towards Islam and Muslims in the UK. Elaha talks about how she was grateful that her mother stopped her from wearing a hijab, while Bahar mentions that she will reconsider whether she wants to stay in the UK in the longer term:

> When I was 12, I saw a bunch of hijabis in school, I like the idea of expressing myself as a Muslim because I lacked the knowledge of how to pray etc. So, I told my mother that I wanted to wear a hijab. She argued and said 'No' and to go back to Afghanistan and wear them. I genuinely regret laughing back at her and telling her to go back to Afghanistan. Now that I'm an adult, I came to my senses and actually agree with my mother in terms of not allowing me to wear a hijab, simply because of protection. British people are still hostile towards hijabis, whether it be finding a job or in public transport. (Elaha)

> Mainly because of some Islamophobia, it kind of makes you question whether you would want to stay here. I'm Muslim, and I do feel like I'm very religious and God conscious, so it does upset me. (Bahar)

Elaha and Bahar's awareness of the marginalisation and exclusion they have experienced highlights the importance of Brickell's (2012) arguments about being alert to the negative characteristics of home and the politics of home, domestically and structurally, in understanding the role of London as a place to call home. Religion intersects with migration on a number of scales, from personal embodied practices such as wearing a hijab or engaging with religious institutions across transnational space. Sheringham (2011: 70) argues that the study of religion in the domestic spaces of migrants points to the permeability of boundaries between the sacred and the everyday and, moreover, to how belonging and identity become imbued with religious meanings. Recent research on migrants and discrimination in the UK

(Fernández-Reino, 2020), argues that adult children of migrants may be more likely to see inequalities through the lens of discrimination than the foreign-born population, as the former have higher expectations of equal treatment in UK society. In this way, protracted exposure to a society that espouses the values of tolerance and equality has an effect on how the individual perceives their place within that society, changing expectations of what 'belonging' should entail.

Home as a site of emotions

Home, for some, is a complex mosaic of different, and possibly contradictory, emotions, filled with safety, fear, loss and hate. Home is thus an imaginative and emotional space as well as a physical location (Blunt and Dowling, 2006). For the overwhelming majority of participants, home was where they felt safe, confirming Boccagni's (2017) argument that safety and security, alongside control, are two of the three elements of home. Maryam's accounts of where home is illustrates this, 'Home is simply where I feel safe and comfortable and I have a sense of community'.

For others, serenity and comfort were features of home. Boccagni (2017) argues that making sense of home in migration is partly constructed through constant comparisons between countries of settlement and countries migrated from. Therefore, in this study, when participants mention comfort, they may be relating their understanding of home today to Afghanistan, a place of conflict and instability from which they (and/or their parents) fled. Numerous respondents mentioned that home, for them, meant comfort:

> Home is … what it means to me is a comfortable space where I've got my family. Where I can have my friends over and it's like a comfortable, fun, relaxing, serene environment where I'm just chill. (Aria)

> Being happy and comfortable. Not feeling different or not understanding the surroundings. The familiarity. (Bahar)

> I wouldn't say home is a physical structure. Somewhere where you feel really comfortable. Family, somewhere where you feel a sense of belonging – feeling of comfort. (Omid)

Despite the emphasis on home as a place of comfort, Manzo (2003: 50) calls for a recognition of the full range of emotions and experiences that influence people's relationships with place, acknowledging that home may be a place of insecurity, rather than love and care. This study understands that it is challenging to create feelings of home, security and belonging in the context of mobility and the lifelong impact of losing one's home in a background of war and displacement and therefore it is also important to recognise home as a site of identity.

Home as identity crisis

Research has theorised home as a site of identity and also as a process in which home and its inhabitants transform each other (Dovey, 1985; Miller, 2001; Mallett, 2004). Studies focusing on refugees argue that refugees can experience 'double displacement', whereby home is lost both temporally and spatially, and is no longer experienced in the present (Kabachnik et al, 2010). Such feelings of displacement and confusion regarding participants' identity and where they belong were found in this study, as seen in the following statement from Alia:

> I don't want to be completely Afghan, but I also don't want to become completely British. At home we have certain rules, the moment you step into home you can't speak English. Family gatherings, we need to be available. But when going out with friends, I also needed to be aware of what's going on in society, so I kept up to date with my British side.

Alia's wish to retain aspects of her Afghan identity while also being British relates to Walter's (2001) argument that one can feel 'at home' in one location, in this case, London, while retaining significant identity outside it, in this case, Afghanistan (206). Alia went on to state that her interest in both Afghanistan and the UK was due to her father's approach to her upbringing, highlighting the importance of flexibility and independence in the parents' generation: 'If my dad was too strict on me I would have completely lost my Afghan roots, but because of the balance it made it possible.'

Interest in the 'homeland' and where one has migrated from is the approach taken to socialise the second generation. When looking at what contributes to a sense of belonging, it is important to reflect on the approaches taken by each family to the country of birth and the current place of residence. In Alia's case, 'homeland' has not been left behind, but plays an active role in shaping her identity through providing her with 'emotional, relational, sociocultural and political anchoring' (Kinefuchi, 2010: 244). Roxanna argued that you can have a dual identity, and that an insistence on seeing the way of life from your 'homeland' as the only one would not make you happy:

> I think it's just adjusting to the Western way of life. I mean it doesn't mean you have to forget your culture, your background, but still you need to integrate, umm, or you won't ever be happy and it's a lot different. You might not agree with the people who live in the UK,

but as you have come to this country, so you are going to have to respect them as well. Because they respect you and you live here now. Yeah, I feel it's not one issue. It's about not letting go of your values. Especially Afghans. They are very, this is how it's meant to be.

These examples suggest the importance of understanding identity development among the second generation, given the complexity of how they relate to 'homeland' and the place where they are currently living, in this case London. Although research has demonstrated that identity development continues throughout life (Kroger et al, 2010; Meeus, 2011), few previous studies have examined identity status during young adulthood (Kroger, 2015) but clearly this can be a significant period.

Conclusion

This chapter reveals the importance of religion as a site of safety, home and belonging for the second generation, with religious sites providing a space to connect with people from similar backgrounds. Participants may, however, also have been subtly coerced into attending religious services, as a way of holding on to their norms and values. For participants who came to the UK after a significant time in transit, London was a place of diversity and acceptance, with participants expressing positive views about the presence of religious sites and living in this city. However, my research also uncovered that some participants also felt hostility directed towards Muslims in London, with one participant questioning whether she can continue to live in London in the longer term.

Comfort and safety have emerged as important attributes of home. Given that the majority of the participants are living in London because of war and instability, this choice of qualities could be due to comparisons being made between countries of departure and the country of settlement. The complexity of identity is also evident for the second generation, with some participants stating that they identify as both British and Afghan and others feeling a need to adjust to a Western way of life. For the second generation, who were young adults in this research, it is a period of uncertainty where it is common to question one's identity. The focus in much research has been on home as a site for security but what is left to explore is narratives of home as a site of conflict, which can be framed within literature that emphasises a geopolitical understanding of home, shaped by wider power relations, focusing on gender and generational dimensions.

References

Anderson, B. (1991) *Imagined Communities: Reflections on the Origin and Spread of Nationalism*, London: Verso.

Al-Ali, N. and Koser, K. (2002) *New Approaches to Migration? Transnational Communities and the Transformation of Home*, London: Routledge.

Bloch, A. (1999) 'Carrying out a survey of refugees: Some methodological considerations and guidelines', *The Journal of Refugee Studies*, (12): 367–83.

Blunt, A. and Dowling, R. (2006) *Home*, London: Routledge.

Blunt, A., Bonnerjee, J. and Hysler-Rubin, N. (2013) 'Diasporic returns to the city: Anglo-Indian and Jewish visits to Calcutta in later life' in J. Percival (ed) *Return Migration in Later Life: International Perspectives*, Bristol: Policy Press, pp 141–60.

Boccagni, P. (2017) *Migration and the Search for Home: Mapping Domestic Space in Migrants' Everyday Lives*, New York: Palgrave Macmillan.

Braakman, M. (2005) *Roots and Routes: Questions of Home, Belonging and Return in an Afghan Diaspora,* Amsterdam: Leiden University Press.

Braakman, M. and Schlenkhoff, A. (2007) 'Between two worlds: Feelings of belonging in exile and the question of return', *ASIEN*, 104(1): 9–22.

Brah, A. (1996) *Cartographies of Diaspora: Contesting Identities*, London: Routledge.

Binnie, J. and Skeggs, B. (2004) 'Cosmopolitan knowledge and the production and consumption of sexualised space: Manchester's Gay Village', *The Sociological Review*, 52(1): 39–61.

Brickell, K. (2012) 'Geopolitics of home', *Geography Compass*, 6(10): 575–88.

Change Institute (2009) *The Afghan Muslim Community in England Understanding Muslim Ethnic Communities*, Available from: https://webarchive.nationalarchives.gov.uk/20120920001132/http://www.communities.gov.uk/documents/communities/pdf/1203127.pdf

Chong, K. (1998) 'What it means to be Christian: The role of religion in the construction of ethnic identity and boundary among second-generation Korean Americans', *Sociology of Religion*, 59(3): 259–86.

Chopan, G. (2000) 'Das Lebensgefühl afghanischer Jugendlicher in Deutschland' in *Afghanen im Exil. Identität und politische Verantwortung. Tagung der Evangelischen Akademie Iserlohn im Institut für Kirche und Gesellschaft der EkvW*, 15–17 December, Iserlohn: Evangelische Kirche von Westfalen, pp 95–8.

Conradson, D. and Latham, A. (2005) 'Transnational urbanism: Attending to everyday practices and mobilities', *Journal of Ethnic and Migration Studies*, 31(2): 227–33.

Crul, M., Schneider, J. and Lelie, F. (2012) *The European Second Generation Compared: Does the Integration Context Matter?* Amsterdam: Amsterdam University Press.

de Certeau, M. (1984) *The Practice of Everyday Life*, Berkeley: University of California Press.

Den Boer, R. (2015) 'Liminal space in protracted exile: The meaning of place in Congolese refugees' narratives of home and belonging in Kampala', *Journal of Refugee Studies*, 28(4): 486–504.

Dovey, K. (1985) 'Home and homelessness' in I. Altman and C.M. Werner (eds) *Home Environments*, New York and London: Plenum Press, pp 33–64.

Erdal, M.B. and Oeppen, C. (2013) 'Migrant balancing acts: Understanding the Interactions between integration and transnationalism', *Journal of Ethnic and Migration Studies*, 39(6): 867–84.

Faist, T. (2000) *The Volume and Dynamics of International Migration and Transnational Social Spaces*, Oxford: Clarendon.

Fernández-Reino, M. (2020) 'Migration and discrimination in the UK', Migration Observatory Briefing, Oxford: COMPAS.

Fischer, C. (2018) 'Reframing transnational engagement: A relational analysis of Afghan diasporic groups', *Global Networks*, 18(3): 399–417.

Gilao, M.A. (2008) 'Second-generation connections, rejection and possibility: Being 'home', *International Journal*, 63(1): 116–22.

Glick Schiller, N. (2004) 'Transnationality' in D. Nugent and J. Vincent (eds) *A Companion to the Anthropology of Politics*, Malden: Blackwell, pp 448–67.

Glick Schiller, N. and Çağlar, A. (2009) 'Towards a comparative theory of locality in migration studies: Migrant incorporation and the city scale', *Journal of Ethnic and Migration Studies*, 35(2): 177–202.

Hirsch, M. (2008) 'The generation of post memory', *Poetics Today*, 29(1): 103–28.

Hitchings, R. (2012) 'People can talk about their practices', *Area*, 44(1): 61–7.

Kabachnik, P., Regulska, J. and Mitchnek, B. (2010) 'Where and when is home? The double displacement of Georgian ideas from Abkhazia', *Journal of Refugee Studies*, 23(3): 315–36.

Kibria, N. (2002) *Becoming Asian American: Second Generation Chinese and Korean American Identities*, Baltimore: Johns Hopkins University Press.

Kinefuchi, E. (2010) 'Finding home in migration: Montagnard refugees and post-migration identity', *Journal of International and Intercultural Communication*, 3(3): 228–48.

Kroger, J., Martinussen, M., and Marcia, J.E. (2010) 'Identity status change during adolescence and young adulthood: A meta-analysis', *Journal of Adolescence*, 33: 683–98.

Kroger, J. (2015). 'Identity development through adulthood: The move toward "wholeness"' in K.C. McLean and M. Syed (eds) *The Oxford Handbook of Identity Development*. New York: Oxford University Press, pp 65–80.

Ley, D. (2004) 'Transnational spaces and everyday lives', *Transactions of the Institute of British Geographers*, 29(2): 151–64.

Loizos, P. (2007) 'Generations in forced migration', *Journal of Refugee Studies*, 20(2): 193–210.

Mallett, S. (2004) 'Understanding home: A critical review of the literature', *The Sociological Review*, 52(1): 62–89.

Manzo, L. (2003) 'Beyond house and haven: Toward a revisioning of emotional relationships with places', *Journal of Environmental Psychology*, 23(1): 47–61.

Martinez, A. (2014) 'Locality and journeying in migration' in H. Moeller and A. Whitehead (eds) *Landscape and Travelling East and West: A Philosophical Journey*, London: Bloomsbury, pp 35–44.

Masten, A.S. and Narayan, A.J. (2012) 'Child development in the context of disaster, war, and terrorism: Pathways of risk and resilience', *Annual Review of Psychology*, 63: 227–57.

Meeus, W. (2011) 'The study of adolescent identity formation 2000–2010: A review of longitudinal research', *Journal of Research on Adolescence*, 21: 75–94.

Miller, D. (ed) (2001) *Home Possessions: Material Culture Behind Closed Doors*, Oxford: Berg.

Nawa, F. (2001) *Out of Bounds: Afghan Couples in the United States. A study of Shifting Gender and Identity*, San Francisco: Aftaabzad Publications.

Office for National Statistics (2009) *Migration Statistics 2008 Annual Report*, London: Home Office, Office of National Statistics and Department for Work and Pensions.

Portes, A. (1996) 'Transnational communities: Their emergence and significance in the contemporary world system' in R.P. Korzeniewicz and W.C. Smith (eds) *Latin America in the World Economy*, Westport, CN: Praeger, pp 151–68.

Sandercock, L. (2003) *Cosmopolis II: Mongrel Cities of the 21st Century*, London: Continuum.

Seale, C. (2004) *Researching Society and Culture*, Thousand Oaks: Sage Publications.

Sheringham, O. (2011) *'Thanks to London and to God': Living Religion Transnationally among Brazilian Migrants in London and 'Back Home'*, Unpublished PhD Thesis, Queen Mary, University of London.

Simonsen, K. (2007) 'Practice, spatiality and embodied emotions: An outline of a geography of practice', *Human Affairs*, 17(2): 168–81.

Smith, M.P. (2001) *Transnational Urbanism: Locating Globalization*, Oxford: Blackwell.

Sürig, I. and Wilmes, M. (2015) *The Integration of the Second Generation in Germany: Results of the TIES Survey on the Descendants of Turkish and Yugoslavian Migrants*, Amsterdam: Amsterdam University Press.

Taylor, S. (2015) '"Home is never fully achieved … even when we are in it": Migration, belonging and social exclusion within Punjabi transnational mobility', *Mobilities*, 10(2): 193–210.

Tolia-Kelly, D. (2004) 'Locating processes of identification: Studying the precipitates of re-memory through artefacts in the British Asian home', *Transactions of the Institute of British Geographers*, 29(3): 314–29.

Timmerman et al (2003) 'The second generation in Belgium', *International Migration Review*, 37(4): 1065–90.

Valentine, G. (2008) 'Living with difference: Reflections on geographies of encounter', *Progress in Human Geography*, 32(3): 323–37.

Vertovec, S. (2007) 'Super-diversity and its implications', *Ethnic and Racial Studies*, 30(6): 1024–54.

Walter, B. (2001) *Outsiders Inside: Whiteness, Place and Irish Women*, London: Routledge.

Young, C., Diep, M. and Drabble, S. (2006) 'Living with difference? The 'cosmopolitan city' and urban reimaging in Manchester, UK', *Urban Studies*, 43(10): 1687–714.

PART II

Crucial voices

This second section of the book, 'Crucial voices', foregrounds the narratives and journeys of refugees and migrants themselves, bringing their voices to the fore. In economic, political and academic discourse, such voices are often overlooked and yet are crucial to understanding how policies and practices are experienced by those to whom they are ascribed. Intimate attention to these crucial voices must be central to research, policy development and, ultimately, to shaping meaningful practice interventions. The section brings together chapters that draw on these voices and journeys through the authors' experiences of migration as well as activism, practice and research that directly engage with refugees and migrants, building on the research in the previous section. As such, the section further draws on the voices and experiences of both migrants themselves and the practitioners and activists working on the ground with these communities internationally.

These often-marginalised voices are crucial to understanding refugee and migrant communities. With the authors of the chapters being former migrants and/or activists themselves, they recognise the ethical and power dynamics in drawing directly on the voices of refugee and migrant communities, and they represent a wide range of intersectional identities and experiences.

Rohina Sidiqi and Pearson Nkhoma explore the experiences of unaccompanied minors from Afghanistan in Chapter 6. In Chapter 7, Sarah Crawford-Browne considers trauma-informed responses to migrant journeys, highlighting the need for such interventions to reflect the intersectional and complex experiences of those in her case examples from South Africa, Sierra Leone and Pakistan. Eric Harper and Angela Rackstraw, in Chapter 8, reflect on the narratives of African refugees, based on three decades of work with these communities, framing their discussion in a consideration of issues of relationships, power and intersectionality. In Chapter 9, Pearson Nkhoma draws on his participatory research with child migrants in Malawi, moving within and across borders, and with lived experience of trafficking for prostitution.

6

Unaccompanied Afghan minors in the UK: integration dilemmas in retrospect

Rohina Sidiqi and Pearson Nkhoma

This chapter explores the integration challenges faced by young asylum seekers from Afghanistan and the Middle East into British society. The increase in youth migration due to conflicts has brought the issue of integration to the forefront of Western policy making. The Office of the United Nations High Commissioner for Refugees (UNHCR) (2023; 2025) notes that the world is currently witnessing the highest levels of displacement on record and estimates than 139 million people are forcibly displaced worldwide because of 'persecution, conflict, violence or human rights violations'. UNICEF (2023b) estimated that around 40 per cent of the world's displaced were children and that nearly 450 million children were living in or fleeing from conflict zones and enduring 'unimaginable suffering'. The true global figure could be significantly higher, as data from Palestine, Sudan, Ukraine and the Democratic Republic of Congo had not been fully integrated by either UNICEF or UNHCR by the time this chapter was finalised. As such, these figures could merely be underestimates of the reality.

Afghanistan is one of four countries with the largest displaced populations (UNHCR, 2021), the other three being the Occupied Palestinian Territory, Ukraine and Syria. In Afghanistan, the resurgence of the Taliban and ongoing civil unrest have forced millions of Afghans to leave their homes and seek refuge elsewhere (UNHCR, 2021). The number of internally displaced persons (IDPs) in Afghanistan reached 1.2 million in 2021. It is further estimated that there are more than 2.6 million Afghan refugees and asylum seekers worldwide. Against this background, the UNHCR describes the situation in Afghanistan as dire, with violence and human rights abuses reported daily, leading to an influx of people leaving the country.

Evidence documented by UNICEF (2023a) shows that children and young people remain the most vulnerable and among the worst impacted by displacement, leading to forced child migration as people escape various forms of conflict. Among those forced to leave Afghanistan are unaccompanied minors; that is to say child immigrants arriving in any country without any accompanying adult relatives. With half of the country's population being under the age of 18, it can be inferred that there are more children displaced, both within and outside the country, than are currently documented.

Migration has a significant impact on a child's life. While discussions on migration often focus on the experiences of migrants, from the causes of their departure to their lives as immigrants, this chapter focuses more on their integration into the countries where they seek asylum and refuge. As Elizabeth Hoyt (1961) noted, discussions on integration often prioritise societal integration over cultural integration. This research, however, focuses on the integration of Afghan unaccompanied minors (UMs) into British society. The study will examine the retrospective experiences of individuals who arrived in the UK from Afghanistan as minors, reflecting on their integration journey. This study particularly focuses on the asylum-seeking process for Afghans in the UK, with the goal of understanding the process and challenges Afghan minors face when seeking asylum and how this shapes their integration process. It is worth noting that the UK has accepted a relatively lower number of refugees compared to other European countries. As such, by highlighting their experiences of the integration process, this study could foster more effective integration policy and practice. It is worth noting that the UK has accepted a relatively low number of refugees compared to other European countries.

Intersectionality and cultural identity theory

This chapter is anchored in two core theories: cultural identity theory and intersectionality. Cultural identity theory focuses on the process of forming a sense of self, particularly in relation to cultural and social factors (Syed and Fish, 2018; Zolfaghari et al, 2016). Erikson's theory, presented in *Identity: Youth and Crisis* (1968), and Phinney's *Stages of Ethnic Identity Development in Minority Group Adolescents* (1989) burrow into the process of identity formation across various domains during adolescence. These theories suggest that individuals pass through several stages of identity development, including unexamined identity, exploration and commitment. Both Bestor (1996) and Coutin (2018) suggest that this process takes place through externalisation, deconstruction and reconstruction based on global standards of authenticity.

Using cultural identity theory to analyse the integration dilemmas of Afghans in the UK could involve exploring how these individuals negotiate their sense of self in a new cultural context. The theory is applied to demonstrate how individuals can experience a sense of crisis or confusion as they try to reconcile their cultural heritage with the expectations and norms of their new community. Cultural identity theory can be used as a framework for understanding the experiences of asylum seekers and refugees as they navigate the integration process in a new cultural context. It allows for a deeper understanding of how individuals negotiate their sense of self in relation to cultural norms and expectations, which can inform more effective interventions and support systems.

Kimberlé Crenshaw's (1991) 'Mapping the margins' emphasises intersectionality and how layered oppressions based on different identities such as race, gender, sexuality, class, and nationality or immigration status uniquely impact women of colour. Crenshaw explores the experiences of violence against women of colour who occupy these intersecting identities. She argues that the distinct forms of oppression experienced due to one's intersecting identities converge to produce a unique and complex lived experience that cannot be understood by examining each identity in isolation. The argument is that oppression, exploitation or experience cannot be fully understood without considering all the intersecting identities and the subsequent experiences at the point of their convergence and beyond.

Crenshaw situates violence against women of colour within a larger context of structural inequality and contends that legal remedies and policies must reflect the complex ways that different forms of oppression intersect. Crenshaw's work is relevant to this study because it emphasises the importance of comprehending the complex matrix of identity that underlies different layers of exploitation. While Crenshaw primarily addresses women's experiences, the intersectionality approach is broadly influential and suggests the need to consider multiple forms of oppression when evaluating the experiences of child refugees (Collins, 2019). This is significant for the study as successful integration requires positive relationships, social interactions and a sense of belonging, along with consideration of various intersectional layers of identities and the subsequent experiences of oppression and exploitation.

The relevance of intersectionality in this chapter is particularly evident in an ethnographic study by Thompson et al (2022) with women migrants and refugee women, half of whom were also from Afghanistan. However, Thompson et al's study, grounded and informed by principles of community-based participatory research (CBPR) to explore the lived experiences of migrants, asylum seekers and refugee women, was not primarily centred on the participants experiences as UMs. Nonetheless, the study provides rich insights into the traumatic and intersectional vulnerabilities and experiences of the refugees and migrant women within the UK because of their gender, race and ethnicity, and immigration status.

However, the question that remains unanswered is 'what experiences of the asylum-seeking process do UMs endure?' Thus, in this study, we extend Thompson et al's focus with an exploration of integration for UMs. A synergy of cultural identity and intersectionality further provides a platform to burrow into the experiences of UMs facing multiple forms of discrimination, vulnerabilities and exploitation requiring unique policy and practice intervention. As such, these theoretical frameworks shed light on the integration issues faced by Afghan UMs in the UK and offer best practices for facilitating their smoother assimilation into the society at large.

Research design

This retrospective study was enriched with a qualitative design. Silverman (2022) argues that qualitative research explores the meaning of a phenomenon that occurs in natural settings with the goal of emphasising the importance of how people interpret their own experiences and understand their worlds. The goal for this study was to generate valuable insights into the experiences of unaccompanied Afghan minors and how the participants retrospectively made sense of those experiences, with a particular focus on the integration process. Nine adult Afghan former asylum seekers who arrived in the UK as minors were interviewed for this study. Of the nine respondents, three were females and the rest were males, all who arrived in the UK as minors. Six held British citizenship, one had an indefinite leave to remain visa, and the status of the last respondents was unclear. Most were familiar with the asylum and integration processes, underscoring their understanding of the associated challenges.

Data was iteratively analysed (Charmaz and Bryant, 2018; Silverman, 2024), aiming to reveal patterns and themes. Interviews were transcribed in verbatim, including pauses and stutters. After familiarisation with the data and the identification of initial themes, a codebook was created. Responses were coded based on identified themes. Codes were refined and organised into broader themes, and narratives were developed to represent key findings. This methodology of analysis provides a robust framework for examining the intersectionality of the participants. Participants were given the opportunity to review the final transcribed data. As emphasised by Kline (2017), these steps were crucial for obtaining findings which were accurate in reflecting participants' own accounts.

Ethical considerations were paramount in this study considering the sensitive nature of the topic. Participants freely gave their consent by signing an informed consent form. Their right to withdraw at any point of the study was always emphasised. This was critical considering that nearly all unaccompanied and separated children, as Li et al (2016) point out, have to live with the trauma. Participants were assured that no harm was intended, following the guidelines of Graham and Phelps (2016). This was important in building trust with participants; as Bowen (2008) highlights, trust is critical in the research process as it can positively influence participants' willingness to share their experiences. A tenth participant withdrew from the study without pressure when he felt uncomfortable sharing his experiences as an unaccompanied child asylum seeker. One potential respondent declined participation, fearing that the researcher was a government agent. All participants were also given a contact card, signposting them to a range of service providers as participation in the study could evoke traumatic memories during or after their participation. Ethical approval was obtained from Goldsmiths, University of London.

Findings and discussion
Being an unaccompanied Afghan minor in the UK

Afghan minors encounter unique hurdles, including the ongoing conflict in Afghanistan, cultural and linguistic differences, and limited resources. Many arrive in the UK either to reunite with their families or to escape the hardships they faced in Afghanistan. Upon arrival, they are typically accommodated in foster care or with other young people, and have access to education and healthcare. It is critical to understand the baggage the young Afghans arrive with and the reasons why they are fleeing Afghanistan. Youth in Afghanistan face forced marriages, human rights violations and trauma resulting from the ongoing armed conflict. The increasing influence of the Taliban has led to internal displacements, with many seeking refuge in neighbouring countries or embarking on perilous journeys to European countries like the UK.

Some of the children die prematurely before reaching a safe place or the moment they embark on their journey of 'leaving' (see Nkhoma's chapter, in this collection). But even those who make it to such countries are further subjected to inhuman conditions (see Harper and Rackstraw's chapter in this collection). While young girls have suffered gross violation of their rights, an age-old practice entailing sexual abuse of young boys has evolved into boys being kidnapped, trafficked and raped by wealthy and powerful men in Afghanistan. This involves young boys dealing with *bacha bazi* (boy play). The core of *bacha bazi* comprises prepubescent boys dancing for and entertaining a group of men, including transgenerational same-sex relationships between younger men (the *bachas*) and older men (the *bacha baz*). It has evolved into the kidnapping, trafficking, rape of these boys and abuse by wealthy or powerful individuals in Afghanistan (Prey and Spears, 2021). Thus, while escaping the armed conflict, there are other factors that force children to escape. The conflict has worsened these factors.

In the UK, Afghan asylum seekers often grapple with several challenges. To understand these challenges, participants identified several issues. Many cited cultural and language differences as primary obstacles. Some recalled experiencing loneliness in their early years. Asela, a female participant, reflecting on this, said:

> To live between two worlds, two cultures. To fit in with my friends in school and college and to please my parents, who were part of the

Afghan community. It's extremely hard for young girls to grow up in the West and yet satisfy the communities they came from, which remain conservative in the West.

The experience of racism was prevalent among all participants. They mentioned frequent cases of terms like 'terrorists' being used against them. Some respondents persistently experienced subtle forms of derogatory jokes about refugees. Bullying was also one of the critical issues participants mentioned, capturing the extent of hostility they faced as minors and continued to face into adulthood. This is how Sara, a female participant, explained her experience of racism in the UK and within the asylum-seeking system: 'While I haven't faced explicit racism or discrimination, I have encountered a lot of implicit racism in the form of jokes about refugees or "terrorists" made at work, school, or university. Despite not being directed at me, these made me feel uneasy'.

There were a few participants, like Shamas, who believed they didn't face racism, noting the respect they received during festivals like Eid and Christmas: 'I only know about Christmas; I have never encountered prejudice. I observed that they respected our Eid. Thus, I don't think I encountered any racism.'

Trauma, heightened by separation from family, was profound for some participants like Masum who shared harrowing experiences of his journey from the onset of his journey and near-fatal experience in both Iran and Europe. But arriving in the UK was even muddled with uncertainty and a strong sense of anxiety as a child with limited support:

> I was the youngest one from the group, all boys. I saw that the [Iranian] police started firing at us I could see people got injured, saw a lot of people die, lots of blood. I saw three people die. I then noticed lots of blood in my shoes and clothes. I was not injured but by other people. Then in Greece jungle, I spent five days without food and water. The journey was by tube, not boat, with 42 people. The tube had gone down because it was not able to carry 42 people. The boys called the Greece police then they took us. We almost died but the police came and rescued us. It took two years for my papers to be processed for me to come to the UK. I lived with my uncle for some time, but his house was very small, so social service put me in a shared house where I now live. I am still terrified by my own memories when I think about the journey.

Despite these traumatic experiences, Masum indicated he had not received any support for his trauma experienced during dislocation. This is an observation that has also been made by other scholars (see Li et al, 2016). This was despite the clear mental health issues that resulted from the journey, further complicating his integration. To navigate this situation, most of the participants indicated detaching themselves from their childhood memories, preferring rather to share their experience of integration in young adulthood or adulthood.

In addition to mental health being unattended, housing and schooling remain problematic for UMs as Masum highlights. Many participants found it hard to locate suitable living spaces and schools that accommodated their needs due to a lack of specific referral services. Asela added: 'As a young girl seeing my parents went through an extremely hard time trying to find their way around as new arrivals (housing, to find schools for my siblings and me as we were all at different stages of education from primary to high school).'

The respondents indicated that finding a place to live was challenging, and those already of school age struggled to find institutions where they could easily fit in.

The integration process for Afghan minors

Respondents highlighted deficiencies in the system for integrating UMs. Rauf, one of the male participants, stated:

> Those arriving with family have family support, while unaccompanied minors do not have this support and are often lost in the system. They are allocated social workers, but most of the time, these professionals are not trained well to handle children and young people from different ethnic and cultural backgrounds, especially from countries like Afghanistan, where many young people experience trauma and violence and bring such experiences with them when they come.

It is therefore not surprising that all participants described the integration process as increasingly challenging. This, they said, was due to limited time and financial constraints, with local authorities under pressure to meet their needs. On this, Rauf explained:

> I think that the experience of young people arriving in the UK has become less positive and more difficult because of a lack of resources and the pressure on local authorities to meet the needs of many refugees and asylum seekers. It's not just about providing them with basic accommodations; it's about offering comprehensive support for their integration, including mental health services, education, and employment opportunities.

It is evident that the integration of Afghan minors seeking asylum in the UK is a complex and multifaceted process, marked by numerous challenges. In essence, Afghan minors in the UK grapple with issues like language barriers, loneliness, bullying, discrimination, racism, the lasting effects of trauma, and access to social services like housing and schooling.

Overlooked vulnerabilities and systemic failures

Developing effective strategies to assist asylum seekers in rebuilding their lives in the UK is crucial. Ehntholt and Tsoucalas (2017) conducted a review of 11 studies of the mental health of Afghan refugees in the UK. They found prevalent issues such as depression, PTSD and cultural barriers. Such findings form the basis of the argument that Li et al (2016) make in their critical piece. Participants' intersectional vulnerabilities, tied to their multiple identities, were often overlooked, with support limited to their asylum eligibility. Mental health issues were rarely addressed in the services they accessed, and there was minimal acknowledgement of their cultural diversity, as if their cultural identities were invisible. As York et al (2018) rightly note, the free language sessions that the UK government offers to support the development of asylum seekers' language skills are generic and hardly tailored to the specific needs of the people based on age and other intersectional complexities. Yet, effective integration, as has been shown, is something that requires a deep understanding of the children's culture, values, systems as well as the intersecting causes for them fleeing their countries. Similar to our findings, research by Zaman and Khan (2017), which analysed the experiences of 15 Afghan refugees in the UK using interpretative phenomenological analysis (IPA), identified four key challenges: social isolation, language difficulties, employment and education obstacles, and a lack of trust. According to participants, the focus is primarily on getting the children integrated, with little consideration for the cultural value they might bring to British communities. Despite this emphasis on integration in the local communities, there is limited support to make it happen. Many participants reported being housed in shared estates and relocated frequently, disrupting their integration process. For some, like Masum, this disruption brought back memories of their escape, making them feel as though they were 'escaping' again – only to another unfamiliar community where they had to start the integration process once again.

These results emphasise the importance of culturally informed policies for the integration of Afghans. Moussaoui and Al-Ali (2018) conducted a study on the role of social networks in the integration of 32 Afghan and Iraqi refugees in the UK. Their research highlighted three key social networks: extended family, co-ethnic networks and mainstream networks, which offered vital support and fostered a sense of belonging. Likewise, Mahmoodi (2018), like Harris-Hogan and Konecny (2017), further explains that some communities in the UK view Afghans as threats to British culture, identity and community cohesion, leading to hostility and violence against them. These challenges can be daunting for children, especially UMs, seeking asylum.

The responsibility of integration is often left completely to those who are seeking asylum. This further exerts pressure and leads to a double burden on the UMs. They are expected to navigate discrimination and lead a resilient life with limited or no support at all for their mental wellbeing. Effective integration would therefore require training for service providers and sensitivity to cultural diversity. Additionally, it is crucial to treat an UM as a child in line with the Children's Act that demands safeguarding children regardless of their immigration status. Sara explained:

> I was a separated child, living with my sister, who was only 19 at the time. It was very challenging to convince the government to allow me to stay with my sister. Beyond the legal steps, little further was done to show support for integration. Once I was granted leave to remain, I had access to child support and then attended school, and my sister helped us find housing, etc. There was no additional support. I am not sure what additional support refugees are eligible for and what distinguished my situation from that of a family.

Considering cultural identity and using intersectionality as a theoretical lens, best practices for integration may include fostering cultural exchange, providing language and job skill development opportunities, and offering psychological support. Due to a lack of referral to available services, many UMs felt cut off from the community and concerned about the future. On this, Asela stated: 'In the UK, you must integrate yourself into society; there is no program in place to make you aware of services or provide information about what to do and where to go if you need help with services such as health, education, employment or housing.'

All participants in this study revealed that the administrative system for integrating UMs has not been sufficient to handle the numerous difficulties; and considered it as largely ineffective for UMs. Cultural identity theory highlights how these challenges can arise from the wider social and cultural contexts in which Afghan minors seek asylum. For example, housing and schooling problems may result from inadequate resources and support. Additionally, discrimination and racism can stem from negative stereotypes and attitudes towards refugees in the host country. Cultural identity theory also emphasises that these challenges can lead to individual and collective action, such as seeking support from informal networks or engaging in activism to change policies and attitudes towards refugees.

It is with this understanding that some of the participants felt that the integration process was being made harder and nearly impossible to engage with. One participant identified austerity as a driving factor for the reduction in support. Like others, this participant viewed the age assessment process as complex and less child friendly. One male participant recalled how the age assessment spiralled to episodes of medicated depression:

> In the beginning, the Home Office accepted my age. I started to go to school then they told me we don't accept your age because there was a fight at school; boys brought knives to school, that's why they sent a lot of us for age assessment, and I was one of them. I was not part of the fight, but teachers and families complained that they are over 18. I have gone through an age assessment, and they accept me as a minor, then the school again said he is not underage. Again, I have gone through the age assessment, and it was very scary, the age assessment took three hours, and five people were there. I was very scared of what would happen. They have put me under pressure. They have asked many questions about Afghanistan. I told them I didn't live in Afghanistan. I lived in Peshawar (Pakistan). But still, they pressured me to answer the questions. From 2017 to 2019 I was on depression medication because the age assessment matter was like a trauma for me.

Experiences such as these fuelled their anxiety of the whole asylum system and impacted their mental health. Barret et al (2019) and Li et al (2016) also found that asylum seekers reported an absence of support during integration processes, regarding their traumatic experiences and for their mental health. This particularly impacted UMs in Barret et al's study and left them feeling lost in the system.

Based on this, it is concerning that practitioners such as social workers responsible for guiding minors through the integration process are not well-trained in dealing with diverse backgrounds, particularly those who have experienced trauma and violence. This calls for more specialised training for professionals working with minors from different cultural backgrounds. The fact that most minors have used integration as a path to academic success shows the potential benefits of successful integration. However, it is crucial to identify and address the barriers that prevent successful integration, which appear more systemic than individual. This highlights the need for more holistic and coordinated support for UMs, involving key stakeholders such as schools, social services and community organisations.

Overall, this chapter provides valuable insights into the challenges and opportunities of integrating unaccompanied Afghan minors into UK society. The findings should inform policy and practice to ensure these vulnerable young people receive the support they need to thrive in their new homes. Similar to Hamilton's (2020) argument, integrating young Afghans into UK society is a complex process requiring both language proficiency and an awareness of cultural norms and nuances. Hamilton (2020) contends that successful integration into a new context necessitates an understanding of local culture, values and processes.

For Afghan minors, who come from a culture vastly different from that of the UK, developing a cultural identity can be a challenging process. Our findings suggest that the social workers responsible for guiding these minors through the integration process need to be better trained in dealing with children from diverse backgrounds. This lack of training can make it difficult for social workers to assist Afghan minors in navigating the complex cultural differences between their home country and the UK. As a result, some minors may require additional support to succeed in the integration process. To this end, successful integration requires a comprehensive approach that addresses both the individual needs of Afghan minors, such as their cultural identity development, and the systemic factors impacting their integration, such as access to resources and supportive social services. There is also the need to further invest in the services devised to support and safeguard UMs while supporting integration.

Conclusion: Addressing complex needs

This research provides invaluable insights into the myriad challenges confronted by Afghan minors, whether accompanied or unaccompanied, during their journey through the asylum application process and their pursuit of integration within the UK. Many of these young individuals have escaped harrowing violence and conflicts in Afghanistan, seeking refuge and safety in the UK. However, upon their arrival, they frequently encounter rights violations, abuse, discrimination and limited access to essential services, resulting in profound mental trauma. Despite the UK's efforts to facilitate integration, Afghan minors continue to grapple with numerous obstacles, especially in the context of an ever-evolving socio-political landscape. This chapter emphasises the urgent need for targeted policies and practices to address the multifaceted challenges faced by Afghan minors seeking asylum in the UK.

While this chapter has provided valuable insights, it is essential to acknowledge some key limitations experienced in undertaking this study. Firstly, we only involved a relatively small sample of participants, which may not fully represent the broader community of UMs, let alone all those from Afghanistan. Secondly, we have only explored participants' retrospective experiences as UMs. There is, therefore, a need to explore the experiences of integration for UMs at an earlier stage of their settlement.

References

Barret, E., Löfgren, E., Upthegrove, R. and Welander-Vatn, A. (2019) 'Challenges faced by refugees and asylum seekers in accessing mental healthcare: A literature review', *BJPsych International*, 16(2): 33–5.

Bestor, T. (1996) 'Competitive festivals and the structuring of tradition in Japan' in T.J. Csordas (ed) *Embodiment and Experience: The Existential Ground of Culture and Self*, Cambridge: Cambridge University Press, pp 238–62.

Bowen, G.A. (2008) 'Building trustworthiness in qualitative research: The listening and relational credibility tasks', *Journal of Personality Assessment*, 90(4): 312–25.

Charmaz, K. and Bryant, A. (2018) 'Grounded theory and credibility' in D. Silverman (ed) *Qualitative Research: Issues of Theory, Method and Practice* (3rd edition), London: SAGE, pp 291–309.

Collins, P.H. (2019) *Intersectionality as Critical Social Theory*, Durham, NC: Duke University Press.

Coutin, S.B. (2018) *The Culture of Legality: Immigration and the Legal Process in the United States*, Cambridge: Cambridge University Press.

Crenshaw, K. (1991) 'Mapping the margins: intersectionality, identity politics, and violence against women of color', *Stanford Law Review*, 43(6): 1241–300.

Ehntholt, K.A. and Tsoucalas, G. (2017) 'Mental health needs of Afghan refugees in the UK: A review of the literature', *Journal of Immigrant and Minority Health*, 19(3): 705–11.

Erikson, E.H. (1968) *Identity: Youth and Crisis*, Toronto: Norton & Co.

Graham, C. and Phelps, R. (2016) 'Ensuring ethical integrity in educational research involving human participants', *International Journal of Research & Method in Education*, 39(1): 4–18. https://doi:10.1080/1743727X.2015.1082579/

Hamilton, T. (2020) 'The role of social workers in facilitating the integration of refugees and asylum seekers: A systematic review', *British Journal of Social Work*, 50(7): 2071–90.

Harris-Hogan, S. and Konecny, P. (2017) 'Refugees, terrorism and violent extremism: From misconceptions to empirically-based strategies', *Journal of Ethnic and Migration Studies*, 43(9): 1466–84.

Hoyt, E.E. (1961) 'Integration of culture: A review of concepts', *Current Anthropology*, 2(5): 407–26.

Kline, R.B. (2017) *Principles and Practice of Structural Equation Modelling* (4th edition), New York: Guilford Publications.

Li, S.S., Liddell, B.J. and Nickerson, A. (2016) 'The relationship between post-migration stress and psychological disorders in refugees and asylum seekers', *Current Psychiatry Reports*, 18: 1–9.

Mahmoodi, M. (2018) 'Challenges faced by refugees and asylum seekers in the UK', *Regional Science Inquiry*, 10(1): 111–15.

Moussaoui, L. and Al-Ali, N. (2018) 'The role of social networks in the integration of Afghan and Iraqi refugees in the UK', *Journal of Refugee Studies*, 31(4): 526–46.

Phinney, J.S. (1989) 'Stages of ethnic identity development in minority group adolescents', *The Journal of Early Adolescence*, 9(1–2): 34–49.

Prey, E. and Spears, K. (2021) 'What about the boys: a gendered analysis of the US withdrawal and Bacha Bazi in Afghanistan' (24 June 2021), Washington DC: New Lines Institute, Available from: https://newlinesinstitute.org/gender/gender-as-an-analytical-tool-for-foreign-policy/what-about-the-boys-a-gendered-analysis-of-the-u-s-withdrawal-and-bacha-bazi-in-afghanistan/

Silverman, D. (2022) *Doing Qualitative Research* (6th edition), London: Sage.

Silverman, D. (2024) *Interpreting Qualitative Data* (7th edition), London: Sage.

Syed, M. and Fish, J. (2018) 'Revisiting Erik Erikson's legacy on culture, Race, and ethnicity', *Identity*, 18(4): 274–83. https://doi.org/10.1080/15283488.2018.1523729

Thompson, N., Nasimi, R., Rova, M. and Turner, A. (2022) *Community Work with Migrant and Refugee Women: 'Insiders' and 'Outsiders' in Research and Practice*, Bingley: Emerald Group Publishing.

UNHCR (2023) 'Refugee data finder', Available from: https://www.unhcr.org/refugee-statistics/

UNHCR (2021) 'Afghanistan situation', Available from: https://www.unhcr.org/en-us/afghanistan-emergency.html

UNHCR (2025) 'Global appeal 2025', Geneva: UNHCR, Available from: https://reporting.unhcr.org/global-appeal-2025-executive-summary

UNICEF (2023a) 'Child displacement and refugees', UNICEF DATA, Available from: https://data.unicef.org/topic/child-migration-and-displacement/displacement/

UNICEF (2023b) 'For every child: UNICEF Annual Report 2023', New York: UNICEF, Available from: https://www.unicef.org/reports/unicef-annual-report-2023

York, H., Punton, M. and Kullman, K. (2018) 'Exploring the role of ESOL classes in refugees' lives in the UK', *Journal of Refugee Studies*, 31(2): 178–96.

Zaman, H. and Khan, H. (2017) 'Integration experiences of Afghan refugees in the UK: A qualitative study', *Journal of Ethnic and Migration Studies*, 43(13): 2234–50.

Zolfaghari, B., Möllering, G., Clark, T. and Dietz, G. (2016) 'How do we adopt multiple cultural identities? A multidimensional operationalization of the sources of culture', *European Management Journal*, 34(2): 102–13.

7

Evolving paradigms: witnessing refugees' unstable passages to safety

Sarah Crawford-Browne

The journeys of people travelling in search of refuge or opportunity are perilous. For most, experiences of dangerous home circumstances are exacerbated by treacherous departures, risky flights, and survival on the margins of an unfamiliar, inequitable society. Hearing the stories of family remaining at home extends these stresses. Many travellers return to rebuild in ongoing volatility. There is little stability or safety within these passages, but rather ongoing adversity and danger, particularly for those in the Global South.

Over the years, humanitarian workers have witnessed these journeys using evolving paradigms. Horrified by events and concerned about potential post-traumatic stress, responders initially drew on psychiatric concepts and trauma counselling approaches. Fear for children's wellbeing strengthened ecological interventions. The central humanitarian agencies combined these into triaged mental health and psychosocial support guidelines in emergency settings. However, divisions remain between those advocating for 'trauma-focused', 'psychosocial' or 'global mental health' approaches.

This chapter reflects on these developments drawing on case examples from Pakistan, Sierra Leone and South Africa, derived from personal reflections on two decades of work within post-conflict communities and humanitarian emergencies. It considers the diverse impact of complex emergencies across populations and offers critical reflections on the concepts of 'psychosocial', 'trauma-informed', 'trauma-focused', 'mass trauma' interventions, and 'post-traumatic stress' within humanitarian responses. It concludes that, while witnessing these threatening journeys prompts action, supporting people to reach psychological and physical safety requires complex, intersectoral, multi-layered and resourced interventions grounded in intersectionality and reflexive practice.

My journey started with community work in my home country, where I learned to negotiate power and positionality within a recently democratising South Africa. Yet in post-conflict Sierra Leone it was difficult to find my voice while navigating powerful international organisations, conflicting intervention approaches, disempowered communities and my own intersecting identities as a white African. I was relieved to move to a locally-led disaster response organisation in Pakistan but, as a lone foreigner, found lessons in listening, teamwork and task-shifting. Our travels as humanitarian workers in complex international spaces and emerging paradigms require deep reflexivity.

Witnessing refugees' unstable passages to safety

Natural disasters, war, economic hardship and exile disrupt lives with experiences that are hard for those witnessing to imagine. These disruptions affect individuals, but also their families, communities and societies, causing further dislocation for the person. Initially, humanitarian mental health programmes drew on the individualised psychiatric and trauma counselling approaches developed in more stable contexts. More recently, psychosocial, population-based mass trauma, trauma-informed and trauma-focused interventions jostle in emergency settings.

The three cases presented in this chapter illustrate that people respond differently in contexts of shared trauma, and recovery occurs within social systems. Integrating trauma recovery principles while providing basic needs strengthens the supportive social milieu. Community storytelling that witnesses injury and perpetration rebuilds ruptured community narratives, facilitating collective and individual reconnection. Collective recovery is supported or hindered by the political and economic structures embedded within societies. Therefore, recognising that people in shared crises are part of disrupted social systems offers additional opportunities for support.

Building a camp on trauma intervention principles

Tasked with setting up an emergency camp, I sat on a pile of 200 tents in the middle of a cornfield. Surrounded by the austere mountains of northern Pakistan, we were experiencing frightening aftershocks every few minutes that would gradually dissipate over the next 18 months. Three days earlier, a destructive earthquake had flattened the nearby scenic village of Balakot and shaken tenant farmers' homes and livelihoods from the surrounding terraced mountain slopes. Later, we learned that the 2005 South Asia Earthquake had killed at least 75,000 people in Pakistan, Kashmir and India, with a further 3 million losing their homes and livelihoods.

People's facial expressions spoke of shock, anxiety and grief. Groups of men and boys stood at the roadside or distribution points, waiting. Piles of donated blankets, clothing and food lay on the pavements, but they were looking for tents. There were not enough tents. Survivors were sleeping in the open and, every night, temperatures were plummeting. Snow was expected soon. Families were separated as many men had migrated to work in urban Pakistan and the Middle East and were now desperately trying to connect with family members deep in the mountains. Women led many of the secluded households on the surrounding slopes despite the strongly patriarchal traditions. Their young sons were negotiating village resources. The stress was tangible.

Witnessing great suffering while sitting on that huge pile tents, I considered my clinical social work toolbox. Like those who had sent clothes and food on the generous truck convoys snaking up the Silk Road, I felt compelled to help. I had arrived a month earlier to facilitate training on the impact of traumatic stress on Afghan refugee children. Witnessing the horror of Balakot's destruction, I assumed that my experience as a trauma therapist would be helpful. However, these circumstances were far from a stable counselling space. I knew nothing about running a camp for displaced people or the customs and languages of northern Pakistan.

Drawing on my trauma therapy toolbox, I designed the camp as a supportive, safe social milieu for psychosocial recovery while providing basic needs. Guided by Judith Herman's (1997) classic trauma recovery pathway, my colleagues and I ensured that consciously caring relationships and safety underpinned every activity within the camp. Safety is understood as an innate human need, with the establishment of physical and psychological safety accepted as a requirement for recovery after traumatic exposure and the first step in trauma recovery (Briere and Scott, 2014; Herman, 1997). Assuming that people may be struggling with traumatic stress, the work with remembrance, memories, reconnection, and commonality would follow as people were ready (Herman, 1997).

Clearing the cornfield, erecting tents and digging latrines were the priorities. The Pakistani army agreed to provide this logistical support. Once they erected all 200 tents, my colleagues and I realised they had created a military-style camp with the tents less than a metre apart. This closeness would not be safe or comfortable for most communities, but my colleagues explained that it would be even worse for Hindko women who live by codes of honour and rarely relate to people outside their families. Despite the urgency to provide accommodation, the first task was to convince the military officer to re-erect the entire camp with well-spaced tents and room for each family to have a hearth and for children to play. This was the first of many heated debates over the next 18 months.

As part of designing the camp as psychosocially supportive and culturally sensitive, we carefully welcomed each family and delivered materials to their tent. Beyond meeting subsistence needs, we sought to create infrastructure and a social environment that was emotionally supportive, spiritually and culturally appropriate, and psychologically safe. We consciously worked towards providing all basic needs and sharing information in a manner that maintained dignity, routine, participation and caring relationships. A corner in the camp was set aside as a playground and school to return children to routine as quickly as possible. Men could pray and meet in a tent dedicated as the mosque. On the back mountain slope, we set aside a tent initially for counselling groups. When it became evident that residents were not seeking counselling, it was used for women to breastfeed, relax privately or share green tea, enabling informal support. This space allowed us to facilitate meetings with resident representatives to build participation in managing the camp, offer brief psycho-information and support, and share information about resources, government plans and the stabilisation of the mountain passes for their return home. This approach directly speaks to the intersectionality approach that acknowledges the societal power structures and differing needs of people related to their age, gender, ethnicity, religious and cultural diversity (Collins, 2019). Returning to routine, understanding physiological arousal, regaining personal control, and strengthening personal and social efficacy are all recognised elements of trauma recovery (Briere and Scott, 2014; Herman, 1997).

Within the first weeks, we employed ten trilingual local young women as psychosocial workers within our base and the surrounding camps to work alongside me as the only foreigner. Their training ran over a week and included Rogerian listening, traumatic stress, children's needs, parenting and problem-solving. Divided into teams of two to protect their honour and safety, we used the 'Lady Health Visitor' model familiar to the community. Team members systematically visited each tent, regularly connected with struggling or particularly distressed families, and linked people with others from their home region. While listening to the families' challenges, the psychosocial workers shared information about the earthquake, services and psychoeducation about common trauma responses. The team worked closely with the camp doctor, who quickly realised that our consultations would consider the psychosocial and psychiatric elements. Every evening, the team gathered to complete notetaking and debrief, giving opportunities for supervision, training and feedback around the residents' emerging needs.

Many people in the camp believed that the Almighty determines every part of life; hence, the disaster was part of the divine plan. Those with more traditional beliefs held that the world balances on a cow's horn, and when tired, the cow shifts the earth from one horn to another. And the world shakes. Understanding the subjective experience and interpretations of the population is essential in acknowledging what may be perceived as traumatic (Miller et al, 2008). Although the families embraced the local psychosocial workers, most avoided formal counselling or mental health interventions as these were unfamiliar. While accustomed to 'Lady Health Visitors' who provide home visits to provide maternal and child health care, support for emotional distress such as counselling was unknown. Our visits allowed us to slowly build relationships, observe, support, respond, become part of the camp social networks and offer informal counselling processes. Residents valued the immediate sense of safety and relative security, and this seemed to be their focus. Although I was generally preoccupied with camp logistics, such as water and food supplies for 2,500 people, the team referred a person or family to me for (co)counselling about once a week.

In the spring of 2007, the government decided people needed to return to their leased tenant farms. For many, this decision triggered fears of ongoing rock- and landslides during their journey home and on their farms, reflecting real danger and traumatic responses. For others, the liminality of camp life was coming to an end. There was a greater need for counselling as people reconnected with the earthquake-related trauma, grief and what had been lost, and started to think about the challenges and fears of returning. Our caseload ballooned. Gradually, the camp emptied as the men and boys returned to rebuild, with women following.

Relying on Herman's (1997) trauma recovery principles for designing the camp was a lifeline. We created a community based on respectful and caring relationships, psychological safety, participation, information and efficacy as an active therapeutic milieu that moved beyond counselling. In hindsight, our approach reflected the psychosocial-ecological recommendations of the Mental Health and Psychosocial Services Working Group of the Inter-agency Standing Committee (IASC, 2007), where the humanitarian agencies agreed on a universal population-based, triaged approach to mental health services in emergency settings (see Figure 7.1).

Figure 7.1: Intervention pyramid for mental health and psychosocial support in emergencies

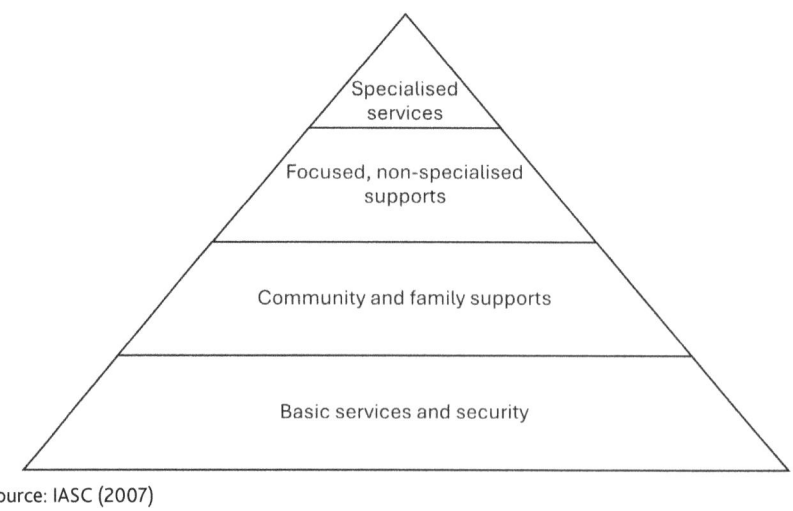

Source: IASC (2007)

Within this approach, providing essential services such as accommodation, food, sanitation and child protection is undertaken in a manner that contributes to psychosocial recovery. In explaining the 'Basic services and security tier', the recommendations include: 'influencing humanitarian actors to deliver them in a way that promotes mental health and psychosocial well-being. These basic services should be established in participatory, safe and socially appropriate ways to protect local people's dignity, strengthen local social supports and mobilise community networks' (IASC, 2007: 11–12). Tol et al (2015) argue that providing basic services using a psychosocial lens offers a mental health promotive approach that may reduce further distress.

Sharing psychoeducation messages during camp management meetings, enabling the mosque, and facilitating a child friendly space would be considered universal prevention from a public health standpoint (Tol et al, 2015) and as strengthening natural networks for 'community and family supports' (IASC, 2007). The psychosocial workers would be viewed as part of the next level of 'focused, non-specialised supports' that drew on local capacity as knowledgeable within the context as suggested by the IASC (2007) recommendations or selective prevention strategies from a public mental health perspective (Tol et al, 2015). Fortunately, the camp had a doctor and a clinical social worker (me), available for more specialised mental health services, but these were rarely used.

Linking these layered services provided a unique opportunity to form a therapeutic milieu. Commonly, key elements within mental health promotion and prevention activities include intervening to create a supportive socio-ecological environment, involving intersectoral collaboration, adapting to meet developmental stage needs, and building on and with each community's strengths (Tol et al, 2015). The services within the camp worked with these different elements to create a supportive context.

Despite horrific experiences, most people in the camp were able to function in daily roles. Even though extensive mental health epidemiological studies within humanitarian and post-conflict contexts have found dose-exposure related levels of post-traumatic stress and depression across diverse cultures (Wilson and Drozdek, 2004; Charlson et al, 2019), it is crucial to note the diversity of response (Tol, 2015). Typical of many humanitarian contexts, only a minority of camp residents were explicitly deeply distressed, and only a few were open to counselling.

As researchers of traumatic stress and resilience in post-conflict and culturally diverse contexts, Miller and Rasmussen (2010) advocate for post-modern approaches that centre affected people's processes of meaning construction as the core explanatory element of the traumatic experience. In this, the appraisal of the meaning and chronicity of life-threatening exposure is considered crucial for understanding what people perceive as traumatic, thereby framing an understanding of their responses. Despite the emphasis on psychosocial safety within the camp, being forced to live in a shared space with other families in a way that undermined honour and dignity was construed by many as the most threatening experience of the earthquake. Rather than a safe destination, the camp represented a temporary interlude, with a perilous and challenging return ahead. This resonates with emerging discussions of continuous traumatic stress, where trauma is anticipated rather than in the past (Kaminer et al, 2018).

Community conversations in post-conflict Sierra Leone

As Sierra Leone's 11-year civil war ended in 2002, I joined a psychosocial programme in a regional centre working with Sierra Leoneans in towns and Liberians in refugee camps. Using long-term apprentice partnerships between an expat clinician/trainer and local psychosocial counsellors, the programme revolved around standardised eight-session counselling groups with men, women and children that drew on local music, metaphors and rituals. The goals were to provide mental health care, train local counsellors, and raise awareness of trauma within the community (Stepakoff et al, 2006). With peace returning, Sierra Leonean colleagues living and working in Guinea's refugee camps were eager to return home to the far eastern Kailahun district. I agreed to accompany 24 team members in buses loaded with a decade of refugee life as they returned with their families.

Occupied by the Revolutionary United Front and cut off from the rest of the country by fighting, most of Kailahun's residents had crossed through the jungles to the refugee camps in neighbouring Guinea and Liberia. Those who stayed were forced into battle or tortured. Kailahun had been stripped. Most houses stood naked without roofs, window frames or doors. Rebel graffiti was scrawled in blood on walls and rocks. It was rare to hear birds, as the people who had stayed had foraged on what was available. As we arrived, the town felt tense, with radios tuned to the Sierra Leone Truth and Reconciliation Commission (TRC) district hearings in the local church hall. School was starting again under temporary palm and bamboo structures, rice fields were being reclaimed from the encroaching jungle, and the small market was selling tomatoes, ground nuts, flip-flops and batteries. Life was returning.

Over the next year, the team rebuilt their homes, settled their families and established offices in the district's four largest villages. Their communities looked to them as well-paid and trained, at a time when there were multiple personal, cultural and social needs. In hindsight, I realise that pressured to deliver an internationally designed programme and meet targets while managing my own emotions, I had not sufficiently appreciated the complex emotional demands on my colleagues as they returned from exile to listen to the stories of what had happened while they were away. Children flocked to the centres to play soccer and games. However, the conflict in Kailahun had ruptured relationships at multiple levels. It took time for the community to make sense of formal counselling activities and, initially, only the most vulnerable joined the group counselling programmes, including unaccompanied children, combatants and older women who had stayed through the conflict. Some people had stayed and experienced, witnessed or participated in multiple atrocities. Others had escaped into exile, but often only after directly experiencing the war or fraught journeys. As peace stabilised, neighbours needed to create a shared meaning of what had happened, reorganise their relationships and recreate an everyday social milieu that could be trusted.

Two years later, the atmosphere was still tense. Our team accepted a contract to host discussions of *Witness to Truth*, a film of the Sierra Leone TRC's report (Caldwell, 2012) which had been translated into Krio and Mende. Knowing the horrific experiences, I feared community conversations would trigger flashbacks, prompt dysregulation, re-traumatisation and even restart conflict. However, my local colleagues were confident they could hold the conversations safely, urged that we create spaces for community dialogue, and negotiated the programme with the district chiefs. Together we held 24 dialogues that connected the district with the national conversation, weaved a local narrative about war experiences, and provided a step towards community reconnection. We drew on the west African traditions of palaver, or open community conversations to create a shared sense of what had happened and community reconciliation (Scheid, 2011).

Initially, we started in the towns and villages where we had a presence, using halls to host separate events with the local leadership, men, women and youth. We then carefully negotiated access with the smaller surrounding villages, where we arrived in the early evening, propped up a huge home-made collapsible screen against a house, and set up a generator, digital projector and sound system. Curious people gathered, bringing chairs. After a shared meal, the team carefully framed the event by explaining the evening's programme, the TRC and that the film was a visual record of the report. As part of this introduction, team members described typical trauma responses, demonstrated exercises to regulate emotions and arousal, and outlined referral resources. During the screenings, the audiences became particularly engaged during the testimonies of the RUF commanders who had controlled the Kailahun area. After the film, the audience typically talked for two or three hours using the microphone as a talking stick, with the facilitators listening, reflecting and occasionally facilitating exercises for emotional and physiological regulation. The clinician was always in attendance, and counsellors checked on the wellbeing of those who spoke, just after the dialogue and a week later. People found the opportunity to talk helpful, and everyone who had spoken was glad they had, although Hamber (2009) notes the complexity of linking mental health work with community truth-telling. In this, our teams stepped out of traditionally therapeutic spaces to build community-wide dialogues for peace and population-based mental health processes. During these community and village-based dialogues, people responded to the film but more often recalled their own experiences. Victims of the most horrendous violence were acknowledged and afterwards said it was meaningful for them to tell their stories to contribute to peace. Neighbours involved in violence gave explanations and sometimes asked for forgiveness. Those who had recently returned learned of what had happened. People wanted to be heard, to share their stories and to rebuild their community, resonating with similar processes elsewhere (Somasundaram, 2007; Hamber, 2009). Most sessions were spontaneously concluded by an elder saying that this must never happen again while outlining the community's future path. People actively participated in the dialogues, connecting and resonating with the process. The psychosocial counsellors felt that through the dialogues, communities came together to acknowledge what had happened and build a shared understanding that allowed them to move forward together, echoing Schneid's (2011) observations of west African palavers. In parallel, more people joined the counselling groups, recognising this was a different, more focused process.

Sharing the film at a district level reflected Staub's (2013) approach to preventing further violence through building a collective understanding of the origins of the war while promoting truth, justice and the creation of a collective history. The post-film dialogue created opportunities for sharing narratives, strengthening understanding of other people's experiences, and extending group boundaries to include others. These processes are part of building reconciliation and peace (Staub, 2013). Reflecting on the perceptions that South Africa's TRC contributed to healing, Swartz and Drennan (2000) appropriately question whether psychological healing occurs for those participating in cathartic public discussions. These local dialogues were more intimate and informal than the judicial processes of TRCs, making comparison difficult. Hamber (2009) questions the concept of post-conflict communal healing and whether TRC processes prevent future violence. However, the dialogues provided a platform for building awareness of the impact of war on mental health and of strategies for managing arousal and difficult feelings with a wider constituency. This would be considered as building community support at the second level of the IASC (2007) pyramid (see Figure 7.1 earlier in this chapter) and a mental health prevention activity (Tol et al, 2015). The services and structures put in place went on to endure and support the distress of both the outbreak of Ebola in 2014 and then COVID-19. This is testament to the IASC model, those who support it and the resilience of local communities.

Overwhelming care

South Africa is home to large populations of Zimbabwean, Somali, Congolese, Cameroonian, Rwandan, Angolan and Malawian people seeking safety or a better life. They live alongside a local population burdened by an apartheid and colonial past, current inequity and deep poverty. In May 2008, national tensions led to xenophobic riots, 12 deaths and great fear. Overnight 20,000 people sought safety in local town halls and churches in Cape Town, requiring support for several months. Recognising that the halls were unsuitable, the municipality moved people to five large recreational campsites and military bases. Ill-equipped and poorly structured for providing emergency shelter, these sites were not adequate. People were distressed and fearful, living conditions were squalid and safety was not assured. The city's disaster management programme called on a local psychosocial organisation to provide support. The non-profit organisation had built a robust psychosocial disaster response capacity and had responded to relatively small events, including aircraft incidents, informal settlement fires and terrorist bombings. Without extra resources, it suddenly needed to provide much more substantial psychosocial support.

Remembering the enormous generosity of the first weeks of the Pakistani earthquake and the valuable role of psychosocial workers, I invited psychologists and social workers from across the city to join the team. We adopted Hobfoll et al's (2007) formulation that mass disaster responses should include creating: a) a sense of safety; b) calm; c) a sense of self and community efficacy; d) connectedness; and e) hope. These volunteers were briefed and trained in Hobfoll et al's model, coordinated in camp-based teams led by a staff member, and invited to weekly debriefing sessions. While the city was managing the camps, I anticipated that the psychosocial teams would contribute to the camps' management capacity, identify vulnerable people needing protection, connect with those who were distressed, provide information and psychoeducation, and support problem-solving.

It took six months before the provincial government could negotiate a safe return to the neighbourhoods. The psychosocial teams visited the camps daily, connecting with camp administrations and resident leaders. In many camps, each nationality had a leadership structure, with whom the psychosocial team engaged to problem-solve and advocate for arising needs and concerns. Although it was evident that people were distressed and in crisis, most camp residents focused on meeting daily needs. They feared returning to communities with high levels of criminal violence and ongoing xenophobic threats. Few participated in the information, psychoeducation or counselling sessions. Evidence-based protocols responding to post-traumatic stress were inappropriate where current safety was not assumed, and further danger on neighbourhood return was anticipated. Conceptualisations of continuous traumatic stress may be more helpful (Kaminer et al, 2018).

At that time, the province and the city were governed by competing political parties. The provincial government's approach focused on urgent reintegration and peacebuilding. The city was concerned with meeting the displaced people's basic needs. Although both approaches were needed, each administration remained convinced of their approach. Building safety and hope, or sharing clear information, became impossible when the political leadership was focused on scoring political points in an election year.

Not only had the societal structures led to xenophobic violence against African refugees and economic migrants, but political competition made it impossible to create safety, calm, connection, hope or efficacy as a milieu to redress the events. Gradually, immediate fears subsided, the city closed the camps, and people returned to live in the margins of an unstable society with an ongoing fear of xenophobic violence. After the COVID-19 pandemic, Hobfoll (2021) critiqued their own mass trauma intervention model by recognising that ecological and political factors impact significant scale events and the capacity to respond. Governments are mandated to respond to complex emergencies affecting their citizens, but foreign nationals are vulnerable as governments cannot allocate scarce national resources and political parties play on their constituencies' fears. The needs were overwhelming in this situation, and no agency could meet the needs of a marginalised population. The people affected had few resources before being displaced and were further impoverished by this crisis.

While filling an essential role in identifying the real challenges that people were experiencing and enabling advocacy to improve camp conditions, the volunteer psychologists and social workers felt frustrated in an unfamiliar, diffuse milieu with unspecified roles and a context where they could not provide counselling or therapy. The camp residents were primarily concerned about creating psychological safety by meeting basic subsistence needs and could not focus on traumatic past experiences. While incredibly generous and well-meaning, most volunteer mental health workers were more used to working with privileged clients in individual spaces and found population-based care uncomfortable and difficult. They struggled emotionally with being confronted by the extreme inequities within the city. The organisation's team shifted to supporting the volunteers as they reflected and debriefed their experiences of the camps. To this end, this case study illustrates the significance of designing and shaping policy and practice responses to crises around a myriad of factors such as the political and contextual interests, as well as age, class, ethnicity, gender and sociocultural factors.

Conclusion

Most professional practice in emergency settings takes place outside of the academic gaze. This chapter has shared insights into these experiences and considered the value and challenges of supporting social systems in complex emergencies. It provides an important reflection on the influences of power and intersecting identities in our journeys of offering and engaging with interventions, necessitating innovative approaches. Managing a camp in Pakistan using trauma recovery principles showed the value of understanding the impact of traumatic stress and the potential of working with the social milieu to create a supportive social context. This could be described as a 'trauma-informed approach' and a form of mental health promotion or prevention within emerging terminologies. The social milieu within the camp provided a sense of psychological safety and predictability that allowed the residents to build a sense of self-efficacy and control. The capacity for trauma-focused, specialised counselling strengthened the supportive milieu. The work in Sierra Leone illustrates the opportunities in connecting national transitional justice conversations with traditions of local dialogue in rebuilding social connection and trust at neighbourhood level. This population-based community support intervention was supported by focused specialised services for those needing trauma counselling, strengthening the supportive milieu. Finally, the South African case scenario reminds us that social contexts are themselves held within wider political and sociological systems that may support or challenge work within social systems. Within stressful contexts, the wider social milieu may moderate, exacerbate or cause distress, thereby influencing mental health (Miller and Rasco, 2004).

When working at a community or population level rather than focusing on individuals, it becomes clear that social relations may be affected by large scale events, and that people experience traumatic events very differently, with some deeply distressed with post-traumatic or depressive symptoms and others coping with the distressing situation. When trauma-focused interventions focus on only the core symptoms of post-traumatic stress disorder (PTSD), the diversity of responses or cultural variations may become invisible. Trauma-focused interventions may be also problematic within majority world conflict environments if it is impossible to assure safety and the traumatic exposure is ongoing or continuing in other forms (Summerfield, 1999; Miller and Rasco, 2004; Miller and Rasmussen, 2017).

Witnessing suffering in complex emergencies requires reflexive awareness, seeking to understand the experience and carefully managing power (Weingarten, 2003). It is crucial to be deeply aware of how people experience situations and to have the courage to evolve new paradigms of practice as needed. While certain situations may demand trauma-focused interventions, a trauma-informed practice may be more appropriate in others. Witnessing these threatening journeys prompts us to action, yet supporting people to reach psychological and physical safety requires complex, intersectoral, multi-layered and resourced interventions grounded in reflexive practice and nuanced understandings of intersectionality.

It is evident that complex needs must be met by developing and supporting individuals within a communal and social milieu that reflects the IASC model (Figure 7.1). What's more, to provide such a holistic approach that goes beyond the trauma paradigm, counselling and social work requires the integration of local, national and transnational agents. From the traditions of the displaced communities, be it women's privacy or palaver, to the understanding and respect of the varied respondents on the ground, themselves connected to national and international entities, the implementation of 'natural' networks for community and family supports is a complex, yet capable, global effort that must be enabled. However, as the South African case shows, such efforts are easily undermined by local, national and international politicking and regressive approaches. As we continue to evolve, challenging such obstacles will be critical.

References

Briere, J.N.D. and Scott, C. (2014) *Principles of Trauma Therapy: A Guide to Symptoms, Evaluation, and Treatment*, Thousand Oaks, CA: Sage Publications.

Caldwell, G. (2012) *Witness to Truth: A Video Report on the Sierra Leone Truth and Reconciliation Commission*, Available from: https://www.youtube.com/watch?v=fJbLHAX4k8Q

Charlson, F., van Ommeren, M., Flaxman, A., Cornett, J., Whiteford, H. and Saxena, S. (2019) 'New WHO prevalence estimates of mental disorders in conflict settings: a systematic review and meta-analysis', *The Lancet*, 394(10194): 240–8. https://doi.org/10.1016/s0140-6736(19)30934-1

Collins, P.H. (2019) *Intersectionality as Critical Social Theory*, Durham, NC: Duke University Press,

Hamber, B. (2009) *Transforming Societies After Political Violence: Truth, Reconciliation, and Mental Health*, New York: Springer Science & Business Media.

Herman, J.L. (1997) *Trauma and Recovery*, New York: Basic Books.

Hobfoll, S.E. (2021) 'Five principles in context: We have been blind to ecological principles and politics', *Psychiatry*, 84(4): 347–50.

Hobfoll, S.E., Watson, P., Bell, C.C., Bryant, R.A., Brymer, M.J., Friedman, M.J. et al (2007) 'Five essential elements of immediate and mid-term mass trauma intervention: empirical evidence', *Psychiatry*, 70(4): 283–315. https://doi.org/10.1521/psyc.2007.70.4.283

IASC (2007) *Guidelines on Mental Health and Psychosocial Support in Emergency Settings*, Available from: https://www.who.int/publications/i/item/iasc-guidelines-for-mental-health-and-psychosocial-support-in-emergency-settings

Kaminer, D., Eagle, G. and Crawford-Browne, S. (2018) 'Continuous traumatic stress as a mental and physical health challenge: Case studies from South Africa', *Journal of Health Psychology*, 23(8). https://doi.org/10.1177/1359105316642831

Miller, K.E., Omidian, P., Rasmussen, A., Yaqubi, A. and Daudzai, H. (2008) 'Daily stressors, war experiences, and mental health in Afghanistan', *Transcultural Psychiatry*, 45(4): 611–38. https://doi.org/10.1177/1363461508100785

Miller, K.E. and Rasco, L.M. (2004) 'An ecological framework for addressing the mental health needs of refugee communities' in K.E. Miller and L.M. Rasco (eds) *The Mental Health of Refugees: Ecological Approaches to Healing and Adaptation*, London: Taylor & Francis, pp 1–64. https://doi.org/10.4324/9781410610263

Miller, K.E. and Rasmussen, A. (2010) 'War exposure, daily stressors, and mental health in conflict and post-conflict settings: Bridging the divide between trauma-focused and psychosocial frameworks', *Social Science and Medicine*, 70(1): 7–16. https://doi.org/10.1016/j.socscimed.2009.09.029

Miller, K.E. and Rasmussen, A. (2017) 'The mental health of civilians displaced by armed conflict: an ecological model of refugee distress', *Epidemiology and Psychiatric Sciences*, 26(2): 129–38.

Scheid, A.F. (2011) 'Under the palaver tree: Community ethics for truth-telling and reconciliation', *Journal of the Society of Christian Ethics*, 17–36.

Somasundaram, D. (2007) 'Collective trauma in northern Sri Lanka: A qualitative psychosocial-ecological study', *International Journal of Mental Health Systems*, 1(1): 5. https://doi.org/10.1186/1752-4458-1-5

Staub, E. (2013) 'Building a peaceful society: Origins, prevention and reconciliation after genocide and other group violence', *American Psychologist*, 68(7): 576.

Stepakoff, S., Hubbard, J., Katoh, M., Falk, E., Mikulu, J.-B., Nkhoma, P. and Omagwa, Y. (2006) 'Trauma healing in refugee camps in Guinea: a psychosocial program for Liberian and Sierra Leonean survivors of torture and war', *American Psychologist*, 61(8): 921–32, Available from: http://psycnet.apa.org/journals/amp/61/8/921/

Summerfield, D. (1999) 'A critique of seven assumptions behind psychological trauma programmes in war-affected areas', *Social Science and Medicine*, 48(10): 1449–62. https://doi.org/10.1016/S0277-9536(98)00450-X

Swartz, L. and Drennan, G. (2000) 'The cultural construction of healing in the truth and reconciliation commission: Implications for mental health practice', *Ethnicity & Health*, 5(3–4). https://doi.org/10.1080/713667455

Tol, W.A. (2015) 'Stemming the tide: promoting mental health and preventing mental disorders in low- and middle-income countries', *Global Mental Health*, 2, e11.

Tol, W.A., Purgato, M., Bass, J.K., Galappatti, A. and Eaton, W. (2015) 'Mental health and psychosocial support in humanitarian settings: a public mental health perspective', *Epidemiology and Psychiatric Sciences*, 24(6): 484–94. https://doi.org/10.1017/S2045796015000827

Weingarten, K. (2003) *Common Shock: Witnessing Violence Every Day: How We Are Harmed, How We Can Heal*, New York: Dutton/Penguin Books.

Wilson, J.P. and Drozdek, B. (2004) 'Introduction' in *Broken Spirits: The Treatment of Traumatized Asylum Seekers, Refugees and War and Torture Victims*, New York: Routledge, pp 1–4.

8

In the refuge of the wake: intersectional considerations in therapeutic practice with African refugees

Eric Harper and Angela Rackstraw

Introduction (of the wake)

Our intention with this piece of writing is to demonstrate the therapeutic and political necessity of creating links when they are broken, through the physical act of stitching together within life-affirming one-to-one, group and community relationships. Human rights violations involve an attack on life sustaining links. Perpetrators of human rights violations often attempt to isolate the victim through inducing a sense of shame, internalised self-oppression and silencing. The key lesson is to co-construct a relational healing and political space using the stitching process, thereby enabling individuals as part of a group and community to find their own voice. This stitching together creates intra-psychic links and interpersonal bonds that function as a network of internal and external life-affirming resources.

This piece is focused on work with African refugees which took place over a 30-year period for both of us. It is an experience that was not going to have been written; firstly, due to the lack of space, time, and distance from the work; and secondly, our reluctance to remember, reflect and revisit the terrible experiences others have endured. At the same time, without giving voice to this experience, there can be no honouring of the humanity that can prevail after the most brutal of circumstances or learning from these experiences.

We present our stories and the stories of others, which became a co-constructed narrative. We have used direct quotations from some of those we have worked with to underscore the affective tones and music of the visual images they created, encapsulating key elements of their journeys following their exodus from their countries of origin. At the same time, we present images produced in a therapy group throughout this chapter. The images show something of the wake work of a group of refugee mothers who had experienced unspeakable traumas and numerous losses. The examples of our work and those we have worked with that we discuss in the chapter draw on a wide range of our experiences and interventions with people from refugee backgrounds.

Our position as the therapist while proclaiming a therapeutic neutrality is framed by intersectional considerations that influence what happens within the therapeutic setting. Intersectionality speaks to crossing over of power play, positions of taken-for-granted privilege, the therapists as white, middle class and the different modes, or 'matrix of oppression' based on identity (Collins, 2019; Sanchez, 2017), for example, race, class, gender, sexuality, religion and ethnicity. Reflexivity calls upon us not to shy away from the difficult conversation of privilege, us being white and middle class at the time when the racial relations in South Africa were volatile. As such, this had the potential to reinforce the clients' overlapping experiences of oppression.

To situate the concept of intersectionality alongside the psychoanalytic concepts of transference, counter transference and projective identification is to accept both therapist's and client's personal and political affects (unconscious biases) into the encounter regardless of how it is professionally framed. It aims to both think about and acknowledge the intersection of these different modes of oppression, for example, race and gender, which shape experiences as well as how these relationships of power overlap make visible what is often erased.

The stories we engaged in are framed by what is unrepresentable, acts of extreme cruelty. After much consideration, we have decided not to describe these events in any detail in the chapter, though some brief quotations from those we worked with are included. Our aim is not to shock but speak of humanity and life that comes into being even when the shock of cruelty attempts to erase life and its stitches to other life. We are engaged in what to us feels like an impossible task, witnessing peoples experience of suffering as reported by them as well as not creating a 'pornography of suffering' (Halttunen, 1995). In this case, while we want to give voice to those we have worked with, we do not see this chapter as the place to give voice to their most traumatic experiences.

Wakes and stitches

Our position is that refugee work such as ours with African descendants can be conceptualised as 'wake work':

> Wakes are processes; through which we think about the dead and our relations to them; they are rituals … But wakes are also "the tracks left on the water's surface by a ship; the disturbance caused by a body swimming, or one that is moved, in water; the air currents behind a body in flight; a region of disturbed flow …" (Sharpe, 2016: 21)

The concept of wake work underlines how the reception centres that refugees encounter when crossing borders have echoes of the holds of the slave ships and '[w]here those who arrive never have arrived' (Sharpe, 2016: 69). In the context of this chapter, we use the word 'wake work' to describe the vigil process we have experienced – in both one-to-one work and collectively within groups – of bearing witness to and being alongside what feels dead, frozen and cast out. This is a brotherly and sisterly holding in mind, through one-to-one, group and community relationships; a creation of a network of hospitality and care of that which mentally and physically does and does not survive the holding centres.

Our own addition to the concept of wake work is stitching. Stitching is often about repairing or mending something that has been broken or destroyed or lost. Women have used stitching going back many generations, and it is still used as a way to give voice to what is often unspeakable. Sewing in community is an ancient practice and indeed people in different countries at different times have used and/or use stitching when their voices have been forcefully silenced, or when they are unable to find the words to express the unspeakable. Story cloths made by Chilean, Argentinian and South African women (to name just a few) have depicted human rights abuses, political strife, gender-based violence, losses and other life-changing events. Over and over again, the women whom we journey alongside have confirmed our own and others' experiences: that using needle and thread brings about a deep connection to and reparation of self, to those parts of oneself that have been numbed, lost or disconnected as a result of trauma and/or bereavement.

The concept of mirroring helps us understand both the act or experience of stitching, as well as the stitched cloth or object 'affirms the self as a being with agency, acceptability and potency' (Parker, 2020). The stitcher sees a reflection of herself in her work, and then in the reception of her work by other women in the group. Additionally, women have not only been able to feel seen and heard, and to see and hear one another as they sew together and share a collective grief, but also by connecting to themselves as they quietly and rhythmically push the needle and thread through the fabric, they have often described a feeling of deep connection to their lost loved one. They are thinking, reflecting and remembering as they work on their pieces of fabric, and this is mirrored back to them. The fabric or cloth serves as a container of sorts, a second psychic skin, holding these memories and emotions in some way. When these story cloths or heirlooms are looked at by other embroiderers, their work and their stories are witnessed and validated.

The women sometimes make small fabric dolls, which become part of their stitched landscapes. Sometimes they make these dolls on their own; in this way telling their individual stories through another dimension of themselves, telling it in the third person.

One woman who did this and then wrote down her story, was a 35-year-old mother. She had fled from the Democratic Republic of Congo (DRC) with three of her children. She endured terrible human rights violations. She eventually arrived in South Africa where she found herself feeling completely alone and isolated, and where her children experienced xenophobia in their school.

She too felt unsafe due to xenophobic and community violence, and was suffering from deep depression. She was visibly fearful of talking about her experiences but wanted to share them with us through writing after she had made her doll. She found the making of the doll (originally for her daughter, but the doll became a self-portrait of sorts) very evocative and, through it, she found her voice and told her story. As a result, she was able to reach out and ask for help in various areas at the refugee centre. This included help for her children. She continued to stitch and, during our last encounter, was working on a story cloth which illustrated her journey. Sadly, we had only been able to offer the women a limited number of sessions from the onset, which was why we included writing as a way for the group members to continue with their storytelling and serve as an additional container of sorts. Later we heard how she had become a counsellor and started supporting other women who came to the centre.

Stitches, like *Kintsugi*, are the 'scars in gold', which, as Leila Zaki (2020) underlines, is the 'healing act in the narratives of loss and recovery, breakage and restoration, tragedy and fortitude'. In the women's stitching groups, we begin every session with each woman having the opportunity to light a candle, in order to honour a lost loved one. This has become a ritual that unites the group members in a sometimes unspoken act. The act of being alongside allows for a healing relationship and a process – such as ritual – that enables a sense of coming to the support of life: the stitching together of life-affirming links. Stitching placed alongside wake work needs to include a political dimension, a co-constructed healing that invites the community to speak back. Figure 8.1 shows the women's candle ritual.

Listening to images

> Do I stay in my country with those I love and where I feel alive, but face certain death, or do I come here where I know I will not be killed but feel dead?

The young man, who spoke these words, had walked from Somalia to Cape Town with a bullet in his leg. It was a journey of chance encounters: the unasked-for kindness of strangers, alongside the loss of homecoming. It was a pilgrimage of survival, hope and vulnerability, also framed by 'limits of emancipation' (Hartman, 1997: 6). His future included a sense of capture, and uncertainty and foreboding as people from Somalia living in the informal settlements of Cape Town were often subject to 'scenes of subjection' (Hartman, 1997), such as normalised xenophobic attacks. This young man

Figure 8.1: Candle centrepiece

wanted to stop (stillness), to no longer be on the run, but feared for his life. Sharpe (2016: 126) describes the possibility of stillness as to be haunted by past and present 'breaking points', including the possibility of neither returning or arriving, since a return would be marked by violence and homelessness, while arrival is haunted by the unhomely kin(ships) to the slave voyages.

Therapy with this young man, over a four-month period in 1998, ended abruptly as he had to work during the day at the same time as the sessions. One morning, I found a letter from him under my car's windscreen wiper. This image evoked a feeling of something interminable and a fixity, what Sharpe (2016: 48–9) calls 'marking'. The marking of his and other refugees' failed passage. Sharpe (2016: 21) describes this as 'the track left' by somebody marked: someone who wanted to make his mark and tell his story. At the same time, 'listening to this image' (Campt, 2017: 9), by looking beyond the scarred body, we are touched and connected to an unspoken moment 'that emphasizes mobility, resistance, and expressiveness' (Campt, 2017: 9).

Years later, a chance encounter between a human rights lawyer and I took place on a London bus. We conversed as follows:

'You think you have heard the most shocking and extreme thing ever, only a few weeks later to hear another story with the same intensity.'

'Yes, when it comes to inflicting pain, people have so much more creativity and imagination than when it comes to kindness.'

This is 'recognising antiblackness as total climate' (Sharpe, 2016: 21) of the experience of those seeking refuge. We know that not all refugees are treated in the same way as has recently been seen in Ukraine. This is not in any way to diminish the struggle each person goes through, but rather to call attention to a layered dimension of struggle that some will endure.

Another chance encounter occurred, this time in Denver, Colorado in 2001, between two fathers from opposite sides of Africa in a therapy group that included talking therapy, art and dance. Both men were haunted by their lived experiences of being forced to watch terrible human rights violations, as well as by their own multiple experiences of torture. The effect of their experiences and 'memories' was a violent breakdown in representation and, paradoxically, too much representation. As a refugee who had endured torture put it: 'I often have the images right in front of my face, but I cannot remember anything. Images in front of me but no memory of them.'

A key bonding moment in the group occurred when both men shared detailed descriptions of a horrific event outside everyday experience. At the end of the group there was a bonding moment brought about by a dance ritual. As a result of this shared experience, which got embodied through the dance, the group became a communal body, no longer isolated and alone with the haunting images. As one member of the group stated, today the ancestors were present.

While we have chosen against sharing these horrific details in this chapter, the experience of these group members sharing those experiences with each other was part of the act of healing. The *process* of sharing – including the group dance and witnessing – was more significant in this than the specific content shared. The act of sharing became a vital life-link between the two men and the group.

These links invite vitality and life: a state in which one's body is no longer only subject to a state of reduction to an object, marked and cast overboard. Alongside the sense of excommunication from a sense of community and without a sense of an interlocutor, there is now a link to others and life. This is what is meant by stitching and wake work. It is an ongoing conversation with both the dead and that which feels dead but is actually defrosting. It is a dance in the presence of the ancestors: the inclusion of witnesses that were absent within the original experience.

Refugee work is a monumental struggle to find a voice. Danticat (1996a: 12 in Sharpe, 2016: 70) describes it thus: 'I tried to talk to you, but every time I opened my mouth, water bubbles came out. No sounds.' Bubbles of sound, laughter and tears of the ancestors invite other images and questions, what Khanna (2003) calls a form of critical melancholy, as seen in the questions of what the two men wanted to happen to those who killed their families.

One of these two men resumed his career as a journalist and the other started a family, but only after both men had spent many hours remembering the intimate and tender gestures of their children, wives, mothers, and brothers: all the dead buried without their respective [cultural] funeral ceremonies. The journalist helped the treatment centre create a newsletter that gave voice to refugees' stories and in so doing helped support the creation of a community. He also published in the newsletter his own personal account and he attended the social gatherings. The co-construction and intersection of these one-to-one, group and community relationships was their/our wake work. Figure 8.2 shows refugee women stitching together dolls – this 'stitching' is also an allegory for the connections made among refugees in the examples in this chapter.

Figure 8.2: Assembling parts

A stitch is like a bridge to a community

> I am not just a refugee. What I have learned from our group is that I am not just a refugee. I am my mother's son. I studied at university, play football, dance and I have loved and will love again. I am leaving the group today with thanks but want you each to know you are not just a refugee!

The young refugee man quoted above expresses the joy in becoming defined by more than the experiences that led to their displacement. As part of a team of psychologists, therapists and social workers at the Trauma Centre for Victims of Violence and Torture in Cape Town in the late 1990s, we attempted to construct bridging activities to reach out to ex-political prisoners from within South Africa, as well as refugees from other parts of Africa. We began to learn that we risked the danger of holding people ransom to treatment frameworks that were containing for us but alien to them. As such we attempted to co-construct the space and through outreach work. We hoped that this would support people and help overcome barriers to asking for help. The work included a blend of various kinds of relationships, such as social work, therapy, activism, advocacy, case management and assisting with the establishment of community initiatives and different forms of therapy.

We learned that sometimes people in pain are unable to name what is going on. The connecting thread of their life story may be cut due to multiple losses. Sometimes the work is simply helping the person re-construct the thread of their life story. At other moments, it is creating a map and trying to find resources that enable the person to get through the week. As such a key therapeutic element is not being seduced by the horror that results in a one-dimensional reality that collapses lives and problems under a psychiatric diagnosis. The only relevant 'diagnosis' is knowing when getting through the day or week or month can no longer be taken for granted, when it becomes one day or week at a time.

With South African ex-political prisoners and returning exiles/refugees, we learned the importance of drawing upon ritual dimensions used in the days of the struggle against apartheid. For large community gatherings, we drew upon oral narratives, singing, dance, candle lighting and moments of silence remembering the dead/ancestors. The group documented the stories in a newsletter which was then shared with each member of the group and others who could not attend the meetings. Some people only contributed to the sense of community via the newsletter. The group, as a community, created their own political advocacy forum. At first, we tried to bring together South African political prisoners and returning South African exiles with people (refugees) from other parts of Africa, but this only worked as a yearly celebration, being the International Day for Torture Survivors. Separate refugee groups were created. However, as part of these international events, members from both groups spoke out and shared their stories.

The work problematised what we thought was therapeutic. Not everybody benefits from talking about the most horrific things that have occurred in their lives; and doing so can be damaging and voyeuristic. For some, what is most important is to be able to have a relationship with another once again, for example, to function in a group or community setting. This is a huge ask, as acute pain makes having a relationship with oneself exceedingly difficult, let alone having a relationship with another. Here, alternative healing forums like art, music, dance, sport and social gatherings can provide vital channels for relationship building. For others, the work was about financial and legal reparation and recognition. This was clearly seen in the women's stitching groups. Although the candle lighting at the beginning of each session was a unifying ritual, the honouring and remembering was initially an individual act. The women stitched quietly, immersed in their own worlds and realities. Gradually, however, the stitching became a collective and unifying act, and women started talking and sharing together. They were able to listen deeply, and this meant they felt less isolated. The repetitive, almost meditative act of sewing with needle and thread helped facilitate this.

The healing work often involves physically reaching out to people, as was the situation with a man in a darkened shack in Cape Town who I was brought to see. He lay on the floor moaning, deeply disorientated. His brother told me he had never been right since the death of their father. After the recall of this traumatic event, I invited him to tell me about his father, a carpenter, a life that exists beyond the shocking cruel violent death. He shared his memory of the sounds of chipping away at wood and the smells of the work shed; then the feeling of holding the objects his father made for him, his father's smile, voice and the touch of his hand. Remembrance of these images enabled him to once again internalise something good as opposed to being left with an identification with images of horror.

Following this encounter, our sessions moved from his home to my office. He read the newspaper in the waiting room before the session, eating a sandwich I would make him. He educated me about the conflict in Angola and told me about his first love, his family and the challenges of living in South Africa.

There was laughter, crying and rage. Sometimes he was incredibly sad, desperate, but there was also hope as he found a way to resume his life. It was sad for us to say goodbye as we had become close. In doing this work, we learned the art of stitching images of refugee life and life beyond the branding of the refugee identity. We had learned the importance of not prioritising one kind of conversation, the narratives metaphorically consisting of high-frequency horror images. We created a montage of what Campt (2017) calls low-frequency images composed of 'haptic form of sensory contact' (Campt, 2017: 6). For this young man, it was the sensory contact and images of mealtimes at home or walks with his white German lover.

He missed the sound of her voice and the smell of his mother cooking. All manner of topics were voiced, offering the sense of an affective dream field composed of a flickering montage of moving images, allowing the blurring of past and present relationships to find new threads. This space was framed by the fusion of the 'shock or vibration, which gives rise to thought' (Deleuze, 2013: 171) alongside those 'quiet soundings of the grammar of Black Futurity' (Campt, 2017: 9). This allowed for the opening up of space for 'another thinker in the thinker' (Deleuze, 2013: 173) and a coming together – a relationship – that could stitch together the ghosts of the past that had had no resting place.

'You are not just a therapist to me, you are my African brother'

On leaving East Africa, a young woman ended up as a childminder in Saudi Arabia. She was raped and fell pregnant. After six years, her child was taken from her and she was deported, eventually seeking asylum in the US.

When I met her there, the story she wanted to tell – the one that kept her awake at night – was the memory of her child. But the story we knew she had to tell the asylum judge was not this story, but rather the one of her imprisonments as a young person and what she witnessed: the torture of her father and sister; the death of her sister and brother; and not knowing what had happened to her father. Her story needed to be told in a coherent and detailed way to evidence that she was indeed traumatised by human rights' violations.

This is what Hartman (1997: 3) calls the reinforcement of the 'spectacular' character of Black suffering and the way asylum seekers and those supporting them are 'called upon to participate in such scenes'. To demonstrate suffering and subjection was not the only parameter of a successful case: a lawyer needed evidence that country conditions still presented a risk to her, and a doctor needed to evidence the damage to her body. Even if she were able to tell the story in the way required, with scars evidencing her testimony, she could still be sent back under some pretext, like safe country conditions.

Our therapy space was framed by her upcoming asylum hearing. I spent many therapeutic hours helping her to be able to tell, that is to remember the story of violence she did not want to remember. We can think of this as akin to the slave market, a body-memory that could be handed over to the legal judges so that they could display their mastery and legal rights over this body. This was the story she had tried to erase from her mind for fear of the madness contained in the re-remembering but the story the nation-state demanded as part of its citizenship rite of passage. Under such circumstances, court hearings, even those with the best of outcomes, always have something of the slave market and Kafka about them. The corridor of escape is the one that pushes you back towards those rooms you attempted to dissociate from.

The most touching outcomes – as was the case in this example – are those in which the person is not only granted asylum, but in which they walk away with a profound sense of having somebody (being the law) bear witness to the violence which, at the time it was experienced, was without witness. This then also serves as a challenge to those who acted as law unto themselves.

After this young woman was granted asylum, she continued to see me. Now she could talk about what was important to her. We spoke about her day-to-day activities, her child and her faith. Now it was no longer a case of getting through the day, for she had found a way of taking one week at a time, despite one or two nights of terrors each week. She began to dream, something of a miracle as the holy trinity of night, sleep and dreaming had been taken from her in the darkness of the prison and loss of her child. She liked to swim; it was meditative for her. She liked to go to church; it provided a community and something familiar. She found a job in a nursery, and she attended our community gatherings, making the coffee for the events using a traditional coffee-making ritual. She never spoke much at the community gathering or at the international events, but she told me how meaningful it was to hear the stories of others, how it helped her overcome a sense of isolation. She laughed and stated that maybe she would speak one day, but she was worried she might speak so much that no one else would get a chance. She gave me a ritual coffee mat and a deeper understanding of the importance of ritual and the role that faith plays for some.

When it came to us saying goodbye, she again referred to me as her African brother, as she often had before. As a white man who identified as somebody part of Africa but also part of the oppressive system, it was a moment of recognition of my attempt to contribute something. I could simply have said it was this transference of her dead brother and sister, but this would have minimised the gift in her recognition of me. Perhaps this African brother is akin to what Jessica Benjamin (2018) refers to as 'the third', a moment of mutual 'recognition' 'beyond doer and done to'.

What we learned is that therapy continues to fail refugees or simply pays lip service to them in its reluctance to be open to the political dimensions needed as well as new and creative 'cultural' approaches to reaching out to those who do not come knocking. The approach of being open is not something that can be known beforehand. It is something that is co-constructed and something that both changes as it unfolds and challenges what we understand therapy and ourselves to be. The work impacts upon the client but also changes our sense of being-in-the-world pushing up against taken-for-granted sites of privilege, such as white privilege, of deciding whose life is deemed to matter, or not. The work is re-finding those networks of relationships that survive this erasure of life. This is the repertory of stitching: embracing how the person is embedded in their community and reinforcing personal, group and community resources, offering a mix of verbal and non-verbal therapies and community-building initiatives, and creating political platforms, like newsletters or international events.

These communal gatherings, then, are opportunities to create the space to think, dream, play and transform with the support of others through past and present repertoires. The community bears witness to the process, and provides access to dreamtime, good internal objects and attachment that facilitate the slowing down of a client's inner process, which is often in inner turmoil, to allow resourcing to occur (Gray and Harper, 2001).

The concept of dream space and ritual is a transversal of atomised, individual testimony. What is required is a body-memory that is in relation and linked to the extended family, community and ancestors. It is common for people to gather, in community or in ritual, in some form of collective process, and dance, drum, mourn or wail. This 'becoming' – as described by Deleuze and Guattari (2004) – is a collective experience. Related to this, it is accepted in many cultures that an injury to one member of the community impacts the entire community. Moreover, as argued by Graham Bull (2000), the loss of ritual in modern culture is traumatic, as there are no longer communal support forums in which people can express deep psychic pain.

Stitching happens in community partnership

> You are on the run, you keep going. You see terrible things, but you keep going. Then when you get to safety, your body catches up, you fall apart. Now I have a room, but I am even more alone and back in solitary confinement with nowhere to go. Worse still, I have the keys to my own cell but cannot use them.

The refugee quoted above took a great migration north only to find himself trapped. After his arrival in London in the early 2000s, most of his days were spent shut up in a room. His doctor diagnosed him as depressed and prescribed a cure through taking a course of selective serotonin reuptake inhibitors (SSRIs), a type of antidepressant, to alter the serotonin and noradrenaline neurotransmitters linked to his mood and emotions. He wanted to sleep all the time, while at other times he could not fall asleep. He spoke of feeling 'powerless', saying 'things just happen[ed]' to him. Everything he experienced felt meaningless, hopeless and futureless. He wondered why he was alive and what the purpose of his life was.

The onset of his depression came about when he came to London, but he felt the contributing factor was imprisonment. The first occasion that he was imprisoned was the same year that his mother – to whom he had been very close – died. On the second occasion, he was regularly interrogated and tortured, sometimes up to ten times a day.

The details he had as evidence to support his asylum application included descriptions of interrogation sessions. The story he wanted to tell was how different life was in the UK compared with Africa. Growing up, he slept in a large room with other children. When discipline occurred, it included members of the community, for the community brought up one another's children, not a single family. Now living in London without a sense of community, having his own room felt like 'prison' because it reminded him of solitary confinement when he had been imprisoned.

He began to assist me with an attempt to create a community for the refugees living in an exceptionally large homeless hostel as well as the creation of a newsletter for the hostel, which was not limited to just refugee stories. At an event to celebrate Refugee Week, he was one of the speakers. Although only six people turned up at the event, they formed a group that would meet weekly. We also continued to do outreach work – namely door-to-door visits – within the hostel. Slowly others joined the group. Some would stay for only one meeting, while others would drop in from time to time.

At least half of the group suffered from alcohol or *khat* addiction. As the referrals increased, we decided to work in partnership with an addiction service that specialised in cross-cultural work.

The need was expressed for refugee representation within the hostel. This was followed by an election campaign in which a letter was given to all the refugee and asylum-seeking residents to vote. All three representatives got elected. Another area of much discussion and concern was around racial and religious abuse within and outside the hostel. Many examples were recited of being verbally abused and/or seeing derogatory graffiti insulting Muslims. Some of the group found this abuse distressing and called for a meeting with management, while others said that an understanding of the factors fuelling such hatred on the basis of race or faith was needed: many residents in the homeless hostel had mental health problems and it was thought that racism was an expression of frustration and a way to feel better about themselves. A meeting with the management took place and diversity training, open to both staff and residents, was run by staff and some of the group members.

Two other major areas of discussion were people not being able to eat food that was consistent with their religion and not having a place for praying. The group requested that Muslims be given a place to cook for themselves, also noting that the only religious festivals acknowledged were Christian celebrations. Again, tensions and opposing views around how to proceed dominated the group discussions. A few individuals repeatedly expressed that they did not like the focus on refugees and Muslims and wanted activities to involve more integration with other residents. Others did not feel this way. The result was another meeting with management. The outcome was that a room was provided for Muslims to pray, cook their own meals and break their fasting during Ramadan.

The weekly group meetings took on a new format: a discussion followed by a meal. The group decided to open the doors to other cultural groups. Black British, Caribbean and white Irish men entered the space. The story of 'No Blacks, Irish or dogs' became a bridge. The Irish spoke of English imperialism. Intersecting narratives pushing up against each other, sometimes with laughter and at other times with anger, sadness or compassion. As these sites of intersectionality intersected, a community gathered. Some of the stories were published in a newsletter which was used as an outreach tool as well as a way to inform other residents in the hostel about the experiences that refugees endure. The refugee who had initially been isolated in his room played a leading role in creating a newsletter that included the story of anyone in the hostel who wanted it to be told. This produced a new sense of interfacing communities. The result was a more horizontal playing field: stories about torture alongside stories about addiction, child abuse, neglect and acute poverty, as well as celebratory stories of survival.

The group sang together and shared personal stories. They spoke of being a family. Members of the group undertook visits to the British Museum and British Library, the irony of which was not lost. Discussions outside the Museum on British colonisation took place. Another activity was playing football in the park.

No longer using SSRIs, the refugee who had initially been isolated in his room had now become the link person who welcomed people into the group. He was key in doing outreach and preparing for the build-up to International Torture Day. Figure 8.3 shows a refugee woman stuffing her doll, an illustration or allegory of the practices described in this chapter that reflect people building new lives and experiences.

Marked migrations

'Wake work' (Sharpe, 2016: 17) is tied to 'shippability and containerization' (Sharpe, 2016: 30) of those who 'inhabit the Fanonian "zones of non-Being"' (Sharpe, 2016: 20). It is a condition of the chokehold – what Sharpe (2016: 108–13) calls aspiration. In the forced exodus from their homeland, refugees face the risk of doors closing before they reach the shores of the European fortress. There is a risk of a failed asylum application, criminalising those who dare to dream. There is risk of endlessly waking at sea, caught within the currents of Fortress Europe's 'death-dealing policies' (Sharpe, 2016: 57). There is risk of accepting the branding of the name 'refugee', bringing simultaneous hyper-visibility and invisibility.

A young unaccompanied minor from north Africa saw his parents die in a brutal manner. His dream was to visit Old Trafford. I wanted to take

Figure 8.3: Filling in

him, but I was told there was no budget and that other priorities prevailed. The demand was paperwork: to present a story of child protection that conformed to timelines but in truth involved minimal or no contact with the young unaccompanied minors.

The young man came to trust me and, in doing so, to trust re-connecting to images of the father who taught him to play football and watched Manchester United on television with him. I liked him a great deal and wanted to maintain contact with him when I left the agency but was told it was not professional to do so. He told me about the gangs in his area and shared his vision for the future – yes, a future, even as I and we failed him.

Another young person seeking asylum shared, 'I am not under 18'. It was a huge risk for her, an unaccompanied minor from west Africa, to tell me this. I was supposed to report this, in effect supporting deportation, but I kept her secret and invited her to join the youth football team that the young man had joined. Both she and the young man were exceptionally good at football. She trusted me and her church, while I wondered whether I had betrayed her by supporting her capacity to once again trust and dream.

Her lawyer, who only met her once and yet called her 'sister!' did not bother to obtain a medical or psychological report of the abuse she endured. She shared with me that there was an attempt to kill her for *juju* purposes, following which she was placed in a sex trafficking syndicate and repeatedly raped. She then endured a system that did not believe her and a judge who wanted her sent back. Perhaps she was better off not trusting, as once again she had to flee and go into hiding. Yet, sadly, without some trust, where would she hide? Was her body a sign of 'immi/a/nent death' (Sharpe, 2016: 71)?

There was no doubt in my mind as to the truth of her story. Where doubt lay was with the system claiming to support these young people. All the staff at this facility were agency workers, a cheaper option than permanent staff. Among those who had been working there for a longer while, it was rumoured that the young people were not given the services to which they were legally entitled and that the money for such services was redirected to other services. The focus of the system was on trying to catch out young people, evidenced by the excitement accompanying the introduction of a tooth examination to prove the person was over 18, and thus deemed not to need care.

In contradiction to the pieces of work described above, creating a political platform for these young people, or a newsletter, seemed unimaginable. At best some sense of community and an attempt to fight for the legal right to receive the services the state claimed they were entitled to was all that seemed possible. Young people clearly in deep distress, bewildered and unaware of their rights would not be placed in foster care, but in group homes. Another rumour was that the person who ran the group homes, little more than a dumping ground, was friends with one of the managers and received financial rewards for placing them in these so-called homes. The primary aim of the system was to spend as little money as possible while ensuring that no paper trail of negligence emerged. As such paperwork was policed, creating a parallel process of staff subjected to 'interrogation' in a similar way that the young people were. The aim was to ensure the notes reflected the prescribed version and the story looked good.

After eight months, I left with a sense of cowardliness for not exposing what was going on. I never did take the young man to see the football stadium. The consoling memory I have is that for a brief time I had created community groups, a football team and African youth club that walked along the South Bank, visiting art galleries and other parts of London, far from the London they knew located in council estates in remote settings. I left wondering what kinds of images they would have wanted to display in the art galleries. Another consoling memory was my discovery later that some of the corruption did become known and that a manager was dismissed. But I was still left with a sense that the system was holding the children to ransom to the masquerades of care, and I had not spoken out. Figure 8.4 shows the parts of a doll not yet stitched together, representing the feeling at times that the work is left unfinished and people let down. Figure 8.5 shows 6 dolls in various stages of completion, again an allegory that demonstrates the work is ongoing even as this chapter concludes.

Conclusion: (Re)fugue work

> Coming to this group I have started to see what I saw without seeing what I saw.

This piece of writing, this story, also speaks of the fatigue, emotional labour and risk of pausing and reflecting as evidenced with a reflective practice

Figure 8.4: Stitch together

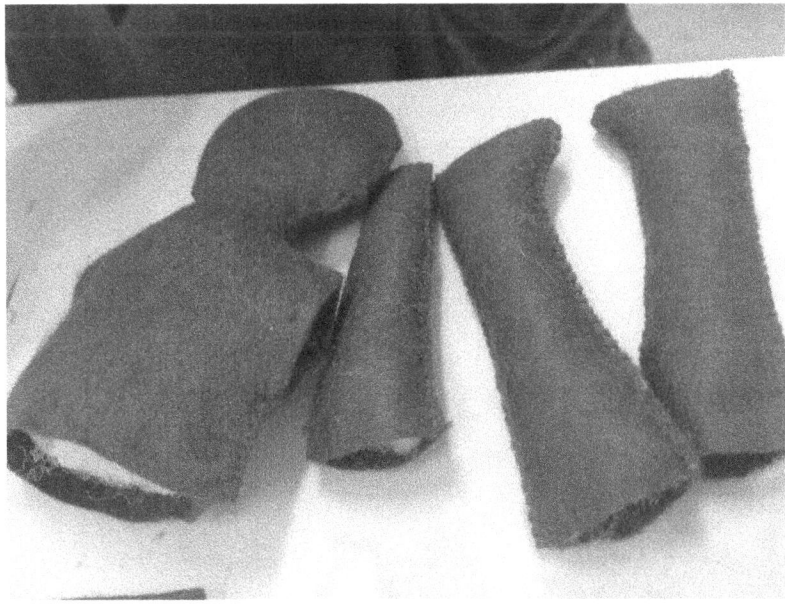

Figure 8.5: Remade

group in London. Four of the people that attended the managers' reflective practice groups facilitated in London worked with refugees. Their services provided various kinds of relationship possibilities that went beyond simply medicating clients, but that also relied on staff going the extra mile, doing at least two jobs, and filling multiple roles. But as the group started to reflect, so questions emerged around the extra mile that staff had to traverse:

'The boundaries of our roles are often blurred.'

'Sometimes we like to be the heroes stepping in, feel we must help out or things won't get done.'

'We are doing more and more things that are not part of our job role/ scope of practice. This blurring of job role boundaries can leave us feeling stressed and overwhelmed, but only if we choose to take on these extra responsibilities.'

Creating reflective groupwork allowed for a slowing down and the creation of an interval between the sensory and motor. When still – pausing in this way – two of the refugee managers became aware of being burnt out and left their jobs. Another manager was able to experience a sense of getting patched up through respite before going back out onto what one of them referred to as 'the frontline'. The other manager found the group resourceful and it helped him to continue the work.

In parallel with this, it has taken us 30 years to pause and reflect on what we saw without seeing what we saw. It is by chance meeting with the editors of this book that we find ourselves writing this piece, pausing and reflecting on stories which have become part of our story. Stories that live on in our body, some stories thankfully forgotten and others which mark what we know about the limits of human experience. Working in this field, we are asked the question: 'Is it not difficult working with people who have been tortured?' It would be difficult if we only worked with torture or with refugees, but we work with people for whom being a refugee is just one of their experiences.

Stitching talks to the different parts of who they are: somebody's son or daughter; someone who has likes and dreams; and someone who had a life that began before they fled their country. This approach, as Hartman (1997) underlines, is more than simply recounting the violence of seeking refuge: it is about approaching a face, voice, story, song, dance and community and a celebration of life alongside the extreme outrage. Outrage that people are supposed to move on, or worse forgive, for at best there can only be granting pardon but never forgiveness.

The intersection of political, ritual and therapeutic relationships can produce something paradoxical, which can be described as a state of (re)fugue. Why (re)fugue? The word 'fugue' has both meaning as a musical term and as a description of a psychological state of dissociation. In the individual's quest to survive there is a necessary state of dissociation to keep going, to stay alive when parts of them psychologically feel dead. But when intimate healing spaces are found (one-to-one and group work), and community is co-constructed and rituals and political mobilisation are created, there is a listening to images of unsayable trauma, the music of the 'haptic form of sensory contact' (Campt, 2017: 6) that moves people to celebrate a life that resisted death and speaks back, thereby reclaiming a body, including the body-memory of the ancestors. Within these paradoxes, for example, the singing at the end of community gathering, wake work occurs and comes to the support of life.

What is seen is barely audible. This is what Butler, Athanasiou and Campt refer to as the 'refusal to stay in one's proper place. … It is a refusal I equate with a striving for freedom that Ruth Wilson Gilmore articulated as the "possibility to live unbounded lives"' (Campt, 2017: 32). It is the collective gathering and ritual observances and political statements of those who are passing over into new lands (Sharpe, 2016: 10). This is the creation of a re(fugue): the interval, musical repertories and refrains that stitch those non-representable traumatic imprints on the flesh but that also refuse to limit the tale of re(fugue) to the recounting of the violence involved in seeking refuge. This gives disassociation a new kind of association: a place within the intersections of one-to-one, group and community relationships – a wake work.

References

Benjamin, J. (2018) *Beyond Doer and Done to. Recognition Theory, Intersubjectivity and the Third*, London; New York: Routledge.

Bull, G. (2000) Personal communication.

Campt, T. (2017) *Listening to Images*, Durham, NC: Duke University Press.

Collins, P.H. (2019) I*ntersectionality as Critical Social Theory*, Durham, NC: Duke University Press.

Deleuze, G. (2013) *Cinema II. The Time-Image*, London, New York: Bloomsbury.

Deleuze, G. and Guattari, F. (2004) *A Thousand Plateaus: Capitalism and Schizophrenia*, London: Continuum.

Gray, A. and Harper, E. (2001) 'Reaching underserved trauma survivors through community-based programs', Paper presented at International Society for Traumatic Stress Studies 17th Annual Meeting, 6–9 December, New Orleans.

Halttunen, K. (1995) 'Humanitarianism and the pornography of pain in Anglo-American culture', *The American Historical Review*, 100(2): 303–34. https://doi.org/10.2307/2169001

Hartman, S. (1997) *Scenes of Subjection. Terror, Slavery, and Self-Making in Nineteenth Century America*, Oxford: Oxford University Press.

Khanna, R. (2003) *Dark Continents: Psychoanalysis and Colonialism*, Durham, NC: Duke University Press.

Parker, R. (2020) *The Subversive Stitch: Embroidery and the Making of the Feminine*, London: Bloomsbury Publishing.

Sanchez, G. (2017) 'Critical perspectives on clandestine migration facilitation: An overview of migrant smuggling research', *Journal on Migration and Human Security*, 5(1): 9–27. https://doi.org/10.1177/233150241700500102

Sharpe, C. (2016) *In the Wake. On Blackness and Being*. Durham, NC: Duke University Press.

Zaki, L. (2020) Personal communication.

9

Kwapatakwapata! Young Malawian girls trapped in predatory odysseys

Pearson Nkhoma

Immigration continues to be a significant subject of political and public contention.[1] The link between immigration and politics has become increasingly prominent in recent years, instigating the rise of different political parties and ideologies, both in the Global North and Global South. Immigration can also be described as the lifeblood of Brexit and the election of Donald Trump in the US. In the UK, immigration was one of the recent Conservative government's five priority pillars, with plans to deport illegal immigrants and asylum seekers to Rwanda and threatening not to provide protection to victims of modern slavery merely for 'arriving in the country illegally' (Sunak, 2023).

While immigration remains a topic of both global policy and public interest, the focus is usually on barring 'immigration'. Consequently, the nuances of child migration, as told through the stories of the children and young people themselves, are often overlooked. The experiences of unaccompanied minors and other young migrants are frequently lost in broader immigration discussions, leading to a gap in understanding about unaccompanied minors or child migration in general. Yet, it is well documented that migrants continue to face precarious realities. Media reports highlight the rescue of unaccompanied minors and adolescent girls among those crossing the English Channel and the detention of children in the US (Bhatnagar, 2019). Immigrants continue to be targeted with terror attacks, mob justice, racial and xenophobic fuelled attacks (see Young, 2022). Such anti-immigration attacks have also been observed and reported in other European countries like Portugal, Ireland, Germany, Italy, Denmark and Sweden (Gudrun et al, 2017; Hagelund, 2020; Moller and Cardoso, 2023). These experiences are not only limited to the Global North. Social media footage from recent crises in Afghanistan, Syria, Palestine, Sudan, Democratic Republic of Congo and Ukraine highlight the vulnerabilities of young migrants and how some child migrants are perceived as (or treated as) more equal than others on the basis of their age, gender, class or nationality. Cases of xenophobic attacks have also been recurrent in South

Africa. Recently, Malawi rounded up Black refugees and asylum seekers in different parts of the country despite the country's Constitution supporting integration for migrants who have lived in the country for more than seven years. Overall, the United Nations Human Rights Council (2017) has raised concerns about the growing number of vulnerable migrant children. Despite the appalling reports on the plight of migrants, there is still a lack of literature on the stories and experiences of unaccompanied minors and migrant children and young people especially girls and young women.

This chapter, therefore, seeks to address this gap by examining the lived experiences of child and young migrants, starting from the inception of their journey, partly through the lens of intersectionality (Cho et al, 2013; Collins, 2019; Collins and Bilge, 2020). It positions immigration and asylum seeking as multifaceted phenomena rather than single-journey social phenomena, acknowledging the multiple levels of exploitation and inequalities faced by children and young people. This chapter attempts to bridge the knowledge gap by exploring these lived experiences that result from intersecting identities of girls and young women in Malawi on the basis of their age, gender, *unaccompaniedness* and deprivation or marginalised inequalities.

With the global focus on immigration largely centred on 'barring' outsiders (immigrant people), the chapter will engage with the findings of a study examining the experiences of girls and young women engaged in prostitution since childhood. The chapter explores why they leave their homes unaccompanied; how they experience 'leaving'; and how the chain of their exploitation is often sustained with very limited hope for their safeguarding. This approach creates space for participants' own accounts, enabling a reconceptualisation of social inequality and chronic deprivation as a form of conflict or crisis. Such a perspective supports the case for measures aimed at transforming the structures that perpetuate deprivation and exploitation. This is particularly relevant for children and young people, especially girls, who are often compelled to leave their communities due to constrained choices, or as a result of degrading and undignified living conditions as migrants. At this point, it is therefore important to articulate the research design that guided the study from which this chapter is developed.

Research design

This study employed participatory research (Greenwood et al, 1993; Cahill, 2007; Shamrova and Cummings, 2017) to understand children and young women's lived experiences of prostitution. The study was conducted in two cities in Malawi and involved 20 children and young women. All participants had lived experiences of prostitution since childhood. This chapter centres on two participants, Labani and Loni [not their real names] who shared their experiences using visual and verbal methods of their choice (see Nkhoma and

Charnley, 2018). Using the Malawian language of Chichewa, their narratives were later transcribed into English to make the findings of the study accessible to a wider audience. All transcripts were coded in NVivo and analysed through an iterative process (Coffey and Atkinson, 1996; Silverman, 2024). By focusing on the narratives of these participants, this chapter illuminates their personal migration experiences, both within and across borders. This approach captures the complexity of children and young women's involvement in prostitution while problematising the dominant conceptualisation of sex work, particularly for those whose involvement stems from child commercial sexual exploitation (CSEC) – as defined within the children's rights framework (UNCRC, 1989; United Nations, 2000). However, the children's rights approach is significantly constrained when it comes to safeguarding children in countries where the age of consent is below 18 years.

This limitation necessitates engagement with intersectionality (Collins and Bilge, 2020; Collins et al, 2021) to further explore and make sense of the participants' vulnerability and experiences of exploitation because of their gender, nationality and social class in addition to their age. By expanding the children's rights framework and viewing the children and young women and their experiences through the lens of intersectionality, this study lays bare the layers of exploitation experienced by children and young women involved in prostitution. This permits broader and more nuanced understandings of diverse children's rights as being more than a question of age of consent. This theorisation reframes the stories of the two participants, viewing the 'odysseys' of these unaccompanied minors as a 'crisis' deserving attention comparable to a global crisis or armed conflict; a perspective that goes beyond the conventional discourse on human migration.

The narratives of the two participants emphasise the initial stages of migration for unaccompanied children and young people, before they find themselves in foreign countries where they are subjected to policies that involve separation, detention or deportation without regard for their intersectional inequalities and the consequent vulnerabilities, marginalisation and/or exploitation. This chapter illustrates how approaches similar to the 'rescuing' of children from prostitution, as observed in Malawi (Nkhoma and Charnley, 2018), which lack a nuanced understanding of *intersectional* vulnerabilities, exploitation and experiences, are likely to confine the children to prostitution throughout their lives – further exacerbating their vulnerabilities and exploitation. In such circumstances girls and young women can easily be left with constrained choices leading them to exercise an 'adaptive preference' to engage in sex work as adults (Nussbaum, 2001).

This chapter addresses a notable gap in the understanding of unaccompanied child migration within, and from, sub-Saharan African countries. In contrast to stories of rescue, separation from guardians or detention in the Global North, I focus on the stories of two unaccompanied minors, the causes of family separation, their journeys and subsequent involvement in prostitution. The chapter puts emphasis on the critical need to understand the contexts surrounding child immigrants and their experiences, with some participants likening these to conditions akin to slavery. It questions the rationale behind decisions by countries such as the UK to withhold modern slavery protection from these vulnerable groups (Gadd and Broad, 2018).

Furthermore, the chapter identifies a significant gap in the discourse on child migration: the narratives of children at the earliest stages of their migration journey. The analysis purposively focuses on the lived experiences of two participants, Labani and Loni, whose stories form the core narrative. The goal is to generate rich insights from unique accounts for a deeper qualitative analysis rather than aiming for quantity or generalisation (Clark et al, 2021; Silverman, 2022). However, the experiences of other participants are also considered, contributing to a broader understanding of the reasons behind the migration of children and young people from their homes or countries. The focus is deliberately on girls and young women with experiences of migration within and between countries in sub-Saharan Africa to shed light on an often-overlooked area of child migration and slavery, as the global discussion on this topic tends to focus on people who have left the region for the Global North. However, children and young people face extreme vulnerabilities and exploitation, including sex slavery, death from mob justice and traffickers, and xenophobic attacks in their quest to escape extreme exploitation and severe deprivation within this region. It is therefore important to create spaces from which their reasons for, and experiences of, migration can be heard and understood more widely.

Escaping deprivation, child marriages and child prostitution

In Malawi, since gaining independence, there has been little significant civil unrest or conflict, of a kind which would make 'leaving' or displacement inevitable. However, as defined by Tambulasi (2009), conflict typically involves violent tensions leading to significant displacement and fatalities, often leaving individuals with few survival choices. This backdrop is key to understanding the experiences of Labani and Loni, with experience as unaccompanied minors outside and within Malawi.

Labani's involvement in prostitution began before she was 15, following her father's death. Before she was 18, she left Malawi for South Africa, using her earnings from prostitution to escape further involvement. In South Africa, lacking safeguards, she ended up as a housemaid, a common path for many young Malawians. This pattern of labour migration, with historical roots in pre-colonial times and the era of slavery (Banda, 2017) is not surprising. Labani's story, marked by orphanhood and lack of support, mirrored themes common among other study participants. She shared her experience, providing a personal insight into her life:

Nditalemba mayeso a 8, bambo anga anazamwalira ndiye zinthuno zinayamba kuvuta kwambiri. Ndinakhala pakhomo zaka ziwiri osapita ku school chifukwa fees imavuta. Ndiyeno ndinayamba zibwenzi. Moti nthawi imenoyoyo ndikanakhala kuti mwinanso ndiri pabanja. Ndinali ndi dzaka pakatikati pa 13 ndi 14. Nthawi imeneyo ndikangofuna kuti mwina ndikhale pa bwanja. Ndikawona kuti mwai oti ndizapitenso ku school suzapezekanso ndimene zinthu zinalilili. Ndiye ndimkafuna kukwatirana ndimwamuna wina yemwe amapanga business yogulitsa makala amene ndinapanga naye chibwenzi.

[Soon after my primary school leaving exams, my father died. Following his death, we faced extreme hardships. I had to drop out of school for two years, considering marriage as my only option. At 13 or 14, I entered a relationship, almost marrying a man who supported me through his charcoal business. Unlike marriage, school seemed like an impossibility. So marriage was my focus.]

This narrative, at first glance, appears as a straightforward case of deprivation or orphanhood. However, a deeper analysis reveals a complex interplay of poverty, loss of parental support and subsequent vulnerability, Labani explained:

Ineyo u sex work uja ngakhale ndimangopangira kuti nditani, panalibe chilichose chomwe ndingapange, ndinalibe chilichose choti ndingapezere ndalama. Ndiyeno ndipanga bwanji. Koma ineuyo mmoyo mwanga sizimangisangalasa ai. Ndinalibe choice ndi mmene zinalili. Ichi ndichifukwa ndinapita kwa mzanga uja (ku South Africa), koma kukhalanso kumene kuja kuona ntchito yake ya ukapolo. Basi apa ndinangoti ndizingochivomereza chilichonse chimene chingandipeze.

[I engage in sex work merely because I don't have a choice. What else could I do except this; I did not have anything to earn money. So, upon reflecting over what I could do, I picked prostitution. But that does not mean I like what I am currently doing. I have tried to leave before. This is why I once went to South Africa as I was trying to find things I could do. But even there, I was working like a slave. As such, I returned home and rejoined sex work because I did not have a choice.]

The case of Labani and other participants captures the impact of losing a primary breadwinner and the resultant constraints in meeting daily needs. As an orphan,[2] Labani's life course took a vulnerable turn, pushing her towards difficult choices in the absence of plausible alternatives and ultimately, prostitution. This situation is indicative of a broader pattern in Malawi, where *limited conflicts* have led to different survival strategies, including migration for economic reasons rather than conflict-driven displacement.

Labani's decision to leave Malawi was driven by a desire to escape the cycle of prostitution. However, in South Africa she continued to face challenges. Her story reflects the broader dynamics of labour migration from Malawi, historically shaped by economic needs and the absence of significant conflict-induced displacement. However, there was no safeguarding for her while in South Africa just as there was none in Malawi despite UNCRC's 'obliging' the country to do so. In South Africa, being undocumented and an underage employee within an informal sector heightened her risk of exploitation at multiple levels due to her young age, gender and identity as a 'foreigner'.

The sexual abuse of children especially girls working as maids or house-helpers has widely been documented (Thi et al, 2021). Like most young girls who leave Malawi for South Africa, Labani ended up working as a housemaid. Her choice of South Africa was consistent with formalised labour migration paths dating back to the colonial period when people from Malawi moved to the Rhodesias (Zambia and Zimbabwe) and South Africa to work in mines during the *teba* (The Employment Bureau of Africa) movement. These pathways reflect forced labour movement and slave like conditions that have continued through colonialism and into the post-colonial period.

However, just like many other girls from Malawi and other countries in sub-Saharan Africa who go to South Africa or leave their countries or communities without any guardian, Labani was evidently a victim of child slavery. Illegally employed underage, her future opportunities to lead a dignified life and realise her fullest capabilities were further compromised by her constrained choice (Nussbaum, 2007, 2013; Sen, 2005) to try and earn a living in South Africa. Her choice reflected ambiguous agency (see Bordonaro and Payne, 2012; Charnley and Nkhoma, 2020), associated with decisions made in the absence of any plausible alternative. Working as a house helper in South Africa, Labani was subjected to various forms of exploitation. She described her treatment as that of a 'slave [*ndimagwira ngati kapolo*]', leading her to return to Malawi where she engaged in prostitution or 'survival sex' (Baleta, 2015) as her only viable alternative.

Loni's journey: being trapped in prostitution

Loni's experience in this study stands in stark contrast to Labani's. While most participants, like Labani, did not primarily focus on being trafficked or controlled by pimps, their stories often hinted at a blend of coercion, trafficking and prostitution. Loni's narrative, uniquely captured through a sketch she drew of a girl named Chisk, poignantly illustrates her ordeal

Figure 9.1: A drawing by Loni of an abducted child forced into prostitution

(see Figure 9.1). Twelve year old Loni, who had been lured to work in a brothel by deception under the false promise of employment when trying to escape extreme poverty, conveyed her experiences vividly through a drawing of a girl named Chisk to which she applied the word '*anabedwa* [She was abducted]'. Her detailed account of abduction offered a more intimate glimpse into her experiences. The sketch served as a visual representation, a method used to make the storytelling process more comfortable for participants. Loni shared:

> Anakumana ndi amai enaake omwe anamuuza kuti amafuna mtsikana watchito. Anamuza Chisk kuti awafunire atsikanawo kapena akayambe iwo ntchitoyo. Chisk atakana koma mzake ndiye anamupangitsa. Akadakhala yekha akanakana.
>
> [Chisk met a certain woman who was looking for a maid. The woman asked Chisk and her friend to help find other young girls who she could employ. Her friend convinced Chisk to take up the offer, something she wouldn't have done had she been alone.]

Loni was abducted to the city of Nkhali, one of the main cities in Malawi. Once at the brothel (a combination of a shebeen and rest house) where she was kept against her will, the girls were forced to sell sex to pay for their rooms, food and earn money. Loni explained that she and other girls were not informed in advance about the nature of their job.

Sanatiuze kuti azitipasa ndalama zingati. Tinazindikira titafika ukoko. Titafika anatiuza kuti tidule mowa. Ndinali ndi mantha komanso manyazi. Koma anandiuza kuti ngati sindizidula mowawo ndiye kuti sindizidya. Anthu amanditchula kuti mwana dala.

[We were not informed in advance of the nature of the work or how much we would be getting. We were only told upon arrival to start opening beer for people. I was very shy and nervous. But they said I will not be getting food if I insisted on not working.]

During the six months before Loni managed to escape the brothel, she faced control through physical threats, intimidation and manipulation, including deprivation of food. She endured physical abuse, evidenced by fresh cuts and wounds she revealed as she vocalised Chisk's story. Despite being in need of medical attention and being in touch with health and welfare services, she had not received any treatment and remained largely unsupported.

This theme of coercion and intra-country trafficking, as portrayed through Loni's character Chisk, was a recurring motif in participants' narratives, especially among participants from Mbiya District, Loni's home region. A disturbing trend highlighted by these accounts was the increasing recruitment of young girls by pubs to work as bar girls, mostly through coercion, leading them into prostitution without their knowledge or consent. Mpalini, another participant from Mbiya, confirmed this growing phenomenon. She noted the rising trend of pub operators recruiting young girls from rural areas, often luring them into prostitution under the guise of employment. As Loni conveyed her experiences, it was clearly evident that she had wanted to leave the brothel, fronting as a bar, for a long time. She had been forced to endure sexual activities that damaged her prepubescent body and to hand over her earnings to the brothel owners leaving her dependent on them to access food.

Inducing fear of deprivation of basic needs was a common way through which girls would be forced to engage in sexual acts. Being in a location where they hardly knew anyone, the possibility of seeking alternative support was removed. The only option was to build resilience by attempting to cope with what they were faced with. For Loni, this meant giving in to what Soldier (the male brothel owner) demanded of her, which included having sex with men. Soldier, according to Loni, was an ex-convict, allegedly of murder and widely feared within the area. His demeanour evoked a sense of fear, and the nickname matched the power he projected to abducted girls like Loni.

Loni stated that she had not wanted to engage in the practice as she experienced sex as painful but men would force themselves on her. She expressed being appalled by how she was forced to sell sex by her captors. In addition to being in an unfamiliar location, she was intimidated and instilled with fear upon her arrival, so that there was no opportunity to refuse to engage in prostitution or leave the brothel.

> Ndimaopa mwakuti sindimakana akandituma chinthu. Azawo amawatchula kuti a soldier. Ati anapha msilikali ndipo anamangidwa kwa zaka 30 koma anachita kuthawa. Anali oopsa. Akandiyitana, ndimagwada.
>
> [I was petrified. I never refused whenever the brothel owners asked me to do something. Her husband was called 'soldier' by his friends. It was even alleged that he was an escaped convict jailed for murder. He was scary. I always knelt whenever he called me.]

There was a general consensus among participants that, despite not all children and young people being coerced, abducted and prostituted, the younger the girls, the higher their risk of coercion or manipulation. It also emerged that once involved, children and young people were at a higher risk of being required by clients to have unprotected sex as they could not always negotiate or be in control as regards to how they engaged with clients.

The grim realisation that upon their return, many, like Labani, find themselves resorting to prostitution as a constrained choice, demonstrates the persistent cycle of vulnerability and exploitation. This cycle is not merely a personal dilemma but reflects broader systemic failures. Labani's resignation to her circumstances in South Africa and her eventual return to Malawi – 'I had no choice … But even there, I was working like a slave. With that, there was nothing I could do. I returned home for whatever I would pick [including selling sex]' – emphasises the urgent need for systemic changes to address the root causes of such vulnerabilities.

Labani's near-marriage at 13, followed by her transition into sex work and subsequent migration to South Africa, depicts a relentless search for dignity. Her story captures her ambiguous agency – the willingness to undertake degrading work, only to confront an even harsher reality abroad, illustrates the profound exploitation encountered, compelling a reconsideration of the value of returning home to face another dilemma of constrained choices leading to further exploitation.

Dissecting and reframing conflict

As she spoke through the meaning of her drawing of Chisk, Loni articulated her strong desire to leave the brothel. Yet, being in her own country did not simplify her escape; the unfamiliar urban environment of Nkhali,[3] a relatively bigger city and about an hour's drive from her village, presented considerable challenges. This situation mirrored that of Labani in South Africa, emphasising the recurring theme of unaccompanied minors and young women caught in the snare of exploitation due to systematic inequalities, irrespective of their geographical location. Loni's recounting of her experiences, like other young women in Nkhali who also participated in this study, captures a systemic issue mirroring Labani's constrained choices all of which led to exploitation, whether through child marriage or threats of child marriage, involvement in prostitution, child labour and other contemporary forms of child slavery (McCabe and Eglen, 2022).

The lax enforcement of labour laws in Malawi and other countries like South Africa further exacerbates this issue. While the legal and child protection policy and practice interventions may focus on sectors like tea and tobacco estates, other forms of child slavery, notably commercial sexual exploitation and employment of children as house-helpers, remain untouched. The marginalisation of child prostitution within the country's legislative framework is evident in the 2010 Child Care, Justice, and Protection Act (Malawi Government, 2010), where child prostitution is scarcely mentioned, revealing a significant gap in the safeguarding of children against all forms of exploitation especially child slavery. This legislative oversight is easily exploited by individuals and entities, including pub owners who coercively recruit young girls under the pretence of employment or domestic work, a reality echoed in the experiences shared by Loni. As Labani shared of her experience in South Africa, this is clearly prevalent in other parts of sub-Saharan Africa, albeit under explored as a topic of scholarly research.

Despite Loni's self-rescue from the brothel, her subsequent predicament – a pregnancy at just 15, two years after her self-rescue – further reveals the ongoing struggle and vulnerability she faced and continued to endure. When Loni's situation is examined through a synergised lens of the capability approach, concerned with the freedom of individuals to be and to do what they have reason to value (Sen, 1999), an intersectionality framework and children's rights perspective, the systemic nature of her exploitation becomes glaringly clear. Fieldwork observations suggest that Loni's story, while distinct, is part of a broader pattern of socio-structural inequalities that exacerbate vulnerabilities and risks for young girls like her, seeking escape from these forms of 'conflicts' or 'crises'. Loni's experiences, shaped by her intersectional identity and influenced by structural factors beyond her control, highlight a critical oversight in the childcare and protection system's ability to safeguard vulnerable children effectively.

My observations revealed a lack of initiative by government to alleviate the constraints rendering Loni, and similarly Labani, susceptible to abduction and exploitation. While the social welfare and other organisations working on child protection were later involved, it was evident that Loni was left without support. Safeguarding is reduced to 'rescuing' (from the brothel). Thereafter, the children are left to provide for themselves and the risk that results from different structural factors (such as chronic deprivations, age, orphanhood, for example) that make them vulnerable and at risk of coercion remain unaddressed. Thus, the root causes of their risk for exploitation are left untouched and remain *deep-rooted* in their lives. This failure is emblematic of broader systemic issues, particularly in a context like Malawi, one of the world's poorest countries, marred by significant socio-structural inequalities.

As a result, for most of the children, especially girls and young women, this reality of constrained capabilities to lead a dignified life continues to adulthood. It is commonly understood that being 'rescued' from brothels completes their safeguarding. Yet, involvement in prostitution for unaccompanied minors and young girls results from intersectional factors that further fuel intersectional experiences requiring specific levels of intervention. The inability to address such specific causes at different layers of intersectional identities partly explains why involvement in prostitution for children continues into adulthood. It was therefore not surprising to hear nearly all participants describing their involvement in prostitution in a manner that was normalised with sentiments like 'chikhalidwe' or 'zotengera' to imply something as 'a way of life', 'hereditary' (running in the family), 'adoptive' or 'by blood' from parents or family. In this context, participants' own sentiments suggest that their involvement in prostitution since childhood occurs not out of free choice but due to constrained choices and the absence of dignified alternatives, exercising what Bordonaro and Payne (2012) call 'ambiguous agency'.

Loni's narrative, alongside Labani's, illuminates the intersectional vulnerabilities faced by young girls from rural areas and the normalised yet deceptive practices of child recruitment for exploitation because of their gender, class or nationality (or race for those who travel to countries like South Africa). Such practices persist not only within Malawi but also extend across the region and beyond, affecting unaccompanied minors migrating within and across borders. The stories of Labani and Loni reveal the complex interplay of factors such as orphanhood, poverty and lack of support that shape the life trajectories of children in Malawi. These narratives highlight the desperate paths girls and young women are forced to take, which may include prostitution and migration, in their search for livelihoods or better opportunities, only to find themselves in a cycle of degradation.

The relevance of Labani and Loni's stories for wider consideration of international migration lies in the illustration of circumstances and experiences that are unlikely to meet the standards required for the granting of asylum by global northern policies designed to deter individuals from seeking meaningful lives. Their experiences might well be considered as 'spurious human rights claims' (Sunak, 2023).

Addressing these intricate challenges necessitates an approach that goes beyond the conventional solution of 'rescuing'. The capability approach (Sen, 2005; Nussbaum, 2013), which emphasises enhancing individuals' freedoms and opportunities to lead dignified lives they value, offers a valuable framework for understanding and tackling the root causes of such migrations or supporting unaccompanied minors and young women regardless of their migration status. By focusing on expanding the capabilities of individuals like Labani and Loni, it becomes possible to address the systemic issues that underlie forced migration, including poverty, lack of education and limited economic opportunities for girls due to structural factors and inequalities. This approach advocates for interventions that are not just reactive but proactive, aiming to create environments where people do not feel compelled to leave in search of dignity and safety.

Viewing Labani and Loni's stories through the lens of intersectionality reveals the intertwined nature of unaccompanied minors' journeys, challenging the binary of deserving and undeserving support based on origin and circumstances. This more nuanced lens highlights how narrow understandings of the drivers and meanings of forced migration overlook the complexities in stories like these. A more synergised framework allows us to understand how Loni's plight is deeply entwined with the primary drivers of inequality and deprivation affecting the country. Thus, conflict, when viewed through this lens that focuses on the outcome, is not only restricted to armed unrest. This situation prompts a critical question: if the outcomes of poverty and social inequality render lives as undignified as those affected by conflicts, natural disasters and similar crises, shouldn't these issues be addressed with comparable urgency and resource allocation as defence and disaster response efforts? The necessity for such a paradigm shift is necessitated by the fact that children and young people, even from non-war-torn countries experiencing 'crisis-level' poverty and significant social inequalities, are compelled to migrate in search of better opportunities and means to fulfil their capabilities. Consequently, without adequate support, these vulnerable girls and young women often fall prey to traffickers.

All participants in this study highlighted *mavuto* – a term denoting chronic deprivation or destitution, or the inability to meet basic needs. Almost all participants attributed to poverty or chronic deprivation their decision to leave home, exposing a loss of dignity and the limitations on achieving basic needs that can also be observed among victims of armed conflicts or other forced displacement and/or migration due to varied crises. This predicament often left them facing a grim choice: return to deprivation or venture into uncertain endeavours like prostitution in hopes of finding a semblance of livelihood. The question 'what choice was there for a girl like Loni or Labani?' resonates deeply with their experiences of leaving. I am aware that poverty is deeply contested and relative as the notable debate between Peter Townsend (1985, 2010) and Amartya Sen (1983, 1985) revealed. Walter Rodney's (2018) Marxist analysis of underdevelopment in different parts of Africa lends credence to Loni and Labani's accounts, further explaining why young girls have their bodies commodified and how they become entangled in layers of exploitation akin to modern slavery when faced with *mavuto*. This view opens up the way we can view exploitation of children in prostitution beyond the age of consent, through a complex web of causes and exploitation untangled by utilising intersectionality and capability approaches. The examples of child migration discussed here, while not always leading to the Global North, expose girls and young women to trafficking and further exploitation. Any structural issues that contribute to retaining such levels of deprivation and inequalities can be considered as conduits to child slavery, the result of neo-colonial patriarchal capitalism that ignores the plight of children whose lives are disadvantaged by their race and ethnicity, migration status, class and gender. These children are as deserving as any others of their rights to protection from exploitation as outlined by the UNCRC.

The stories of Labani and Loni, thus, reflect the broader challenges of navigating poverty, exploitation and the quest for a life of dignity in the face of overwhelming odds. It is evident in this study that similar to responses to humanitarian crises or armed conflicts, where nations and regions collaborate and allocate significant resources for prevention and relief, *mavuto* (social inequality, poverty and chronic deprivation) should evoke similar concerted efforts and substantial budgeting. A radical proposition would be for countries to prioritise the fight against poverty and deprivation with commitments at least equal to those made for countering armed conflicts. As such, investing in social services and welfare would be essential if we aim to reverse the current situation and reduce the number of unaccompanied children at risk of trafficking or forced migration.

Conclusion

In summary, this chapter has offered, through a participatory research approach, a critical examination of the lived experiences of unaccompanied minors migrating within sub-Saharan Africa, focusing on Malawi and an example of a disappointing attempt to migrate to South Africa. By centring on the narratives of two participants, Labani and Loni, it has uncovered the intertwining of child prostitution with broader issues of migration, exploitation and systemic failures in child protection mechanisms against child slavery.

This approach has enabled the chapter to highlight the necessity of understanding and addressing the root causes of vulnerability and structures fuelling child exploitation while advocating for comprehensive policy reforms that prioritise the welfare and dignity of unaccompanied minors through more empathetic and effective protection strategies. Finally the chapter offers a poignantly evidenced call for attention, and responses, to global intersectional inequalities based on age, class, gender, race, ethnicity and migration status that continue to deny children their right to protection from harm, abuse, neglect and exploitation.

Notes

[1] Kwapata in Chichewa means 'wandering' or 'nomadic', migrating or moving up and about in search of something. The context of the migration is what determines the Kwapatakwapata, reflected in the title of this chapter. It's deep Chichewa. The voices of testimonies recorded in Chichewa have been preserved throughout the chapter, with translations by the author.

[2] The Malawi government defines an orphan as a child who has lost either one or both biological Parents (Malawi Government National Statistical Office, 2019).

[3] Nkhali is one of the four cities in Malawi.

References

Baleta, A. (2015) 'Lives on the line: Sex work in sub-Saharan Africa', *The Lancet*, 385(9962): e1–2.

Banda, H.C.C. (2017) *Migration from Malawi to South Africa: A Historical and Cultural Novel – Real Life Experiences*, Bamenda: Langaa RPCIG.

Bhatnagar, P. (2019) 'Children in cages: A Legal and public health crisis', *Georgetown Immigration Law Journal*, 34(1): 181–5.

Bordonaro, L.I. and Payne, R. (2012) 'Ambiguous agency: Critical perspectives on social interventions with children and youth in Africa', *Children's Geographies*, 10(4): 365–72. https://doi.org/10.1080/14733285.2012.726065

Cahill, C. (2007) 'The personal is political: Developing new subjectivities through participatory action research', *Gender, Place and Culture*, 14(3): 267–92. https://doi.org/10.1080/09663690701324904

Charnley, H. and Nkhoma, P. (2020) 'Moving beyond contemporary discourses: Children, prostitution, modern slavery and human trafficking', *Critical and Radical Social Work*, 8(2): 205–21. https://doi.org/10.1332/204986020X15945756343791

Cho, S., Crenshaw, K.W. and McCall, L. (2013) 'Toward a field of intersectionality studies: Theory, applications, and praxis', *Signs*, 38(4): 785–810. https://doi.org/10.1086/669608.

Clark, T., Foster, L., Sloan, L. and Bryman, A. (2021) *Bryman's Social Research Methods* (6th edition), Oxford: Oxford University Press.

Coffey, A.J. and Atkinson, P. (1996) *Making Sense of Qualitative Data: Complementary Research Strategies*, London: Sage.

Collins, P.H. (2019). *Intersectionality as Critical Social Theory*, Durham, NC: Duke University Press. https://doi.org/10.1215/9781478007098

Collins, P.H. and Bilge, S. (2020) *Intersectionality: Key Concepts* (2nd edition), Cambridge: Polity.

Collins, P.H., da Silva, E.C.G., Ergun, E., Furseth, I., Bond, K.D. and Martínez-Palacios, J. (2021) 'Intersectionality as critical social theory', *Contemporary Political Theory,* 20(3): 690–725. https://doi.org/10.1057/s41296-021-00490-0

Gadd, D. and Broad, R. (2018) 'Troubling recognitions in British responses to modern slavery', *The British Journal of Criminology*, 58(6): 1440–61.

Greenwood, D.J., Whyte, W.F. and Harkavy, I. (1993) 'Participatory action research as a process and as a goal', *Human Relations,* 46(2): 175–92. https://doi.org/10.1177/001872679304600203

Gudrun, T.J., Weibel, K. and Vitus, K. (2017) '"There is no racism here": Public discourses on racism, immigrants and integration in Denmark', *Patterns of Prejudice,* 51(1): 51–68. https://doi.org/10.1080/0031322X.2016.1270844

Hagelund, A. (2020) 'After the refugee crisis: Public discourse and policy change in Denmark, Norway and Sweden', *Comparative Migration Studies*, 8(13): 1–17. https://doi.org/10.1186/s40878-019-0169-8

Malawi Government (2010) *Child Care, Protection and Justice Act*, Zomba: Government Print.

McCabe, H. and Eglen, L. (2022) '"I bought you. You are my wife": Modern slavery and forced marriage', *Journal of Human Trafficking*, 1–24. https://doi.org/10.1080/23322705.2022.2096366

Moller, I.B. and Cardoso, J.C. (2023) 'When the paradigm shift goes wrong: The case of refugees in Denmark', *Tempo Exterior No 46*, 24(I): 61–75.

Nkhoma, P. and Charnley, H. (2018) 'Child protection and social inequality: Understanding child prostitution in Malawi', *Social Sciences*, 7(10): 185. https://doi.org/10.3390/socsci7100185

Nussbaum, M. (2001) 'Adaptive preferences and women's options', *Economics and Philosophy*, 17: 67–88.

Nussbaum, M. (2007) 'Human rights and human capabilities', *Harvard Human Rights Journal*, 20: 21–4.

Nussbaum, M.C. (2013) *Creating Capabilities: The Human Development Approach*, Cambridge, MA: Harvard University Press.

Rodney, W. (2018) *How Europe Underdeveloped Africa*, London: Verso.

Sen, A. (1983) 'Poor, relatively speaking', *Oxford Economic Papers*, 35(2): 153–69. https://doi.org/10.1093/oxfordjournals.oep.a041587

Sen, A. (1985) 'A sociological approach to the measurement of poverty: A reply to Professor Peter Townsend', *Oxford Economic Papers*, 37(4): 669–76. https://doi.org/10.1093/oxfordjournals.oep.a041716

Sen, A. (1999) *Development as Freedom*, Oxford: Oxford University Press.

Sen, A. (2005). 'Human rights and capabilities', *Journal of Human Development*, 6(2): 151–66. https://doi.org/10.1080/14649880500120491

Shamrova, D.P. and Cummings, C.E. (2017) 'Participatory Action Research (PAR) with children and youth: An integrative review of methodology and PAR outcomes for participants, organizations, and communities', *Children and Youth Services Review*, 81: 400–12. https://doi.org/10.1016/j.childyouth.2017.08.022

Silverman, D. (2022) *Doing Qualitative Research* (6th edition), London: Sage.

Silverman, D. (2024) *Interpreting Qualitative Data* (7th edition), London: Sage.

Sunak, R. (2023) 'If you come to the UK illegally', Twitter, Available from: https://twitter.com/RishiSunak/status/1633158789103747072

Tambulasi, R. (2009) 'Decentralization as a breeding ground for conflicts: An analysis of institutional conflicts in Malawi's decentralized system', *Journal of Administration & Governance*, 4(2): 28–39.

Thi, A.M., Zimmerman, C., Pocock, N.S., Chan, C.W. and Ranganathan, M. (2021) 'Child domestic work, violence, and health outcomes: A rapid systematic review', *International Journal of Environmental Research and Public Health*, 19(1): 427.

Townsend, P. (1985) 'A sociological approach to the measurement of poverty – A rejoinder to Professor Amartya Sen', *Oxford Economic Papers*, 37(4): 659–68. https://doi.org/10.1093/oxfordjournals.oep.a041715

Townsend, P. (2010) 'The meaning of poverty', *The British Journal of Sociology*, 61(s1): 85–102. https://doi.org/10.1111/j.1468-4446.2009.01241.x

UNCRC (1989) *Convention on the Rights of the Child*, United Nations, Treaty Series, 1577(3), Available from: http://www.hakani.org/en/convention/Convention_Rights_Child.pdf

United Nations (2000) *Optional Protocol to the Convention on the Rights of the Child on the Sale of Children, Child Prostitution and Child Pornography*, Available from: http://www.ohchr.org/Documents/ProfessionalInterest/crc-sale.pdf

United Nations Human Rights Council (UNHRC) (2017) *Resolution Adopted by the Human Rights Council on 28 September 2017: 36/5. Unaccompanied Migrant Children and Adolescents and Human Rights*, New York: United Nations, Available from: https://www.un.org/en/development/desa/population/migration/generalassembly/docs/globalcompact/A_HRC_RES_36_5.pdf

Young, S. (2022) 'British Police say immigration centre attack was terrorist incident', Reuters, 5 November, Available from: https://www.reuters.com/world/uk/british-police-say-dover-attack-was-motivated-by-terrorist-ideology-2022-11-05/

PART III

Creative practice

This final section of the book, 'Creative practice', turns towards creative interventions being used in the social, community and therapeutic sectors, building on the implications of the research and practice narratives in the previous two sections. Highlighting the need for values-based practice, these chapters focus on the creative use of arts-based interventions in particular, which overlap social work, community work and therapeutic practices focused on wellbeing and trauma recovery.

Arts-based interventions can provide rich expressive avenues for migrants with low levels of English, and those with experiences of trauma, in expressing and understanding their experiences and working towards recovery. Such creative means of expression allow for participatory practices that equalise power dynamics and enable intersectional identities and differences to emerge. However, they are often overlooked and under-funded by political ideologies that are focused on deficit assumptions and short-term hard outcomes over meaningful long-term recovery. Values-based and creative practices, though precariously funded, challenge problematic discourses about refugee communities and work with them in more positive and empowering ways.

The section starts with a consideration of the need for values-based practice from Finbar Cullinan in Chapter 10, drawing on his research with volunteers engaged with Social Work Without Borders (SWWB). In Chapters 11 and 12, community arts work emerges as particular focus of creative interventions that overlaps social work, community work and interventions focused on wellbeing and trauma recovery. Marina Rova, Claire Burrell and Marika Cohen outline arts-based therapeutic interventions with migrant women in temporary accommodation. Rachel Hughes, Marijke Steedman and Brian Callan explore social work practice through arts work with refugee and asylum-seeking young people. These chapters outline the creative practice examples and explore what they offered to communities in expressing their experiences and supporting their empowerment and recovery. We bring these creative practices to light to raise their profile as effective and meaningful interventions for refugee and migrant communities, supported by the research and engagement with the voices and narratives of these communities in the preceding sections.

10

Social justice and professional values: exploring motivations and opportunities for values-led practice

Finbar Cullinan

Social Workers Without Borders (SWWB) is an organisation engaging with migrants in the UK and in mainland Europe on the UK border (Wroe, 2019). The organisation was formed in 2016 in response to the increased global migration of people to Europe in the 2010s (EU, 2017). Its work, conducted by a network of volunteers, is divided into three pillars: direct work; social work education; and campaigning. Direct work includes visiting people at home and in detention centres in the UK (or online as necessitated by the COVID-19 pandemic) to carry out best-interest assessments in support of immigration cases, and providing practical support and conducting social work assessments for people on the UK border in France or who have been refused entry or return to the UK while in another country.

As a volunteer for the organisation, I undertook a study into why these social workers chose to volunteer alongside their busy day jobs. By drawing directly on the voices and experiences of practitioners, and thus indirectly on the experiences of migrant communities with whom they worked, the study sought to explore what compels these volunteers and consider the group in the context of current practice issues for social workers.

A note on terminology

Despite having specific legal definitions in relation to UK immigration status, the terms 'migrant', 'asylum seeker', 'refugee' and 'immigrant' have been used interchangeably in discourse (Derluyn and Broekaert, 2007). SWWB works with people affected by borders who may fit into various legal categories, from unaccompanied asylum seekers arriving on boats in Kent, to people whose status in the UK is insecure following the 'circus of hoops' that is the immigration system. In this chapter, 'migrant' and 'practice with migrants' are used to describe the people with whom SWWB works and the type of social work, in keeping with the language used by SWWB (Wroe, 2019).

Background

Studies into what motivates people to become social workers reveal the significance of a person's values in inspiring someone to join a profession engaged with improving the lives of individuals within society (O'Connor et al, 1984; Christie and Kruk, 1998; BMRB, 2005; Furness, 2007; Wilson and McCrystal, 2007; Stevens et al, 2012). Considering how these personal values relate to the (often contested) concept of the professional values of social work becomes particularly important when practising with migrants within the context of hostile government immigration policies.

Banks (2008) explores the value base of social work, including discussion of how contemporary neoliberal politics can impact how professional values are formulated and codified. Likewise, Harris (2014) examines how political changes beginning in the 1980s have atomised and degraded the scope of social work in ways that echo to this day. Donovan et al (2017), among others, have argued that this has resulted in what is described as a crisis of identity for the profession, as formerly held or acknowledged values are challenged within the constraints of government policies. As a consequence, social justice has emerged as a value around which to rally in the face of austerity, hostility to immigration and policies that have challenged how many social workers can do their jobs. Higgs (2015) and Solas (2008) discuss social justice in social work and how it can play out in practice. Solas (2008) asserts that any theory of social justice for social workers cannot omit equality, both between individuals and egalitarianism of mutually valued resources. Establishment of this thus becomes a part of the project of social work. Higgs (2015) calls on social justice as a guiding light for social workers within the neoliberal paradigm, who must tread the path of caring and serving while avoiding the trap of oppressing service users.

Social work is inextricable from politics, exemplified by the social workers from SWWB, whose profession is regulated by government policy and legislation – and who support people affected by political decisions. However, Jordan (2004) argues that increased individualism, arising from an ideological shift in politics, has eroded the political context of social work as a profession both in its professional values and how it is practised. Whittington and Whittington (2006) discuss emancipatory social work as the consequent reassertion of social work as political, acknowledging the structural (and thus political) forces influencing the daily lives of those whom social work serves.

Exploring the possible tensions between values and practice, Humphries (2004) examines how implementing immigration policy can conflict with personal and professional values of practitioners. Lipsky's (1980) idea of street level bureaucrats has become a touchstone when considering how individual workers interpret and enact policy at the local level, offering a lens through which to view how social workers (among other professionals) practise within the web of policy.

Work with migrants incurs thinking beyond one nation's borders and can extend to considering international elements of social work practice. The potential for social work as an internationally connected profession with shared values, supporting people globally, is perhaps best illustrated through the work of the International Federation of Social Work and its international definition of social work (IFSW, 2014).

Brief methodology

This qualitative study explored the motivations of individual volunteers and does not claim to represent all of the practitioners within SWWB. An interpretivist/constructivist epistemological approach was taken in the research, reflecting the participants' views as the source of data (Creswell, 2014), acknowledging the impact of my own experiences as a participant researcher who also volunteered for the organisation (Mertens, 2014). Recruitment of participants was by self-selection (Lavrakas, 2008). A notice was posted on the online forum for volunteers, followed by snowball sampling (Walliman, 2006), in which word of the study spread beyond the forum. Five volunteers, based across the UK, were interviewed online or over the phone. Interviews were semi-structured to elicit some overall consistency while allowing insight into the nuanced information constructing participants' motivations and opinions (Denscombe, 2010). Interviews were transcribed and then coded and analysed using thematic analysis (Braun and Clarke, 2006). The study had ethical approval from Goldsmiths, University of London and from SWWB. Participants' names have been replaced with pseudonyms in this chapter.

Findings and discussion
Social justice as a driving force

Human rights and social justice values were central motivations for all participants I spoke with, both to train as social workers and to volunteer for SWWB.

> My values got me into social work: human rights, taking an anti-oppressive approach, also I'm a socialist and wanted to work towards addressing inequality. (Sameera)

> I got into social care work on the principle of social justice and human rights and against a backdrop of Thatcher's government, a lot of economic hardship. (Katie)

> You really feel like you are working for social justice with [SWWB]. (Sameera)

Yvonne spoke of training as a social worker to connect values-led activism with direct work with people – particularly 'around anti-racism and ecological and social justice'.

A critical/radical social work standpoint argues that neoliberal politics has diminished the political scope of social work (Banks, 2008) and argues there has been a concurrent individualisation in recent decades both of social work values and practice (Jordan, 2004). A response to this ideological shift would be the reassertion of the 'social justice mandate' (Higgs, 2015: 115), which motivates many to become social workers and maintains them in their work. It was clear for participants I spoke with that striving for justice on a systemic, humanitarian level, particularly for migrants, was a central part of their vocation.

Practising in the way you know you should

SWWB allowed these volunteers to practice in accordance with their values.

> For me what's important is, is about the values. What resonates with me is what it stands for so if you're thinking about issues of human rights, issues of social justice, issues of equality. (Patience)

> [SWWB] is a chance to do social work that is true to your values, that's why you do it. It inspires me, it's professionally invigorating. (Sameera)

> There's a complete congruence between ethics and practice when I'm volunteering, what I can say to people, the discussions that we can have. (Katie)

There was also a notion that working with migrants in this capacity was liberating from a practice point of view:

> It can be a kind of liberatory model of social work. (Katie)

> It has been liberating in a lot of ways because you actually get to talk to the young people. (Patience)

Being allowed the space for empathetic practice, with capacity for demonstrating that you care, were paramount and for some the social workers, contrasted with their experiences in their 'day jobs'. Frank stated: 'What is important to me is being able to practice in a way that is, you know, the right way to practice.'

Yvonne discussed how their experiences with SWWB interplayed with their values of social justice and human rights:

> The kind of practical things that social workers can do to try and help out, but also how it kind of opened out questions of social justice, ethics of social work and, what we could be doing with our professional skills and voice. (Yvonne)

That personal and professional values were important for these volunteers in choosing social work as a job and then choosing to volunteer is probably unsurprising. It is also broadly in keeping with studies into why people become social workers (O'Connor et al, 1984; Christie and Kruk, 1998; BMRB, 2005; Furness, 2007; Wilson and McCrystal, 2007; Stevens et al, 2012).

While participants certainly reported wanting to support individuals on a personal level, in balance with this there was a stronger adherence to notions of what Stevens et al (2012) call 'societal altruism' than reported in other research. The recurring themes of 'social justice', 'human rights', 'anti-oppressive approaches' and 'equality', along with contextualising practice in terms of political critique, describes this social work with migrants as seeking wider social change, in opposition to politics of exclusion, alongside supporting individuals.

This could suggest that the volunteers I spoke to have a desire and conviction to enact social change beyond the individual in their work that is not necessarily common to all social workers. This would align these participants with the emancipatory stream of social work values (Whittington and Whittington, 2006) and with convictions linked to broader political concepts and analyses of social systems (Higgs, 2015; Solas, 2008), fitting with the experiences of migrant communities traversing frequently oppressive immigration systems. The anti-oppressive approach to practice attempts to achieve material change for people by seeking fair treatment and distribution of social resources (Parrott, 2014). Migrants and those oppressed by borders are a group for whom social workers with emancipatory/anti-oppressive values may well be motivated to support.

Some (notably McLaughlin, 2005) argue that the language of anti-oppressive practice has been subsumed by neoliberal governments, allowing the state to preclude its radical potential and dampen its power. This critical/radical standpoint chimes with the frustration with elements of statutory services reported by some of these volunteers and with which volunteering with migrants was contrasted. Similar to the impact of neoliberal politics since the 1980s (Harris, 2014) and what is described by some as the crisis in social work (Reisch, 2013; Donavan et al, 2017), some of the social workers I spoke to suffered reduced creativity, prescriptive bureaucracy, time restrictions and inefficacies in line with the neoliberal reduction of social work into 'atomised, codified, routinised and calibrated practice, to achieve competitive organisational efficiencies' (Thompson and Wadley, 2017: 5). The view of statutory social work in which procedure has become the guiding force, usurping ideas of making change on a societal level alongside working with the individual (see, for example, Butler and Drakeford, 2001), seems an adequate articulation of the frustrations that some participants expressed, and the salve that their voluntary work with migrants provided.

A critical space for contemporary practice

For one volunteer, SWWB provided an opportunity for collectively challenging policies contrary to social work ethics and values. In relation to the placement of UK Home Office staff in social work offices, Patience found SWWB a space for discussion:

> Why are we allowing immigration officers in the Local Authorities? And that goes to the heart of the knowledge base because if we are very confident in what we know and also very confident in our values then we can challenge those approaches from government. (Patience)

Similarly, on the contentious topic of age assessments on unaccompanied asylum-seeking young people (Crawley, 2007; Cemlyn and Nye, 2012; Preston, 2022), SWWB was also a forum for discussion.

> Because we're really in the middle of theory, politics, campaigning and actual practice we've got the space to explore those things together, you can really get to the [details] of what [new practice] would actually look like. (Yvonne)

A participant with experience of conducting age assessments for local authorities described feeling that time constraints meant that adequate assessment was challenging:

> I think what gets lost in that is the personal experiences these young people have and what may make them much more different from a 14 year old that we are used to seeing in our practice from a 14 year old who has travelled from Afghanistan to Calais. (Patience)

By comparison they reported that SWWB allowed for work that gave time and room for the practitioner/client relationship to develop. SWWB was thus found to be a space contrary to the situation of some statutory social workers, who it is argued are expected to monitor and ration services to migrants in a way that is diametrically opposed to a responsibility for social justice (Humphries, 2004).

A collective voice for a political profession

SWWB was felt to be a vehicle for an openly political collective professional voice on practice with migrants but also on social work generally, in the context of a perceived absence of this in other organisations.

> Politics sit at the heart of social work so actually issues of poverty are the domains of social workers. (Patience)

> Let's politicise this interaction, let's look at what's going on here, let's look at what power is at play … where I can integrate that into my actual social work practice but also, bring anti-racist, no-borders, anti-authoritarian narrative and campaigning into the social work profession as well. (Yvonne)

> We need to collectivise as professionals around our principles and our beliefs and our ethics. (Frank)

In relation to migration, SWWB offered an opportunity to make a collective response that filled a perceived void created by an inadequate response from social work as a profession.

> Then the refugee crisis, I felt that there was no one speaking out from our profession. (Katie)

> We [social workers] seem to be lagging behind when there are what I call human disasters … if you look at our values we should be in the forefront. (Patience)

> There's something really valuable that social workers can bring being in these spaces [migrant camps] and they're not really there. (Yvonne)

Thus, volunteers were attracted to a way of responding to the current situations around international migration that they felt was absent elsewhere in their professional lives.

Similarly, participants were afforded an opportunity to collectively contribute and challenge professional policy.

> We can say 'we do not agree with this policy' and we have a view point, when you're in local authorities I think it's very limited what you can say and cannot. (Patience)

> Wanting to challenge that this was some kind of security crisis, you know the security narrative and say, hold on a minute, this is a massive safeguarding crisis for women and children. And as a profession that works to safeguard women and children we should be saying something about it. (Yvonne)

This collective challenge to policy can be viewed through the lens of street level bureaucrats, with these volunteers (as implementers of social policy) having bottom-up policy-making impact through their active concern for social work with migrants (Lipsky,1980; Gilson, 2015). However, Lipsky's notion of individual discretion (choosing to enact policy in a certain way as a result of personal politics) does not fully capture how these volunteers are taking a proactive approach in using their practice expertise to influence policy.

Perhaps the notion of deviant social work (Carey and Foster, 2011) offers a way of describing social workers who choose to challenge government policy, although the language of subterfuge and sabotage (Carey, 2008; Carey and Foster, 2011) is at odds with the language of the social workers I spoke to. Far from being discrete or hidden, these volunteers are organised as a professional group to advocate for the essentially political nature of social work with migrants and beyond.

Social work with migrants as part of an international cause

Volunteering for SWWB allowed practitioners to align with social workers globally in response to the realities of migration.

> I believe in an international form of social work and I think that is what we are seeing here [through liaising with social workers in other countries], it gives me hope that social workers in the UK are beginning to see that we can play a bigger role, even on the international stage. (Patience)

> Although we do everything that's contextualised by organisations and structures and stuff in the UK, and in a kind of Eurocentric model of social work, otherwise, fundamentally, we share the same profession. (Frank)

By working with and learning from the experiences of people from around the world, these volunteers described the widening scope of their work beyond national boundaries. The participants' inferences to their desire for a profession unified by international values and the feeling that social work needs to extend beyond borders echoes proponents of an international identity for the profession and, again, the importance of unifying social justice values. The International Federation of Social Workers' definition of social work holds notions of social justice on a societal level at its core, above working solely with individuals (IFSW, 2014). Similarly, in *The Global Agenda for Social Work and Social Development: Extending the Influence of Social Work*, a link is made between inequality between nations and 'extensive migratory movements', and the consequent need for a social work response on an international scale (Truell and Jones, 2012: 5).

A growing body of literature (for example, Lawrence, 2009; Blok, 2012; and much of what is published in the journal *International Social Work*) links international migration and the need for social work across borders. Dominelli et al unite social workers globally through the shared values of 'respect for human life and dignity, the struggle to ensure social justice, human rights and the freedom to live life as full members of society' (2014: 91) while Golightley and Holloway (2017) state that, in the face of common challenges, social workers internationally must stand up and fight for shared values such as these.

Likewise, when the volunteers in this study discussed what compels them, their conceptions of the role and responsibility of social workers to seek social justice was, like the lives of the people they volunteered with, extended beyond borders.

Conclusion

The interviews with these volunteers demonstrate that SWWB provided a space for them to enact the values that drew them to social work in the first place. The rights-based practice at the heart of SWWB's work challenges the notion of deserving and undeserving members of our global society, an idea too often propagated by divisionary national immigration policies. Participants in this research described an opportunity to work with migrant communities in accordance with the values that they felt were at the heart of social work as a profession, along with the ability to provide meaningful critique of policies that ran contrary to these values: critical social work in action.

The collective professional voice emerging from organising as SWWB was an empowering chance to assert the necessarily political nature of a profession engaged with eliciting change on both the individual and systemic level. And the collective identity of the profession stretched beyond borders for several of these volunteers, who referred to the international value base binding social workers globally, especially poignant when supporting international migrants and those affected and oppressed by borders, all integrated within a global politically active network of change agents, bound and protected by a humanitarian ethos.

It could be valuable in future to explore whether practitioners for SWWB perceive their work explicitly in terms of the radical, or indeed any other, theoretical strand of social work, as the organisation offers a space for practice that challenges systemic forces facing marginalised people. Similarly, comparing with other practitioner-led groups worldwide may demonstrate alignment depicting a movement, alive in contemporary social work with migrants today, that seeks to use values of social justice and human rights, and to react and respond to restrictive immigration policies.

Apparent from the testimonies of these volunteers is that they are a group of social workers for whom social justice is fundamental to their practice. Their understanding of the social work profession is that it is inescapably political and should be critically engaged with the issues that challenge and oppress marginalised people internationally.

References

Banks, S. (2008) 'The social work value base' in A. Barnard, N. Horner and J. Wild (eds) *The Value Base of Social Work and Social Care*, Maidenhead: Open University Press, pp 24–40.

Blok, W. (2012) *Core Social Work International Theory, Values and Practice*, London: Jessica Kingsley.

Braun, V. and Clarke, V. (2006) 'Using thematic analysis in psychology', *Qualitative Research in Psychology*, 3(2): 77–101.

British Market Research Bureau (BMRB) Social Research (2005) *Motivations for Undertaking the New Social Work Degree*, Edinburgh: Scottish Executive Education Department, Available from: http://www.scotland.gov.uk/Resource/Doc/77843/0018637.pdf

Butler, I. and Drakeford, M. (2001) '"Which Blair project?" Communitarianism, social authoritarianism and social work', *Journal of Social Work*, 1(1): 7–19.

Carey, M. (2008) 'The quasi-market revolution in the head: ideology, discourse, care management', *Journal of Social Work*, 8(4): 341–62.

Carey, M. and Foster, V. (2011) 'Introducing "deviant" social work: Contextualising the limits of radical social work whilst understanding (fragmented) resistance within the social work labour process', *British Journal of Social Work*, 41(3): 576–93.

Cemlyn, S.J. and Nye, M. (2012) 'Asylum seeker young people: Social work value conflicts in negotiating age assessment in the UK', *International Social Work*, 55(5): 675–88.

Christie, A. and Kruk, E. (1998) 'Choosing to become a social worker: Motives, incentives, concerns and disincentives', *Social Work Education*, 17(1): 21–34.

Crawley, H. (2007) *When Is a Child Not a Child?*, London: Immigration Law Practitioners Association.

Creswell, J.W. (2014) *Research Design: Qualitative, Quantitative and Mixed Methods Approaches* (4th edition), Thousand Oaks, CA: Sage.

Denscombe, M. (2010) *The Good Research Guide for Small-Scale Social Research Projects* (4th edition), Maidenhead: Open University Press.

Derluyn, I. and Broekaert, E. (2007) 'Different perspectives on emotional and behavioural problems in unaccompanied refugee children and adolescents', *Journal of Ethnicity & Health*, 12(2): 141–62.

Dominelli, L., Hackett, S. and Ioakimidis, V. (2014) 'Social work: A varied profession with some common concerns', *International Social Work*, 57(2): 89–91.

Donovan, J., Rose, D. and Connolly, M. (2017) 'A crisis of identity: Social work theorising at a time of change', *British Journal of Social Work*, 47(8): 2291–307.

EU (2017) *The EU and the Migration Crisis*, Available from: https://op.europa.eu/en/publication-detail/-/publication/e9465e4f-b2e4-11e7-837e-01aa75ed71a1/language-en

Furness, S. (2007) 'An enquiry into students' motivations to train as social workers in England', *Journal of Social Work*, 7(2): 239–53.

Gilson, L. (2015) 'Michael Lipsky, street level bureaucracy, dilemmas of the individual in public service' in M. Lodge, E. Page and S. Balla (eds) *Oxford Handbook of the Classics of Public Policy and Administration*, Oxford: Oxford University Press, pp 383–404.

Golightley, M. and Holloway, M. (2017) 'Editorial: The voice of international social work', *British Journal Of Social Work*, 47(2): 285–92.

Harris, J. (2014) '(Against) Neoliberal social work', *Critical and Radical Social Work*, 2(1): 7–22.

Higgs, A. (2015) 'Social justice' in L. Bell and T. Hafford-Litchfield (eds) *Ethics, Values and Social Work Practice*, Berkshire: McGraw-Hill Education, pp 112–21.

Humphries, B. (2004) 'An unacceptable role for social work: Implementing immigration policy', *The British Journal of Social Work*, 34(1): 93–107.

IFSW (2014) 'Global definition of social work', Available from: http://ifsw.org/policies/definition-of-social-work/

Jordan, B. (2004) 'Emancipatory social work? Opportunity or oxymoron', *British Journal of Social Work*, 34(1): 5–19.

Lawrence, S. (2009) *Introducing International Social Work*, Exeter: Learning Matters.

Lavrakas, P.J. (2008) *Encyclopaedia of Survey Research Methods*, London: Sage.

Lipsky, M. (1980) *Street-level Bureaucracy: Dilemmas of the Individual in Public Services*, New York: Russell Sage Foundation.

McLaughlin, K. (2005) 'From ridicule to institutionalization: Anti-oppression, the state and social work', *Critical Social Policy*, 25(3): 283–305.

Mertens, D. (2014) *Research and Evaluation in Education and Psychology* (4th edition), London: Sage.

O'Connor, I., Dalgleish, L. and Khan, J. (1984) 'A reflection of the rising spectre of conservatism: Motivational accounts of social work students', *British Journal of Social Work*, 14(1): 227–40.

Parrott, L. (2014) *Values and Ethics in Social Work Practice* (2nd edition), Exeter: Learning Matters.

Preston, R. (2022) 'Home Office social worker guidance unlawful, High Court rules' Community Care, 24 January, Available from: https://www.communitycare.co.uk/2022/01/24/home-office-social-worker-guidance-unlawful-high-court-rules/

Reisch, M. (2013) 'What is the future of social work?', *Critical and Radical Social Work*, 1(1): 67–85. https://doi.org/10.1332/204986013X665974

Solas, J. (2008) 'What kind of social justice does social work seek?', *International Social Work*, 51(6): 813–22.

Stevens, M., Moriarty, J., Manthorpe, J., Hussein, S., Sharpe, E., Orme, J. et al (2012) 'Helping others or a rewarding career? Investigating student motivations to train as social workers in England', *Journal of Social Work*, 12(1): 16–36.

Thompson, L. and Wadley, D. (2017) 'Countering globalisation and managerialism: Relationist ethics in social work', *International Social Work*, 61(5): 706–23.

Truell, R. and Jones, D.N. (2012) *The Global Agenda for Social Work and Social Development: Extending the Influence of Social Work*, IFSW, Available from: https://www.ifsw.org/wp-content/uploads/ifsw-cdn/assets/ifsw_24848-10.pdf

Walliman, N. (2006) *Social Research Methods*, London: Sage.

Whittington, C. and Whittington, M. (2006) 'Ethics and social care: Political, organisational and interagency dimensions' in A. Leathard and S. McLaren (eds) *Ethics: Contemporary Challenges in Health and Social Care*, Bristol: Policy Press, pp 83–96.

Wilson, G. and McCrystal, P. (2007) 'Motivations and career aspirations of MSW students in Northern Ireland', *Social Work Education*, 26(1): 35–52.

Wroe, L. (2019) 'Social working without borders: Challenging privatisation and complicity with the hostile environment', *Critical and Radical Social Work*, 7(2): 251–5.

11

Finding new ground: a creative movement and art group with asylum-seeking women

Marina Rova, Claire Burrell and Marika Cohen

Piecing together a patchwork narrative

In this chapter, we share insights from the development of Moving Space, a creative movement and art group with asylum-seeking women living in temporary accommodation. After successfully establishing and delivering the project between 2018 and 2019 (see Rova et al, 2020) the group was disrupted by the global COVID-19 pandemic. Successive lockdowns and self-isolation measures, in conjunction with the loss of resources and funding, resulted in the group's cessation for two years. The group was re-introduced in 2021 and continues to be delivered in 2024. This chapter draws on the work that took place in 2021 and 2022. By the end of 2022, the Moving Space project had supported more than 100 women from Albania, Iran, Palestine, United Arab Emirates, Pakistan, India, Sri Lanka, Afghanistan, El Salvador, Democratic Republic of Congo, Ethiopia, Somalia, Sudan, Kurdistan, China and Russia.

The material we share here emerged from our evaluation of Moving Space, through a peer supervision process that ran concurrently with the project. Regular reflective meetings facilitated an inquiry into our practice which brought us closer to the lived experience of our group members. These reflections were not set up within a research framework, thus women taking part in the group were not recruited as research participants. Similarly, working (with)in the transient and liminal context of a hostel setting prevented us from establishing a traditional psychotherapeutic frame for the work. Therefore, we locate the Moving Space group within arts-based community practice (Erel et al, 2017; Kaptani and Yuval-Davis, 2008; Vachelli, 2018) supporting physical, creative, emotional and social engagement. The practice enables open, inclusive and collaborative connections through shared movement and art-making. Given the sensitive nature of the themes explored, we have taken care to anonymise group material we write about. We present stories through composite cases to protect the privacy of individuals. The peer supervision and evaluation process involved a reflection on the therapists' experiences working alongside the women, an exploration of the group themes emerging through improvised movement and image, and a broader consideration of systemic, organisational and intersectional dynamics of the process. The chapter is an inquiry into arts-based community practice with asylum-seeking women living in temporary accommodation and recognises creativity as a transformative agent of hope.

We organise the chapter around four themes that emerged through the creative process of the Moving Space group: travelling water, staying afloat, making into being and finding new ground. Not only are these themes creative crystallisations of the women's narratives as part of the group process, they also relate to wider socio-political issues influencing migrants in the 21st century. These four themes reflect the women's experiences of forced journeys, focusing on survival, finding and settling into new ways of being, and finding hope for the future. In addition, these themes serve as a symbolic articulation of the facilitators' experience of holding the group, thus speaking to a parallel process between participants and group leaders. For this reason, the text which follows becomes a patchwork narrative co-created by the voices of asylum-seeking women, two therapists facilitating the work, and one co-explorer, who was not part of the group but supported the peer supervision and evaluation process. All material shared, involving participants' stories, has been altered to protect the women's confidentiality.

Positionality and group structure

The co-facilitators took part in the creative process, their movement and images often tracing, embodying and reflecting the emerging themes of the group. Thus, a shared narrative was created between women's individual stories and the life-cycle of the group. Sessions would begin from a seated circle. Gentle introductions included the sharing of names and often countries of origin or significant places and landmarks encountered while travelling. Surprisingly, this would often reveal that co-residents in the hostel environment, neighbours living in adjacent rooms, were yet to meet. Small globe balls, given out at the beginning of the session, were collectively placed on a large cloth map of the world, on the ground in the centre of the group circle.

Time was taken to tend to the body, offering gestures of kindness to the self, co-creating space in which awareness of both the physical and felt-sense could be fostered. Suffering of physical ailments could be named whereas affective responses took more time to emerge. Women might say, 'it is cold' rather than 'I am sad'. Often, practical tasks would draw the focus away from affective response and moving and naming parts of the body would become an opportunity to practise speaking English in a safe environment.

The therapists would gently expand on bodily expressions emerging in the group (apparent in the shape of gesture, posture and bodily shaping) and movement improvisation would often evoke traditional rituals, cultural practices and steps from folk dances. In turn, these would connect to familiar landscapes and journeys or those left behind. Sometimes, moving through new landscapes into the future would be evoked during the creative explorations. The tension between moving forwards and backwards was always palpable.

During the art-making process, individuals attended to their own space, responding to their needs. They worked on their own images, sometimes in silence and at other times while conversing and sharing with peers. The completed images were then looked at and discussed together. Quite often, the group members decided to take their images with them, perhaps taking control of their future engagement or disengagement with the work. On one occasion, the sole group member asked to keep an image created by one of the group leaders. The group leader's image had evoked a positive memory in contrast to the bleakness of the woman's own images that connected to something more painful that she wished to leave behind (for us to hold).

The art-making, too, offered a way to connect with the sense of home through tracing familiar landscapes. The therapists' images encapsulated this as the images of mountains, lakes and forests (and other important landmarks) emerged across artwork, making connections with something of the past that is known and familiar, stable and protective. We also resonated with other more painful aspects of these symbolic articulations. For example, the image of a molten rock needing containment. The different layers of experience were contained within the images of the group, and emergent narratives were held within the process, not always needing to be revealed or spoken of explicitly.

Due to the sensitive nature of the participants' stories, with respect to their immigration status, we decided not to use their images for the purpose of this writing. The images we include were made by the facilitators spontaneously working alongside the group members. Figure 11.1 is a therapist's image depicting three mountains with steps up to the summit of one of them, representing the journeys that women faced.

In the sections that follow we move through the women's experiences as articulated by the four themes generated in the group: 'travelling water', 'staying afloat', 'making into being' and 'finding new ground'. We move from despair to survival and from uncertainty to safety as new ground is found in the hope of a new horizon.

Travelling water

We gathered to review the work as part of the peer supervision process of the project. Sitting in a circle on mats and cushions in a small dance studio,

Figure 11.1: Mountains (therapist's image)

we placed the artwork on the wooden floor. Pages and pages of images, stories, lived experiences played out before us. The warmth and comfort from which we were reflecting on the images contrasted with some of the isolating and bleak narratives the women were sharing.

We considered questions such as: How do we handle this material? Who are we, looking at these stories that are not (just) abstract metaphors borne out of a creative exploration, but fragments of a lived intersectional history … in the making? Because, though these images were unique to the women who created them, situated within specific time, place and socio-political contexts, they are also part of a larger unsettling picture. Forced migration, or involuntary displacement as it is also described, increased from 41 million affected people in 2010 to 78.5 million by the end of 2020 (Migration Data Portal, 2022).

Whether conflict-induced or disaster-induced, forced migration will continue to affect increasingly more people as the political, climate and cost-of-living crises escalating globally continue. The public view of migration is often shaped by the movement of populations as seen on our TV screens and in our news media ('boats arriving on our shores'). But displacement happens before the treacherous journey is undertaken. Refugees and other migrants are also often lumped into one box, even though their circumstances for fleeing their country vary significantly. People are forced to leave because of persecution due to their race, religion, nationality, political views or social group. Trafficking also forces people into involuntary displacement.

Once the journey of migration begins, people enter a transient state of being. They are neither here nor there, at once moving towards and away. Embarking on the process of migration is like entering a current of travelling water, always moving through space. The notion of home, of belonging, once known, lived and located is now uprooted, afloat. Transported as a somatic memory of deep embodiment, there is potential for grief and loss, an open wound, which migrants might nurse for years to come. But for many there is hope, desire for new locations, safe ground where home might become.

Thus, we may think of our group as a Moving (through) Space. Women arrived in this transient space, as if to rest briefly from their arduous journey before moving on. The group in this sense became a conduit for making visible the invisible experiences of asylum-seeking women. Perhaps, as in a side-road shelter, women who entered the space were able to pause, to be still and to stock up on (emotional) supplies. We nourished body and spirit through movement, art-making and camaraderie. We sat with the not-knowing of what came next. And we listened to fragments of stories. Women spoke of what was left behind and what they carried forwards. Trauma reverberated in the work implicitly and explicitly. We sat painfully holding the absence when no members walked through our open door. After knocking on their hostel bedroom door, women politely declined the invitation to join our session. Their 'no' was both a resounding communication of what it feels like to have a door shut in your face (time and again) and an opportunity to assert one's right to choose.

Looking through the group images, we noticed one element moving through, and joining up, the emerging material: travelling water. Water appeared in the shape of the sea, rivers and streams. There were also images of vessels carried through water, landscapes surrounding watery elements and layers forming below water. Water was present not only as a visual articulation but also as a symbolic narrative in the group material as seen in the following vignette.

Staying afloat

A young woman attended the group for the first time. Finding herself alone in the session, she used the space to speak privately of the imposed restrictions that led to her courageous decision to depart her native country. She defined a sense of necessity in her choice to flee, evoking both empowerment and extreme fear. Alone on foot, slowly moving across Europe, her journey had culminated in the perilous boat crossing across the English Channel from France. She described how the first attempt to cross the Channel had been aborted as the dinghy began to let in water and sink. On making it back to France, the other women in her group, so afraid, abandoned their journey. So, when the group set off for a second time, she was the sole woman on board;

curled up in the bottom of the inflatable boat, eyes closed, exhausted. She described her shut-down state, the disconnection from the men who rowed the vessel, her aloneness as she remained focused solely on her own survival.

Several weeks later, the young woman returned to take part in another session, this time participating with other female residents in a small group. In a guided exploration, the women spent time attending to their own self-care; each woman using a massage ball to explore and make contact with their own bodies, attuning to their felt-sense experience. Transitioning into a group explorative process, the women began working with a large blue stretch cloth; engaging in a billowing movement of the cloth, the group evoked a wavy sea. As one of the massage balls was rolled onto the cloth, the little illuminating ball was instantly dwarfed as it moved wildly across the vast open space of the cloth. The women became focused on following the ball's journey.

Instantly, the interplay articulated a sense of excitement, a freedom of will, while at the same time highlighting an uncontrollable risk as the ball rolled off the cloth several times. The therapists' connectivity to the perilous undertaking of the boat crossing was powerful as they held the young woman and her story in the creative process. The young woman also connected with other women who had made similar boat crossings.

> '6 hours … it took 6 hours', the young woman exclaimed, verbalising her association to the group. Then, pointing at other women in the circle, she continued, 'They came too, on a boat, all the family with their young son.'

Dropping the cloth to the ground, the women sat back into the circle of chairs, back on safe ground but exhausted again, some of them appeared dazed, looking faraway. It was not just an individual story of survival but a group story, miraculously they had all stayed afloat, all survived. Figure 11.2 shows a small boat floating in water, illustrating this theme.

Peter Levine (1997) writes about the importance that movement plays in the healing from trauma, particularly when our physiological response to the perceived threat has been to freeze. He suggests that while this survival strategy serves to protect us from danger, if the person is prevented from moving out of the situation (escaping) they are more likely to somatise the trauma and carry this freezing (blockage) in their psychological journey. In a similar vein, Gabor Mate (2003) suggests that it is not the actual trauma event that causes the damage but the physical and psychological adaptations a person has to make by way of coping, in the absence of adequate emotional holding immediately after the trauma.

Some weeks later, while visiting the art exhibition *Radical Beauty* by Helen Frankenthaler (2022), one of the therapists came upon the image of a

Figure 11.2: Staying afloat (therapist's image)

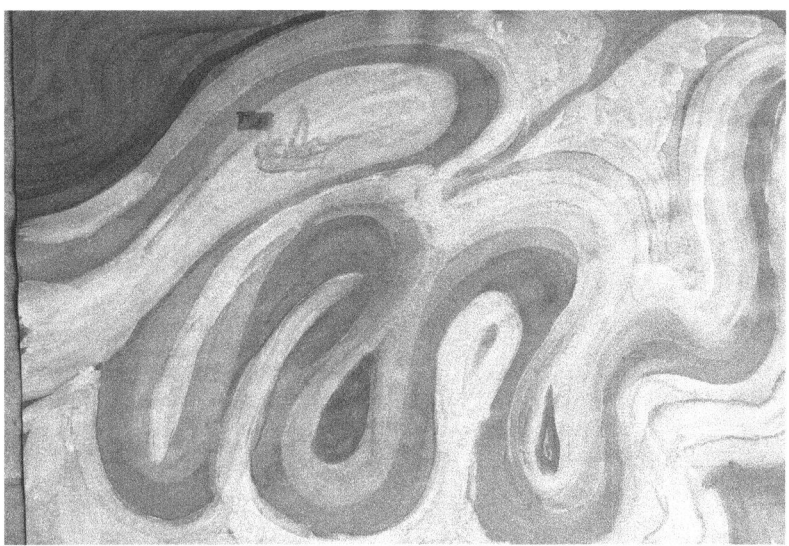

small boat in the vastness of the wood panel prints. Finding herself instantly moved, she sat for a moment, processing a vicarious response that was both physical and emotional, relocated (with)in the art object. The resonance of carrying and yet at the same time being transported by the work of the group had left her feeling afloat. The detail in the gallery artwork resonated with a sense of arrival; the group's boat too had arrived, they were now on safer ground. Remaining deeply touched and searching for words, to step away from this transferential process, the therapist was met by the artist's own words displayed in the exhibition: 'My work is not a matter of direct translation, but something is bound to creep into your head your heart' (Frankenhaler, 2022).

This kinaesthetic entanglement (Rova, 2023) experienced by the therapist and reflected in the artist's work is important in two ways. Attending to our relational moving body promotes empathy and compassion as we are moved to connect with others through a shared intersubjective experience. It also opens us up to vicarious traumatisation as unconscious resonance may lead to merging and over-identification. Holding trauma relationally is complex. Creative embodied process has the capacity to hold the 'unspeakable' (Eberhard-Kaechele, 2020) as the art form provides both a container and a safe distance from which to make sense of the material. The liminal space of creativity involves immersion in uninterrupted flow (see drawing/painting or movement improvisation). This in turn moves us out of fixed or stagnant positions. This may be considered as surviving in the present tense, in that the surviving is happening as it is expressed and experienced in the group.

The group holds a frame for symbolic enactment of the women's lived experiences of displacement and dislocation (see sea and boat enactment in the earlier vignette), while integrating opposites such as leaving and arrival, safety and grief.

Locating the experience of migration in the body can bring forward a sense of having a secure base, relocating a known sense of being and dwelling in a safe place. This might provide familiarity, a continuum perhaps in a time of constant change and unknown transition, thus enabling self-compassion and agency, evoking and consolidating resilience, innate resources and the readiness to take the next steps.

However, we are drawn to ponder what losing one's landscape entails. By landscape we refer to both a socio-political field and the immediacy of significant others, family, loved ones, community and also the actual land, the very physical terrain that one calls home. Indigenous belonging, the timeless traditions handed down through generations, link us to place. One might say … I know who I am because I belong to a cultural set of values, of beliefs, of practices. I know who I am because this mountain rises above me, this river flows past me and this tree gives me sweet fruit in summer. I relate to all that is around me, not only the human but the 'more-than-human' body (Frizell, 2023), which is a bio-system of exchange. Our relational body needs, and seeks to find, the known other, to resonate and exchange. When involuntary dislocation or a radical transition (Dokter, 2023) changes every aspect of our horizon, there is also a need to re-root, to connect again in an exterior way. We might internally hold onto the knowledge that the sun will rise again, but over which mountain will it emerge, over which rooftop, which skyscraper? In London, for example, any horizon at all can be difficult to find. Therefore, a need to shift, to make sense of new perspectives, look across new landscapes, and locate self in relation to new horizons is necessary in the process of making (something new) into being.

Making into being

For a period of time, a small group of women from the same country of origin frequented the group. In one session, two of these women participated, making a small group with the two therapists. While one woman had developed a knowledge of English through her education, the other was completely new to the English language and used the art-making part of the session to explore the diverse alphabet, practising phonetics and shaping letters.

Beginning the session on this particularly cold morning, the therapists supported the women's movement exploration by following a non-verbal patterning through which self-hugging movements and a self-soothing rocking rhythm emerged.

As movement expanded, shrugging shoulders led the women to recall movements from their traditional folk dance. Sourcing traditional music, dance steps were brought forward and the women invited the therapists to join them in a tight shoulder-to-shoulder vigorous and energising line dance. Having danced for some time, attention was drawn to the powerful leg action required in the dance and the woman who spoke English endorsed how women from her culture had 'very strong legs', describing her love of climbing and hiking in the local mountainous landscape.

The women commented on enjoying spending time away from their husbands and the small family rooms which had become homes in the hostel environment. Describing how the sessions gave them space to dance and listen to music without restraint, they placed value on this time for themselves and the word 'freedom' emerged.

Towards the end of the session, percussive instruments were offered and a delicate, gentle music was co-created. The therapists wondered whether any native words might be added or sung and the woman who spoke some English feared she might no longer remember the words to their traditional songs. Then spontaneously she began to sing the soothing words of a lullaby. The group accompanied her with gentle percussive music, as she sang several verses with tears visible in her eyes. The other woman remained silent and the therapists asked whether this song was known to her. 'Yes', she said 'but I do not sing it.' Speaking in their mother tongue, the women then spoke for some time and then translated for the therapists: 'My daughter died, following a miscarriage when my pregnancy was quite far advanced. After this I stopped singing the lullaby, it was too painful.' As the session closed, the woman went on to say that she had lost two daughters this way.

Incomprehensible loss and pain are often difficult to put into words, all the more so when faced with the additional challenges of speaking in a foreign language and navigating forced migration. Thompson et al (2022: 124) suggest that loss is not only a central theme in migrant and refugee women's experience, it is also 'located bodily as women [might be seen holding] their stomach or thoracic area, as they recount … traumatic events'. Building on Vromans et al (2017), who distinguish between the 'normal' experience of bereavement and loss linked to the displacement, Thompson et al (2022: 112) argue: 'Loss may be a universal experience. However, the multiplicity of how it is experienced, expressed and processed individually and culturally is socio-politically complex.' In the above vignette, the experience of loss surfaced after a journey into embodied memory was undertaken (through the folk dancing and lullaby singing). Every week, we arrived at the session not knowing what stories we would encounter. Women's creative and spontaneous engagement in the group gave form to their becoming.

Artistic practice provides a supportive medium for sharing and communicating lived experience. Thus, healthy parts of the self, which have remained intact and defined, are brought forward, carried with the person along their transition. The creative process itself provides an ethical tension for working on the boundary between artistic practice and therapy. Though not established as a psychotherapeutic intervention, the sessions honoured the importance of holding a therapeutic space where all the parts of oneself could come together (Fisher, 2017). Nurturing and modelling movements of self-care cultivated the women's capacity for self-soothing and self-regulation in the present moment. This in turn expanded their tolerance for inner conflict and emotionally overwhelming experiences to be carried forward and named. As Schlapobersky (2015: 410) explains:

> As people in a group construct the picture of a home that was once safe but now lost, they can generate a sense of safety or one of loss and in the group, they come to inhabit the very subject of our theme – safety or grief – through a process of enactment or recreation.

The therapists' own journeys of migration offered moments of connection, validation and hope for the group. The familiar experience of locating oneself between two lands and the sense of home remaining somewhat floating and out of reach were acknowledged. And, yet, despite recognising ourselves in others' stories, honouring women's personal boundaries was a key condition for making the group a safe space. These included respecting cultural and physical boundaries as well as the level of disclosure women chose to bring to the process. Some women struggled to reconcile revealing their emotional pain and vulnerability in the group with becoming overwhelmed by over-sharing.

Holding onto the past while beginning to imagine newness were sensitively considered within the group process. Nature and the elements were often accessed through the creative work providing a material connection between the old and new land. Shared belonging was thus found through the earth, water, air, moon and trees as they emerged as recurrent themes in the art-making. This creative meeting allowed women to explore a common ground and gave them the opportunity to express their difference and unique 'inquiry into future steps and into finding a way forward' (Burrell, 2023: 111).

Finding new ground

The UK Government gives the following definition of 'indefinite leave to remain': 'Indefinite leave to remain is how you settle in the UK. It's also called "settlement". It gives you the right to live, work and study here for as long as you like, and apply for benefits if you're eligible. You can use it to apply for British citizenship' (UK Government, 2023). An 'indefinite leave to remain' – let us consider this linguistic paradox for a moment.

Indefinite suggests either an unstated or unknown length of time or a not clearly defined timeframe. Leave as a verb means to go away from and as a noun it means allowing or causing to remain. Remain on the other hand as a verb means continuing to exist or staying in the place one has been occupying. It also means to be left over or outstanding. We might then ask, what does being 'settled' actually mean? Is there a final destination? Asylum seekers are neither here nor there, at once moving towards and away. They cannot remain so they leave, what remains behind is also left. And then, once they arrive, they need to leave, multiple times in order to … remain, indefinitely. Dokter (2023: 23) reminds us that '[t]he discourse of the in-between cultural subject can be silent on how unequal power relations impact the experience of in-betweenness. Belonging and attachment are complex for intercultural / transnational subjects'.

As an in-between space, the group also paralleled this existential uncertainty. Will the group remain (as a provision in the hostel) or must we leave (end the work)? Reliance on grant funding presented a constant struggle to keep the space alive, to ensure the survival of the work. The pandemic disrupted the group significantly and, yet, once funding was secured and the group re-established, we were challenged by more unpredictability as building works and scaffolding made access to our group room complicated. The constant obstacles we faced in keeping the group going left us feeling demoralised at times. What were we there to achieve?

The women's feedback clarified to us what the group had become for them: 'I met the most kind women in here and have best memories.' Meeting and being met by others is a core psychological and developmental need for all people. Being present in one's here and now, through the transformative experience of the group, connected women to a shared narrative and a mutual recognition rendering the memories of the group hopeful, as one woman stated: 'it helps the mental health'. Though not set up as a psychotherapeutic provision, the group process was undeniably therapeutic as the therapists invited a whole-person approach of holding space for creative expression and reflection. In this way, the conscious and unconscious sharing of lived experience, which materialised in the sessions in the shape of enactment, implicit and explicit memory, sensory stimulation, imagery and symbolism promoted integration of differentiated and often-marginalised parts of a person's psychic experience. Most importantly, this potential for integration was contained within the group process itself in that it supported active shifting of positions and perspective-taking through, for example, the use of different artistic media, witnessing and being witnessed by others, or supporting and being supported by others. Thus, different aspects of the women's resources were tapped into at different stages as they engaged with the creative process physically, cognitively, emotionally and socially. One woman described 'an environment in which you can breathe, very relaxing'.

We consider trauma work relative to 'survival' in the present time context. A present context which is different from the past is key to separating automatic arousal from the memory of the event. The importance of supporting positive implicit memory (for example, dwelling in soothing memory) expands one's capacity to stay with positive re-experiencing rather than the more familiar negative trauma triggers and smoke alarms. Attending to the felt level first, and then the meaning making, gave these women space to embody, communicate and re-vision their story. Creative arts practice transcends linguistic and cultural barriers and enables transformation to materialise in the here and now. As one woman stated: 'it is a group that helps your imagination'.

The journey travelled so far and the unknown destination that follows were recurring themes in the group. We were mapping the crossing of seas and borders, while still on the journey, surviving it. We were 'floating' while being moved by the currents. As well as noting motivated and enthusiastic responses to the group process, we observed some women closing their eyes, disconnecting and falling asleep. There was disengagement. We came to consider (self) isolation as a protective layer, defined and augmented by the impact of the coronavirus pandemic and the consequent restrictions imposed by hostel management. For example, the use of communal spaces or the dining area was not allowed. Activities in group rooms were suspended during lockdown and subsequent resident COVID-19 outbreaks led to clients eating all meals in their bedrooms.

At other times, there were glimpses of hoping for something new. Like the slight opening of a curtain enabling a little light to come in, but not knowing how long to wait until it is time to go again, to move on. The sharing of this vulnerability and fragility would be there in the blink of an eye, the enormity of the trauma, witnessed in a moment, then quickly covered, disconnected from. There was often a tension, a pull in different directions, not knowing which way to go. What is it like to come out of the small hostel bedroom? Is it safer to stay inside? Entering the new landscape involved a kind of negotiation between what is known and what is not known. Figure 11.3 represents this 'push and pull' process through an image of a large moon, which has its gravitational pull on the earth and causes times of low and high tide.

While we might think of trauma as localised in these women's stories, it is important to consider the transgenerational impact forced migration can have upon families and communities. Yet, as Malcolm Rushton (2022) suggests, migration can also be an unconscious motivation to begin one's psychological journey or, as Renos Papadopoulos (2021: 3) argues, an opportunity to 'transmut[e] suffering into transformative potentialities'.

Conclusion

We had come full circle as we (the authors) were meeting again to discuss the final edits of this chapter. We looked at the images that made it into

Figure 11.3: The moon (therapist's image)

this narrative and pondered where we had arrived in our writing process. We remembered one woman's response to our invitation to join the group. She was sitting with uncertainty, her bags packed day after day, waiting patiently for news of more permanent accommodation. Her plans had fallen through on several occasions. She had, on some level, already checked out: 'I have already left' even though she remained. How many more departures, mountains and travelling waters must be survived before a secure ground is found? While there may be no answer to this question, we argue that trauma-informed creative arts practice, as the provision illustrated in this chapter, can act as a form of reconciliation, empathic relating and community building. Most importantly, we have highlighted relationship and creativity as antidotes to adverse life experiences and perhaps a universal language for hope and connection.

References

Burrell, C. (2023) 'Being seen and seeing self. Explorations in the creative process in performance and therapy' in C. Frizell and M. Rova (eds) *Creative Bodies in Therapy, Performance and Community: Research and Practice that Brings Us Home*, Oxfordshire/New York: Routledge, pp 109–21.

Dokter, D. (2023) 'Arts-based research and self reflexive autobiographical performance' in C. Frizell and M. Rova (eds) *Creative Bodies in Therapy, Performance and Community. Research and Practice that Brings Us Home*, Oxfordshire/New York: Routledge, pp 24–5.

Eberhard-Kaechele, M. (2020) 'Dance Movement Psychotherapy. The body tells the unspeakable' in A. Chesner and S. Lykou (eds) *Trauma in the Creative and Embodied Therapies. When Words are Not Enough*, Oxfordshire/New York: Routledge, pp 92–103.

Erel, U., Reynolds, T. and Kaptani, E. (2017) 'Participatory theatre for transformative social research', *Qualitative Research*, 17(3): 302–12. https://doi.org/10.1177/1468794117696029

Fisher, J. (2017) *Healing the Fragmented Selves of Trauma Survivors*, New York: Routledge.

Frankenthaler, H. (2022) *Radical Beauty*, Exhibition, Dulwich Picture Gallery.

Frizell, C. (2023) 'The cat, the foal and other meetings that make a difference: Posthuman research that re-animates our responsiveness to knowing and becoming' in C. Frizell and M. Rova (eds) *Creative Bodies in Therapy, Performance and Community. Research and Practice that Brings Us Home*, Oxfordshire: Routledge, pp 50–61.

Kaptani, E. and Yuval-Davis, N. (2008) 'Participatory theatre as a research methodology: Identity, performance and social action among refugees', *Sociological Research Online*, 13(5): 1–12. https://doi.org/10.5153/sro.1789

Levine, A.P. (1997) *Walking the Tiger Healing Trauma*, California: North Atlantic Books.

Mate, G. (2003) *When the Body Says No*, Nashville, TN: Turner Publishing Company.

Migration Data Portal (2022) 'Forced migration or displacement', IOM Global Migration Data Analysis Centre, Available from: https://www.migrationdataportal.org/themes/forced-migration-or-displacement

Papadopoulos, R. (2021) *Involuntary Dislocation. Home, Trauma, Resilience, and Adversity-Activated Development*, Oxfordshire/New York: Routledge.

Rova, M. (2023) 'Kinaesthetic entanglements and creative immersion in embodied performance' in C. Frizell and M. Rova (eds) *Creative Bodies in Therapy, Performance and Community. Research and Practice that Brings Us Home*, Oxfordshire/New York: Routledge, pp 36–49.

Rova, M., Burrell, C. and Cohen, M. (2020) 'Existing in-between two worlds: supporting asylum seeking women living in temporary accommodation through a creative movement and art intervention', *Body, Movement and Dance in Psychotherapy*, 15(3): 204–18.

Rushton, M. (2022) 'Is there a Jungian approach to supervision?', Lecture, Society of Analytical Psychology, London.

Schlapobersky, J.R. (2015) 'On making a home amongst strangers: The paradox of group psychotherapy', *Group analysis*, 48(4): 406–32.

Thompson, N., Nasimi, R., Rova, M. and Turner, A. (2022) *Community Work with Migrant and Refugee Women: 'Insiders' and 'Outsiders' in Research and Practice*, Bingley: Emerald Publishing.

UK Government (2023) 'Indefinite leave to remain (permission to stay as a refugee, humanitarian protection, Discretionary or Section 67 Leave)', Available from: https://www.gov.uk/settlement-refugee-or-humanitarian-protection

Vacchelli, E. (2018) 'Embodiment in qualitative research: Collage making with migrant, refugee and asylum seeking women', *Qualitative Research*, 18(2): 171–90. https://doi.org/10.1177/1468794117708008

Vromans, L. Schweitzer, R.D., Brough, M., Correa-Velez, I., Murray, K. and Lenette, C. (2017) 'Contributions of loss events to loss distress and trauma symptoms in recently resettled refugee women at risk', *Journal of Loss & Trauma*, 22(4): 357–70.

12

New Town Culture: creative processes in social work with refugee and asylum-seeking young people

Rachel Hughes, Marijke Steedman and Brian Callan

This case study was drawn from a collaboration between researchers and arts and social care agencies in a local authority in London, working with cultural organisations and individual creative practitioners on a culture programme for young people accessing the authority's social care services. The overarching aim of the programme was to explore how artistic and cultural experience can enhance the work of social care practitioners and thus help to support adults and children in need of social care services. The programme pursued three strategies for achieving this aim. Firstly, it increased the arts offer to young people and adults using social care, in one of the most deprived boroughs in London, through the direct provision of new arts-based workshops and projects ('clubs'). Secondly, it embedded this offer within local authority social care, making the activities an integral part of the local authority's provision to support children and young people using support by social care services. Thirdly, it promoted a cultural exchange of ideas and expertise between the arts and social care sectors, with the local authority's culture department and social care practitioners participating in the design of the programme. The programme pursued an agenda of systemic and structural change in addition to one of change for individual participants.

In recent years, a considerable literature has developed which highlights the benefits (and challenges) of socially engaged art (Gibson and Edwards, 2015; Barnes, 2018; Camic et al, 2018). This chapter adds to that literature by providing further data to demonstrate the positive impact of art on the wellbeing and sense of belonging of marginalised people. However, this is not the main purpose of the project. This chapter explores what impact art and creative processes can have on the systems and processes of social care, rather than the impact of art and artists on individual social care users and practitioners – it is a narrative focused on systemic rather than individual transformation. As will be evident, some social care practitioners already incorporate artistic ways of working in their practice and social care leaders have developed their own arts-based projects within their services. However, we are interested more in how art can be integrated into social care, becoming part of the 'core business' of social care practitioners and, put simply, a way of doing social work.

We begin with a brief outline of the research project, which employed multiple methods of reflective and collaborative data generation with a broad range of stakeholders over a two-year period. The purpose of the project was to examine and understand processes for positive change in the provision of social care in an innovative programme in the London borough of Barking and Dagenham, curated by Marijke Steedman, leading to new forms of training and development, including an interdisciplinary form of reflective practice involving cultural and social care practitioners. Five key 'creative processes' emerged as commonalities from across the various creative clubs, tools and activities we observed and participated in. These processes are overlapping, complementary and somewhat fluid categories but all were linked to positive change, both for services users and the teams across the social care agencies. For the first four processes, 'hopeful disruption'[1], 'radical hospitality', 'ceremony' and 'unlocking culture', we present a specific case study for each one, as an exemplar from our data set. For the final process, 'not knowing', we draw together strands of reflections from multiple service providers. The New Town Culture programme offers a model for using creative collaboration with asylum seekers and marginalised migrant communities that centres their own agency and allows social workers to practice in a more open and reflective way which recognises the creativity and humanity of all partners.

The research

In order to complete our work, we attended and participated in art groups with looked after young people, unaccompanied asylum-seeking young people and foster families. In addition, we received data (in the form of the artist's session plan and a recording of a debriefing session) from young women at risk of exploitation. We also attended a workshop run by an artist for social care practitioners from the local authority's Youth Justice Service. We had detailed one-to-one conversations with nine artists and shorter conversations with social care practitioners attending the groups. We attended routine debriefing sessions which took place at the end of groups. We looked at photos from the groups, including photos of artwork. Four of the artists shared written reflections with us, in the form of session plans, reflective diaries and progress reports. We also had a large number of meetings with the programme curators and social care managers and senior leaders, which were instrumental in the identification of the processes discussed in this chapter. As such, the collection and analysis of data falls within a participatory action research paradigm of building relationships, observing, and gathering and generating materials collaboratively (Cornish et al, 2023) between 2018 and 2020, producing a report by the Department of Social, Therapeutic and Community Studies at Goldsmiths, University of London (Hughes, 2020). The research outlined in this chapter was originally presented in that report.

We talked to participants during the course of groups, including, when appropriate, asking them for their views on the groups though we did not speak to them one-to-one as we felt this would be negatively associated with bureaucracy and official power, and could impact on creative processes and spaces. We also felt that one-to-one interviews were ethically problematic, given the fact that a significant number of participants were likely to have suffered traumatic interviews with officials in the past, such as unaccompanied asylum-seeking people's meetings with border officials. The risk of re-traumatising young people through intrusive questioning is highlighted in qualitative research methods literature (see, for example, Hopkins, 2008 and Connolly, 2008, cited in Children's Society, 2018). All participants, or their parents or carers, had given permission for Goldsmiths University involvement when they signed up for the New Town Culture programme. To ensure that participants understood our role as fully as possible, we also distributed picture/symbol-based information sheets in English and four other languages (Arabic, Vietnamese, Albanian and Amharic) and/or gave short talks to participants at the start of the art groups. While artists wished for their names to be used in this chapter, we concealed the identity of the individuals who feature in the case studies, including changing personal characteristics where we felt this was necessary.

Five creative processes

We identified five processes as significant because we saw them happen across all of the groups and settings we observed and because they appeared to be linked to positive change. The processes are overlapping and connected and are perhaps best thought of as different lenses. It is interesting to think about the point of intersection of all the lenses: What can we see if we look through there? What kind of focus does it give us? The names given to them come from the language used by the artists, curators and social care practitioners we spoke to. We hope that gives the terms resonance in the art and social care worlds and enables the ideas behind them to become bridging concepts that facilitate the kind of cultural exchange New Town Culture is aiming for.

Hopeful disruption

At a time of great and dispiriting disruption in the world, it feels odd to be writing about 'hopeful disruption'. We arrived at this term via the term 'positive disruption', to which our attention was drawn by senior social care leaders in the research who use the term themselves and recognised it as a term used in social work internationally. By 'hopeful disruption' we mean artistic acts, carried out by artists or social care practitioners, which challenge conventional ways of talking and acting within both social care spaces and spaces of 'high' culture such as museums and galleries. Such disruption can be orchestrated or spontaneous, but it always emerges from an attitude of hope, and it can generate further hope. To set out to make art and culture part of the core business of local authority social care services is a clear challenge to the current way of doing things in the UK social sector, which is to outsource cultural provision to voluntary sector providers (Hickmore, 2019). 'Hopeful disruption' is also fundamental because, from a socially engaged perspective, all art is, or should be, a form of disruption (Thompson and Sholette, 2004).

In the work of the artists in the programme, there were many instances of orchestrated disruption. For example, in one case an artist supported trafficked and asylum-seeking young people in taking photos of each other's faces. He printed these out and distributed bamboo sticks for them to mount them. Participants carried these placards on a journey on public transport to a museum in central London. At the museum, the artist and young people formed a parade and proceeded to a room full of portraits of the founders and patrons of the museum. Here, they placed their photographic self-portraits alongside those of these wealthy 18th-century philanthropists.

We also observed hopeful disruption in the actions of participants. In the case study below, the activities with the loudspeakers gave the young asylum-seeking people a voice within a public space which is not always open and welcoming to them. The young people played with the boundaries of the activity the artist had devised and he plays along, according them agency within the interaction.

Sound mirrors and loudspeakers

In the morning, Albert Potrony, the artist, shows the young people images of the Second World War giant concrete sound mirrors, precursors to radar, used in the work of artists Amalia Pica and Tacita Dean. He provides the young people with cardboard, tin cans, string, scissors and glue guns and encourages them to make their own communication devices. They engage in this activity with their usual focus and openness.

After lunch we take the DIY communication devices into the street outside the social services building. The young people are relaxed and up for having fun. The sound mirror becomes a hat, which is offered to others, including me, to be tried on. Albert asks the young people to give him words in their own languages to shout into the improvised loudspeaker. One young man causes great merriment among his co-nationals by supplying Albert with words which are almost certainly rude. Albert gamely shouts them out. There are a few amused glances from passers-by. I am not sure if they understand the words or are simply taken by the fun the young people are having.

By playing along with the young man here, Albert showed that he did not see the disruption as problematic. On other occasions, we saw Albert and other artists noting with pleasure instances of disruption initiated by participants. When, at the end of the week's workshop, Kevin, a quiet and apparently shy young man, picked up the sculpture he had made and 'played' it like a saxophone, Albert commented: 'Wow! People surprise you!'

The generative power of 'hopeful disruption' may be similar to the power of a crisis. Crisis intervention is an established model within social work, which still features in textbooks (Trevithick, 2012), but has lacked a recent evidence base for some time (Parker, 2007). The individualisation of risk within society (Beck, 1992; Beck and Beck-Gernsheim, 2002) and the dominance in local authorities of a bureaucratic audit culture where 'new ideas are seen as problematic' (Munro, 2019: 126), may be responsible for the marginalisation of crisis intervention. Hopeful disruption, thus, recognises potential risk but also opens up new relational spaces which we see in the following process of radical hospitality.

Radical hospitality

The ability to convey a sense of being cared for and, more fundamentally, create a sense of safety, is, at root, a tacit, embodied one. It is there in the light touch of approbation on a shoulder, in the steady timbre of the voice and in the beaming smile. The artists we observed were skilled facilitators who possessed this ability. The idea of 'radical hospitality', however, goes further. We first came across the term in an artist's plan for Transform Yourself, a five-day workshop run for young women at risk of exploitation. At the start of the workshop, the artist, Albert Potrony, provided participants with beanbags, duvets, cushions, rugs and gold foil fringe curtains and asked them to transform an area of the room they were working in into a place to relax and take care of themselves. This space was maintained during the whole week as a space for rest and conversation. Reflecting in correspondence with us on how he had come to give this activity the title of 'Radical Hospitality', the artist said:

> I thought that it could be a radical thing to do for these young women at risk of or being abused to experience hospitality in a safe environment, to take care of themselves for the sake of it, without an ulterior motive or benefit to anybody else. By doing so, hopefully, the act of self-care could help them to value themselves for who they are,

in their own terms, and not by what someone else wants them to be. To take control of their own care.

Perfect party

In a three-day workshop for foster families, the artists Rebecca Davis and Alice White gave participants the possibility to control and alter the relationships between themselves as hosts and the participants as guests. The form of collaboration – the preparation and enjoyment of a 'perfect party' – was chosen by the participants at the outset. Activities included the planning and preparation of table mats, table decorations and the food for the party, including a centre-piece of bread dough spelling out 'Perfect Party'. Through these activities, the participants became 'hosts' alongside the artist.

Control over food is a very basic form of agency not infrequently denied to people in state care (McIntosh et al, 2010), and New Town Culture participants appreciated it when it was accorded to them: 'You get food … and the fact that we had a choice … instead of people picking for you … it was nice'.

Choice of food is an important signifier of identity (Fischler, 1988). As part of Your Future, a six-month-long project for young people in the care of the local authority led by the artist Paul Crook, the young people and artists went out into Barking to interview and film members of the public in restaurants and cafes. Paul reflected in his diary that it: 'Was a good experience going out and visiting the restaurants. Faisal took pride in making the introductions and speaking to staff. … We all felt that we had seen parts of Barking we would not normally see.'

Here, one of the participants, Faisal, was able to act as host to the artists and his fellow group members, because he had been placed in a situation where he had something to offer (language expertise and food). Indeed, in this way, Faisal had the opportunity to share and offer something of his very self. This was possible because Paul and his co-worker Dela were willing to relinquish their role as hosts and accept Faisal's hospitality. Derrida holds that 'absolute hospitality' 'emerges when we give up control over our sovereign spaces' (Batchelor et al, 2019: 5) within which he includes ourselves. This is a generosity of the self; a kind of radical openness to others.

In social care both currently and historically there are powerful implicit and explicit rules which govern expressing or sharing anything about oneself with 'service users'. In social care environments influenced by neo-liberalism and an audit culture – that is, most social care environments – these can tend towards avoiding sharing oneself and preserving distance from service users. Warner (2019) frames these issues in terms of proximity, arguing that, from the early 20th century onwards, there has been a tension within social work between practitioners who aim for objectivity and distance, and those who believe in closeness and the value of personal relationships. While social work at the start of the 21st century was in a phase where objectivity and distance were more highly valued, since the mid-2010s, it has taken something of a relational turn. This is evident in the gradual incorporation of models such as 'relationship-based practice' (Ruch et al, 2018) and 'contextual safeguarding' (Firmin and Lloyd, 2020) into practice, as well as in research which suggests that when practitioners are not allowed to show their compassion through touch and self-disclosure they burn out (Tanner, 2020). In this sense radical hospitality may affect positive change for service users and providers alike.

Ceremony, or making moments matter

By ceremony we mean a process of saying, thinking or doing which 1) unfolds in an ordered sequence (while still having room for spontaneity), 2) involves repetition, 3) makes use of objects in a symbolic way, and with attention to aesthetics and 4) has a collective dimension (Moore and Myerhoff, 1977). We might think of ceremonies as large-scale events, such as graduation ceremonies or award ceremonies. Due to COVID-19, these events were not able to take place. However, what we could call 'everyday ceremony' was also an important part of the work the programme artists did with young people in groups and workshops. Some of these 'everyday ceremonies' were familiar ones within Western cultures: for example, the presentation of certificates of achievement at the end of each group, routine 'warm-up' exercises, and 'countdowns', such as this 'jelly ceremony', part of the Perfect Party: 'Are we ready? Five, four, three, two, one – yeah!' (lifts the mould off the jelly).

Ceremonies like this have aesthetic appeal which was recognised by the artists – and they can be fun! This may be why artists sometimes incorporated spontaneous moments of ceremony in their activities. Other ceremonies, like the powerfully evocative Tokens, an activity with unaccompanied asylum-seeking young people, were less familiar in their format and carefully crafted, rather than spontaneous.

Tokens

In a room in the Foundling Museum, we stand in a circle holding our objects. In turn we go forward and place our objects on the floor in the centre of the circle. A small pile accumulates. I see Albert's father's spectacles and a picture of Muhammed's worn wristband woven in the colours of the flag of his home country. It has been on his wrist throughout his journey to the UK. There are the photos of the painted nails of the girls, Celestine and Mahmooda, who had not known what to contribute, because they had nothing to bring. It was their social worker, Amina, who suggested they could photograph their beautiful nails. Ibrahim comes then, and only then, to place his printed-out verse from the Qu'ran on the top of the pile. When it falls slightly to the side, he returns to adjust its position. It is important – essential – that the verse remain on top. The pile looks like a small heap of offerings. In the rooms above us, glass cases contain objects – tokens – left by women as markers of identity for the babies they entrusted to the care of the Foundling Hospital.

There are, in fact, many ceremonies within local authority social care practice; indeed, the work of practitioners is largely organised around them. These ceremonies – local authority processes – include review meetings, case conferences and transition planning meetings. They have their own form of spatial ordering (often, round a table in a local authority office), their own symbolic objects (written documents of pre- determined format) and they unfold in particular sequences, time and time again (Joyce, 2005). One practitioner, reflecting on social care practice in the past, expressed concern about the extent to which local authority processes drive social care and social work practice today. This concern was mirrored in the talk of some senior leaders in the local authority who talked about rooting out 'procedural' practice.

> We weren't as process-driven. We were able to spend more time. It was unheard of if it was a child's birthday not to give them a card and take them out for lunch. We need to get back into that place where children feel that if they're special to anyone then their social worker is among those people.

The point here is that, for some social workers, it feels as if this kind of personal celebration is not central to what they are supposed to be doing. This may have been the experience of some social care users. One New Town Culture participant told us:

> Even though my social worker is nice, it's always kind of 'business'. I feel like they have so many children to care for and look after and sometimes, after a while, you just get tired of going through the same procedure over and over again, loads of kids, can you imagine that.

In Tokens, we see the psychosocial importance of ceremonies: they are processes or rituals that express and reinforce values, assist with life transitions and signify cultures (Laird, 1984). Tokens was a celebration of who the young people were – their identities – as well as where they had come from – their cultures – and their journeys (their transitions from one culture to another, and from childhood to adulthood). Within trauma theory, there is recognition that, 'if transitions are insufficiently marked and integrated, they may continue to be sources of pain, stress and dysfunction' (Laird, 1984: 126;

Levine, 1997). Moreover, it is maintained by some trauma therapists that social recognition of an individual's previously unrecognised transition can be healing, even when it is belated (Levine, 1997). The New Town Culture programme points to the vital importance of ceremonies which celebrate the young person's identity and culture – birthdays and more – and to the importance of social workers being part of these ceremonies. We cannot go without formal 'ceremonies' such as case conferences and review meetings; however, there may be ways, perhaps through new composite ceremonies, which can achieve the same ends while also celebrating the individual whose interest they have been designed to serve.

Unlocking culture/s

By unlocking culture/s, we mean opening people's eyes to new possibilities – to new ways of thinking, doing and being – with the aim of giving them new sources of belonging and self-worth. In the arts literature, this process is sometimes referred to as increasing 'cultural literacy' or 'cultural capital' and the culture referred to is arts-based culture. 'Culture' can also, of course, refer more broadly to a shared set of ideas, practices and material objects, which could be associated with ethnicity or nationality but could also be linked to class, religion, gender, age, sexuality, dis/ability, employment status and a whole set of other variables. The New Town Culture programme has tried to work with and think about culture in both senses. It has also had a concern with unlocking culture not only for participants but also for social care practitioners. Its approach to unlocking culture has entailed both bringing participants and social care practitioners into the many contexts of the arts and taking up opportunities and invitations to enter their worlds. Given all of these different dimensions, it is not surprising that this area is still very much a 'work in progress' for the programme. Nonetheless, there have been some important successes so far.

Your Future

In the Your Future group, participants learnt new skills in filmmaking and production. Two participants, in particular, formed strong relationships with the artist and curatorial assistant leading the group (Paul Crook and Dela Anderson), as well as connecting with the New Town Programme curator. One of these two participants is now very interested in trying to build a career or his own artistic practice in this area. In addition, both participants have both now decided to become part of the Advisory Group for the New Town Culture programme going forward. This is a considerable commitment for one of them, as he has a paid job working long hours in order to meet his daily living costs.

One of the ways in which the programme attempted to unlock artistic culture for its participants was by supporting them to visit prestigious cultural institutions, such as Tate Modern and the Foundling Museum. Another was by supporting them to create their own work and then to make connections between their work and existing and often acclaimed works of art, either directly or through showing films or pictures of them. In the Make Your Own English group, a combination of these strategies was used. Ibrahim was an 18-year-old Somali man who, like all the participants in the group, was polite, respectful and willing to 'have a go' at all the activities. At the same time, like many other participants, he was there because he had been told to attend by his social worker. At the start of the week, when asked why he had decided to come to the group, Ibrahim had seemed embarrassed and agitated: 'I don't know … maybe about training … but still I don't know really about this training still. I don't understand why I come here. Still not explain for me too much. The question, it's hard it … I cannot answer this question.'

Later in the week, along with other participants, Ibrahim made a cardboard and plaster sculpture using similar techniques to the artist Franz West. The following day, the group visited the West exhibition at the Tate Modern. Standing in front of a case of models, Ibrahim commented: 'This is interesting … very interesting. Yesterday was fun, but I thought it was nothing. Now I can see.'

Hearing Ibrahim say this felt like witnessing a small epiphany. Looking back, it was perhaps the moment when Ibrahim shifted from being a young man simply complying with his social worker's instruction to attend the group, to being an active thinker and maker within the project. Of course, there is nothing in Ibrahim's words to tell us whether or not he thought that what he was looking at in that moment – Franz West's work – was of particular worth or not. Perhaps what we can say, though, is that he recognised the 'unlocking' that the artist was trying to facilitate. Ibrahim understood that he was being offered a way of connecting to something that was valued in the new society he found himself in, and he appreciated this.

Engaging in greater depth with the culture(s) of social care services in the borough through discussions with social care practitioners led to new thinking about the continuous professional development aspect of the programme. There is a shift, we suggest, from talking about 'continuous professional development' to speaking instead of a more equal 'knowledge exchange' between social care practitioners on the one hand and artists/curators on the other and we are developing a new methodology for this knowledge exchange, a group reflection method which we call 'interdisciplinary intervision' (Hughes et al, 2020). In addition, the curators and artists are planning more workshops focused on engaging with social care practitioners in their own right. In this way, the task of 'unlocking culture/s' will be progressed in the next phase of the programme.

Not knowing

> We don't know their case history – are they aware of that? Does our not knowing change our approach in how we communicate and interact with them?

With this remark, artist Paul Crook asks, does 'not knowing' the case history of the young people he and his co-worker Dela Anderson are working with change the way he is with the young people? Implicit in his comment is also the question of whether the young people may be different with Paul and Dela because they know that Paul and Dela do not know their case histories. In short, what is the power of 'not knowing'? Paul certainly felt that it was a significant part of the creative process within the Your Future group he ran with young people leaving care. He further commented in his diary: 'Letitia telling us about her experience being in care or Faisal speaking about his difficulties when first living in the UK. These are conversations that could have only happened in the context of the project and were a response to what we were doing.'

Paul is talking here about participants revealing aspects of their identities and their personal histories which were sometimes unknown to their social care practitioners. During the course of the Make Your Own English group, there was another, particularly striking example of this. Celestine, a quietly spoken young woman aged 16, was introduced to the Make Your Own English group by her social worker as a new arrival in the area who spoke very limited English. The social worker explained that Celestine spoke only a minority African language and that the team had as yet been unable to find an interpreter in London who spoke that language. During the course of the week there were a number of activities designed to celebrate the many languages spoken by the participating young people. For example, the young people taught each other the names of animals in all the languages they could think of. They photocopied their hands and then wrote onto the photocopies all the languages they spoke. At the end of the week, they wrote their evaluation of the week on mini-whiteboards, reading out the words so that the different sounds resonated around the council chamber rooms. Through these activities, it emerged that Celestine actually had a good knowledge of two major African languages, as well as her own minority language.

Celestine's social worker, Amina, was quite delighted at this unexpected development. She explained to us that it can be very difficult to find out key information about the young people because they are reluctant to talk about themselves: 'We refer them to CAMHS [Child and Adolescent Mental Health Services] but they don't always want to go or they don't want to talk.'

Sometimes, young people have been explicitly instructed by traffickers not to share information and sometimes they have a mistrust of officials, built up during their journey to the UK. Amina felt that it was due to the nature of the space which the artist had created in the Make Your English group that Celestine felt it was alright to share information about herself. Albert Potrony, the artist who ran both Make Your Own English and the Transform Yourself groups commented that: 'These sessions are a social space in which you can see this person in a slightly different light. A space where another type of relationship can come up … still a professional relationship … (but) where different things can be learned.'

'Not knowing' is a process that may allow young people to be seen in a different way and therefore opens up the possibility for new relationships. The New Town Culture programme curator played a key role in sustaining 'not knowing' because she had to take decisions about what information about young people to share with commissioned artists. In fact, the potential of 'not knowing' in social care practice has been recognised for some time and has renewed prominence as a result of the recent revival of systemic theory within local authority social care practice (Messent and Pendry, 2019). Barry Mason has developed the concept of 'safe uncertainty' (Mason, 1993; 2019) and argues that though 'clients' or social care users want to feel safe, this is unlikely to be a sustainable position. Instead, the practitioner can help the individual to a place of 'safe uncertainty' by using their expertise to open up space for new meaning to emerge. This involves allowing different stories about who the service user is to exist alongside each other.

This was in fact New Town Culture curator Marijke Steedman's position when it came to planning the content of groups and 'experiential encounters' were exactly what the New Town Culture programme art groups were able to offer. In this context, 'not knowing' does not mean ignoring important information about a person but rather not allowing that information to stand for the whole person.

Conclusion

In this chapter we have written about five creative processes which we observed in the work of the 'New Town Culture' programme. The artistic acts, carried out by artists or social care practitioners of 'hopeful disruption' challenge conventional ways of talking and acting within various social spaces. 'Radical hospitality' welcomes others warmly, while also giving place to them though sharing control over relationships and spaces and even the boundaries. The 'ceremony' processes, though sequencing, the use of symbols and attention to beauty, add to the wider social significance of what is being enacted. The act of 'unlocking cultures' opens people's eyes to new possibilities – to new ways of thinking, doing and being, while 'not knowing' allows for different stories about who a person is to exist alongside each other. The New Town Culture programme continues to thrive, offering a radical vision for connecting art practice and various public services of public life. The development and implementation of these innovative processes have fundamentally changed the provision of social work and youth justice in the borough of Dagenham and Barking, to the extent that New Town Culture has now evolved into a platform for 'radical new training', research and tools for social care practitioners, artists, and cultural organisations, including a Creative Social Work course for social work professionals. In this, the project aims to re-imagine the city through the roles of creativity and lived experience leadership in transforming policy design, service delivery and community engagement throughout the UK.

Note

[1] Tim Fisher, a social worker and social care manager, is co-creator with us of the term 'hopeful disruption'.

References

Barnes, S. (2018) *Children Looked After and Arts and Culture*, London: A New Direction.

Batchelor, B., Rackow, H. Valenzuela, D.R. (2019) 'Editorial', *Canadian Theatre Review*, 177: 5–9.

Beck, U. (1992) *The Risk Society*, London: Sage.

Beck, U. and Beck–Gernsheim, E. (2002) *Individualization*, London: Sage.

Camic, P. Zeilig, H. and Crutch, S. (2018) 'The arts and dementia: Emerging directions for theory, research and practice', *Dementia*, 17(6): 641–4.

Children's Society (2018) *Distress Signals: Unaccompanied Young People's Struggle for Mental Health Care*, London: Children's Society, Available from: https://www.childrenssociety.org.uk/sites/default/files/distress-signals-report_0.pdf

Cornish, F., Breton, N., Moreno-Tabarez, U., Delgado, J., Rua, M., de-Graft Aikins, A. and Hodgetts, D. (2023) 'Participatory action research', *Nature Reviews Methods Primers*, 3(1): 1–14.

Firmin, C. and Lloyd, J. (2020) *Contextual Safeguarding. A 2020 Update on the Operational, Strategic and Conceptual Framework*, Available from: https://www.contextualsafeguarding.org.uk/resources/toolkit-overview/contextual-safeguarding-a-2020-update-on-the-operational-strategic-and-conceptual-framework/

Fischler, C. (1988) 'Food, self and identity', *Social Science Information*, 27(2): 275–92.

Gibson, L. and Edwards, D. (2015) *Valuing Participation. The Cultural and Everyday Activities of Young People in Care*, Leicester: University of Leicester School of Museum Studies.

Hickmore, H. (2019) 'Cuts mean arts education is being outsourced to the culture sector – and it's not working', Huffington Post, 16 April, Available from: https://www.huffingtonpost.co.uk/entry/the-government-is-outsourcing-education-arts-education_uk_5ca0eaaae4b0e4e4834dacb1

Hughes, R. (2020) *The New Town Culture Programme 2018–2020, Art, Creativity and Care. Interim Report*, London: Goldsmiths, Available from: https://newtownculture.org/resources/evidence/the-new-town-culture-programme-2018-2020-art-creativity-and-care/

Hughes, R., Steedman, M. and Staempfli, A. (2020) 'The New Town Culture programme: Promoting cultural exchange between artists and children's workers', Youth and Policy, July, Available from: https://www.youthandpolicy.org/articles/new-town-culture/

Joyce, P. (2005) 'The case conference as social ritual: constructing a mother of a sexually abused child', *Qualitative Social Work*, 4(2): 157–73.

Laird, J. (1984) 'Sorcerers, shamans and social workers: the use of ritual in social work practice', *Social Work*, 29(2): 123–9.

Levine, P.A. (1997) *Waking the Tiger: Healing Trauma: The Innate Capacity to Transform Overwhelming Experiences*, Berkeley, CA: North Atlantic Books.

Mason, B. (1993) 'Towards positions of safe uncertainty', *Human Systems*, 4(3–4): 189–200.

Mason, B. (2019) 'Re-visiting safe uncertainty: six perspectives for clinical practice and the assessment of risk', *Journal of Family Therapy*, 41(3): 343–56. https://doi.org/10.1111/1467-6427.12258

Messent, P. and Pendry, N. (2019) 'Editorial: How can family therapy and systemic practice make a difference in front line social care?', *Journal of Family Therapy*, 41(3): 307–12.

McIntosh, I., Punch, S., Dorrer, N. and Emond, R. (2010) '"You don't have to be watched to make your toast". Surveillance and food practices within residential care for young people', *Surveillance and Society*, 7(3/4): 290–303.

Moore, S. and Myerhoff, B. (eds) (1977) *Secular Ritual*, Assen: Van-Gorcum.

Munro, E. (2019) 'Decision-making under uncertainty in child protection: creating a just and learning culture', *Child & Family Social Work*, 24: 123–30.

Parker, J. (2007) 'Crisis intervention: A practice model for people who have dementia and their carers', *Practice*, 19(2): 115–26.

Ruch, G., Turney, D. and Ward, A. (2018) *Relationship-Based Social Work: Getting to the Heart of Practice*, London: Jessica Kingsley.

Tanner, D. (2020) '"The love that dare not speak its name": The role of compassion in social work practice', *British Journal of Social Work*, 50(6): 1688–705. https://doi.org/10.1093/bjsw/bcz127

Thompson, N. and Sholette, G. (2004) *The Interventionists. Users' Manual for the Creative Disruption of Everyday Life*, Cambridge, MA: MIT Press.

Trevithick, P. (2012) *Social Work Skills and Knowledge*, Milton Keynes: Open University Press.

Warner, J. (2019) 'Social work and sociology: Then and now', Presentation to the BSA Sociology and Social Work Study Group Launch Event, 6 September, University of Birmingham.

13

Conclusion: Challenging times and hopeful futures

Brian Callan, Pearson Nkhoma and Naomi Thompson

There is much to take heart from in a volume such as this. Some chapters show people overcoming adversity and uncertainty to develop new spaces of comfort and safety. Often this is assisted by faith-based communities, local youth workers, activists and volunteers who fill in the gaps in the neoliberal austerity economics of deprivation. Despite loss, fatigue and emotional labour, we see new homes, new identities and new lives formed in intimate healing spaces. We see celebrations of lives that resisted death and remembrance of all that was left behind. In this we find shared values that transcend linguistic, cultural and socio-political divisions, supranational networks of people forced from home but also others dedicated to protecting and supporting their very humanity. Testaments, all, to the strength of the human spirit. Yet still, the voices speak of the vulnerability and exploitation of children, the systemic failures of purported protection mechanisms, frequent rights violations, abuse and discrimination. We witness suffering.

To an extent, the demarcation of the different parts of this book – 'Critical research', 'Crucial voices' and 'Creative practice' – is merely a fabrication to facilitate ease of access to a passing reader. All chapters are based on research and the research is of a kind where the voices of the participants are deemed essential. And creativity is always essential when particularly, in the face of overwhelming odds, we endeavour to make the world a safer place. As such, certain themes including intersectionality, power, positionality and participatory methods also run through the chapters. There is thus an emphasis on creative approaches to research and practice that recognise the complex and intersectional experiences of refugee and migrant communities which resist viewing these diverse peoples as a homogenous group or 'problem' to be dealt with. Central to these creative approaches is recognition of the agency, fortitude and creativity of refugees and migrants themselves who, through engagement in research and therapeutic interventions, empower themselves.

This conclusion will bring the different parts of the book together and draw out the key themes from across the chapters. As we have seen in this volume, intersectional identities require holistic interventions, and we argue that the actions taken in attempting to build new lives free from oppression that we see here are inherently political acts of resistance that contribute to a global political movement. However, we also recognise that the work of this movement is increasingly operating within hostile environments in which national governments, particularly those of the Global North and their political supporters, actively seek to deny the rights of refugees and migrants. So, what lessons can we learn and what hope can we derive from the creative research and practice with refugees and migrants presented in this book?

People matter

Time and again, throughout this book, we see the intersection of past, present and future woven through the lives and identities of migrants, their communities and the places they move, they create and inhabit. Rabia Nasimi, who herself threads a complex path within London's Afghan migrant community, sharing language, ethnicity, gender and class with many of the women she works with, has shown the importance of 'home' for her participants. Home is a tapestry of packages from aunts, dried nuts and fruits, trips to Bedford. A spiritual state of mind. Home is a wider community of mosques and shops. Such connections are key to 'Being happy and comfortable. Not feeling different or not understanding the surroundings. The familiarity'. Thus, we see in the chapter by Naomi Thompson, Graham Bright and Peter Hart how faith-based youth and community workers are key to facilitating the familiar in the new. Eric Harper and Angela Rackshaw's work as therapists supports the co-construction of healing and political spaces enabling individuals within groups and communities to find their own voices. The social workers without borders in Finbar Cullinan's chapter act as political agents both supporting individuals and making change on a societal level, staying true to their profession's principles and values, an approach also reflected in Brian Callan's research in the perseverance of professional staff at the UNHCR who struggle against constraints imposed by global neo-liberalism. Throughout this book migrants, communities, volunteers, activists and professionals come together to find 'new ground' (as in Marina Rova et al's chapter) or create 'new town cultures' (as in Rachel Hughes et al's chapter) in defiance of illiberal politics and policies of exclusion.

Such collective collaboration in the public realm is what Hannah Arendt (1958) called Action, which she understood as an inherently political human faculty. Action, she argued, is a denial of the political passivity of modern society in which nationalism, modes of production, capitalism, consumerism and individualism lead to the pursuit of 'life itself' as the highest goal, an unthinking existence solely concerned with the labour of self-satisfaction. Arendt understood that the realisation of a complete human life only occurs within the plurality of humanity's social condition, 'the reality that comes from being seen and heard by others' (1958: 58). Thus, as we see in this volume, the interactions between refugees, migrants, practitioners and participatory researchers in making meaning of their lives offers another strand in the creation of something new 'affecting uniquely the life stories of all those with whom he comes into contact' (Arendt, 1958: 184). Action is therefore the realisation of freedom in which individuals disclose their identities, who they are as distinct from what they are. The critical research, crucial voices and creative practices brought together here are just a small part of a global political movement.

Intersectionality

The significance and utility of an intersectional approach stands out strongly. This applies not only to particular challenges for young female migrants navigating secular Western societies while still trying to satisfy more conservative and religious traditions of their families and the communities they came from in Rohina Sidiqi and Pearson Nkhoma's study. Intersectionality, as Eric Harper and Angela Rackstraw have pointed out here, 'speaks to crossing over of power play, positions of taken for granted privilege, the therapists as white, middle-class and the different modes, or "matrix of oppression" based on identity'. Intersectionality thus becomes an important part of reflective practice where we must examine our own assumptions in the intersubjective encounter where we try to understand an 'other'. In this we may also reflect on Hannah Arendt's concept of Judging not in the sense of criticising but in 'the ability to see things not only from one's own point of view but from the perspective of all those who happen to be present' (Arendt, 1968: 221). Arendt considered Judging to be the most political faculty of the mind in that it is an activity concerned with reflecting on different perspectives and achieving shared understandings that occupy their own intersubjective space. Judging thus produces understanding but this understanding resides neither in the self nor in the other but within a 'third position' of the intersubjective relationship.

In this sense, we have seen Naomi Thompson and Rabia Nasimi negotiating their own fluctuating 'outsider-insider' positionalities as a path to understanding the women they work with. For Eric Harper and Angela Rackshaw it is seen in the examinations of the positions of the therapist within the therapeutic frame, alongside the psychoanalytic concepts of transference, counter transference and projective identification. The creative interventions presented here also seek to access the totality of experiences, vulnerabilities and potentialities that intersect in individuals, using 'hopeful disruption' as artistic acts which challenge conventional ways of talking and acting, as shown by Rachel Hughes, Marijke Steedman and Brian Callan. Hughes and her colleagues deconstruct unexamined assumptions through the enquiring eyes of people from migrant cultures, while still providing 'radical hospitality' and opening people's eyes to new possibilities – to new ways of thinking, doing and being – as new sources of belonging and self-worth. This is done through 'unlocking cultures' which is seen also through the psychosocially supportive and culturally sensitive case examples presented by Sarah Crawford-Browne and through Pearson Nkhoma's recognition of the role of *mavuto* – chronic deprivation or destitution – for young Malawian women in contributing to their decisions to leave home. As Nkhoma points out, a capability approach that emphasises enhancing individuals' freedoms and opportunities to lead dignified lives they value offers a valuable framework for understanding and tackling the root causes of forced migrations and supporting those displaced. Our message is that we must create social environments that are emotionally supportive, spiritually and culturally appropriate, and psychologically safe. We must all find new ground.

A global protection drought

Yet tensions remain in the testimonies in this book. Feelings of not being completely one identity or another in a world where nationality, culture, identity and self are so tightly entwined and valorised as the core of belonging. Rightward political trends in the Global North have been emboldened since the Great Recession of 2007–09 and subsequent austerity economics that denuded public services in many states. Anti-immigrant sentiments in state policy have foregrounded nativist movements in North America and Europe (Goldstein and Peters, 2014; Ybarra et al, 2016). Such movements, which often encompass racism and xenophobia (Guia, 2016), also constitute a global political movement that stands in direct opposition to the actions and lives outlined here. Both Pearson Nkhoma and Brian Callan directly highlight this antagonistic environment which is leading to a 'global protection drought'.

In the UK, former Prime Minister Rishi Sunak (2023a, 2023b) listed immigration as one of the Conservative government's five priority pillars for 2023. This initiative represented the UK's first explicit stance against providing protection to victims of modern slavery. In turn, it framed vulnerable victims as needing additional scrutiny for 'spurious human rights claims' (Sunak, 2023b). Such an approach may leave vulnerable victims, particularly children and unaccompanied minors, struggling to qualify for support designed to prevent their involvement in modern slavery. In the face of such policies and rhetoric, violent attacks on immigrants have been reported in the UK and in October 2022, a terrorist attack on a migrant centre in Dover was attributed to extremist ideology (Reuters, 2022). The purported need for scrutiny of immigration and false claimants remains firmly in public discourse as the new government beds in. The Labour Party's successful election was due in large part to the numbers of former Conservative voters who swung further right to Nigel Farage's Reform UK party, which leads opinion polls as the UK's most popular political party at the time of writing.

After the European elections in June 2024, far-right parties now make up approximately 24 per cent of elected members in the European Parliament, with about half of that number coming from France's Rassemblement National (RN), Fratelli d'Italia, the Polish PiS, the German AfD and Hungary's Fidesz. While the popularity of far-right populist movements is driven by multiple factors to which EU citizens have been exposed since 2008 – the Great Recession, the 2015 refugee crisis, the COVID-19 pandemic and war in Ukraine (Ivaldi, 2024) – a discontent with immigration is a common and central driver. The overall rise in the far-right membership is marginal on 2019 but this reflects, at least in part, the loss of 29 Brexit Party members from the UK who no longer have membership (Ivaldo, 2024). The 2024 results reflect a consolidation of the far-right electorate in almost all EU member states, while in both Hungary and Italy right-wing populist parties form the ruling parties. Regardless of the varying levels of electoral success, xenophobic and often racist discourses have affected the policies of mainstream, traditional parties (Krzyżanowski, 2020). In December 2023, Donald Trump, as part of his successful presidential campaign, made a speech in New Hampshire where he claimed that immigrants are 'destroying the blood of our country' (Lepore, 2023). Such trends are not limited to the Global North, with incidents of xenophobia and violence against foreigners in countries like South Africa, under initiatives like Operation Dudula, and disturbing discoveries such as a mass grave in Malawi (Malawi24, 2022; Nhemachena et al, 2022). The humanistic desire to afford protection to those in need, embodied in conventions such as the Universal Declaration of Human Rights, is under threat from concerted and widespread social and political movements.

Conclusion

We thus have two global political movements: one comprised of a transnational network of major international organisations, migrants and their communities, professionals, local charities and grassroots volunteers and activists dedicated to helping those fleeing deprivation or persecution. The other seeks to scapegoat or demonise those who they deem as 'not belonging' within a given national border due to the colour of their skin, their religion, their culture or lack of wealth. The intersectional approaches and collaborative practices outlined in this volume form part of the former and stand in stark contrast to the simplified and exclusionary political programmes that want to 'STOP THE BOATS' or 'BUILD THAT WALL'.

It would be naive to make predictions as to how the contestation between these two political movements will play out but it is perhaps worth turning again to the work of Hannah Arendt. Much of Arendt's career was concerned with the forms and structures of political oppression that she had witnessed with the rise of Nazism and Stalinism in works such as *The Origins of Totalitarianism* (1951) and on the 'banality of evil' in *Eichmann in Jerusalem* (1963). In her later works *The Human Condition* (1958) and *The Life of the Mind* (1977), she developed the political faculties of Action and Judging used here, which must thus be understood as attempts to resist the rise of such evil in the world. Arendt also offered a third political human faculty, that of Thinking which may 'make men abstain from evil-doing or even actually "condition" them against it' (Arendt, 1977: 5). Here is not the place to delve fully into Arendt's political philosophy, suffice to say that, as a German Jew and political activist, she was arrested by the Gestapo in 1933 and fled her home country soon after. She too was an émigrée, an exile, a stateless person without papers or protection. Just one more of the many crucial voices we need to hear.

References

Arendt, H. (1951) *The Origins of Totalitarianism*, New York: Harcourt, Brace and Company.

Arendt, H. (1958) *The Human Condition* (2nd edition published in 1998), Chicago: University of Chicago Press.

Arendt, H. (1963) *Eichmann in Jerusalem: A Report on the Banality of Evil*, New York: Viking Press.

Arendt, H. (1968) *Between Past and Future: Eight Exercises in Political Thought*, New York: Viking Press.

Arendt, H. (1977) *The Life of the Mind* (1981 reprint), New York: Harcourt.

Goldstein, J.L. and Peters, M.E. (2014) 'Nativism or economic threat: Attitudes toward immigrants during the great recession', *International Interactions*, 40(3): 376–401. https://doi.org/10.1080/03050629.2014.899219

Guia, A. (2016) *The Concept of Nativism and Anti-Immigrant Sentiments in Europe*, Working Paper, EUI MWP, 2016/20, Available from: https://cadmus.eui.eu/handle/1814/43429

Ivaldi, G. (2024) 'EU elections: far-right parties surge, but less than had been expected', The Conversation, 10 June, Available from: http://theconversation.com/eu-elections-far-right-parties-surge-but-less-than-had-been-expected-232018

Krzyżanowski, M. (2020) 'Discursive shifts and the normalisation of racism: imaginaries of immigration, moral panics and the discourse of contemporary right-wing populism', *Social Semiotics*, 30(4): 503–27. https://doi.org/10.1080/10350330.2020.1766199

Lepore, S.M. (2023) 'Trump denies reading Hitler's "Mein Kampf"', Mail Online, 2 December, Available from: https://www.dailymail.co.uk/news/article-12884355/Trump-says-immigrants-poisoning-blood-country-denies-reading-Hitlers-Mein-Kampf-despite-using-language-dictator-recent-speeches.html

Malawi24 (2022) 'More dead bodies found near mass grave in Mzimba Malawi 24 | Latest News from Malawi', Malawi 24, 20 October, Available from: https://malawi24.com/2022/10/20/more-dead-bodies-found-in-mzimba/

Nhemachena, A., Mawere, M. and Mtapuri, O. (2022) 'Operation Dudula, xenophobic vigilantism and sovereignty in twenty-first century South Africa', in A. Nhemachena, M. Mawere and O. Mtapuri (eds) *Sovereignty Becoming Pulvereignty: Unpacking the Dark Side of Slave 4.0 Within Industry 4.0 in Twenty-First Century Africa*, Bamenda: Langaa RPCIG, pp 153–74. https://doi.org/10.2307/j.ctv2z6qdpk.7

Reuters (2022) 'British police say immigration centre attack was terrorist incident', Reuters, 5 November, Available from: https://www.reuters.com/world/uk/british-police-say-dover-attack-was-motivated-by-terrorist-ideology-2022-11-05/

Sunak, R. (2023a) 'If you come to the UK illegally', Twitter, Available from: https://x.com/RishiSunak/status/1633158789103747072

Sunak, R. (2023b) 'PM speech on building a better future: 4 January 2023', Prime Minister's Office, Available from: https://www.gov.uk/government/speeches/pm-speech-on-making-2023-the-first-year-of-a-new-and-better-future-4-january-2023

Ybarra, V.D., Sanchez, L.M. and Sanchez, G.R. (2016) 'Anti-immigrant anxieties in state policy: The Great Recession and punitive immigration policy in the American States, 2005–2012', *State Politics & Policy Quarterly*, 16(3): 313–39. https://doi.org/10.1177/1532440015605815

Index

A

Action, Arendt on 190–1, 194
action research 5
  participatory 15, 19–20, 130, 141
adolescence, identity formation during 82
Afghan minors 9, 81–93
  hurdles encountered by 85–7
  integration process for 87–8
  overlooked vulnerabilities and systemic failures 88–91
  use of cultural identity theory to analyse the integration of 82
Afghanistan
  displaced populations in 81
  migrants in London from 9, 13, 16
  migration to the UK from 63
Afghans *see also* Afghan minors
  conceptions of home for 63–77, 190
  in the diaspora 66
  in England, religious identity of 70
  second-generation, in London 9, 63–77
  in the UK 88
Africa, underdevelopment in 141
African refugees 9, 109
  therapeutic practice with 109–28
  xenophobic violence against 104
age assessments
  impact on mental health 90
  on unaccompanied asylum-seeking young people 152
Al-Ali, N. 88
ambiguous agency 134, 137, 139
Anderson, Dela 184
Arendt, Hannah 190, 191, 193–4
art, socially engaged 174
art exhibitions, Radical Beauty 164–5
art groups 175
  Moving Space *see* Moving Space group
  New Town Culture programme 174–88
art-making 159
  in Moving Space 161
artistic acts 177, 185, 191
artistic culture, unlocking of 182–4, 185, 192
artistic practice 167–8
arts-based community practice 159, 160
arts-based culture 182
arts-based interventions
  with migrant women in temporary accommodation 9, 159–73
  in research and practice with refugee and migrant groups 5
arts-based workshops and projects ('clubs') 174

arts literature 182
aspirations 8, 122
asset-based community development (ABCD) 36, 42
asylum seekers 169
  creative collaboration with 175
  creative movement and art group 159–73
  definition of 5
  hostility towards 35
  integration challenges faced by 81, 85, 90
  in Malawi 130
  'offshoring' policies 46, 50
  treatment of 46
  in the UK 6
  UK government attempt to send asylum seekers to Rwanda 46, 129
austerity 34, 58, 90, 189, 192
  responding to 38–9
  in the UK 32
austerity localism 37
Australia, 'offshoring' policies 50

B

bacha bazi (boy play) 85
Bali Process on People Smuggling, Trafficking in Persons and Related Transnational Crime 49
Banks, S. 148
Barret, E. 90
basic services and security interventions 99
Benjamin, Jessica 119
bereavement 167
Bestor, T. 82
Betts, A. 46, 49
biases 27
  unconscious 110
Binnie, J. 69
black suffering, reinforcement of the spectacular character of 118
Black women, experiences of oppression for 3
Bloch, A. 64
Blunt, A. 65
Boccagni, P. 71
Bonnerjee, J. 65
Bordonaro, L.I. 139
Botterill, K. 25
Bourdieu, P. 19
Bowen, G.A. 84
Braakman, M. 64, 66
Brah, A. 65, 66
Brexit 129
  referendum campaigns 35

Index

The Brexit Party (now Reform UK) 35, 193
Brickell, K. 70
Bright, Graham 8, 13, 22, 190
brothels 135, 136, 137
  being 'rescued' from 138, 139
Buddhists, commitment to intergenerational mentoring 39
Bull, Graham 120
bullying, of Afghan minors 86
Burrell, Claire 9, 145

C

Cağlar, A. 64
Callan, Brian 8–9, 13, 145, 190, 191, 192
camps
  in Pakistan, for displaced people 95–100, 105
Campt, T. 117, 127
capability approach 138, 140, 141, 192
capacity building research 19
capitalism 33
ceremonies 180–2, 185
  everyday 180
  within local authority social care practice 181
  psychosocial importance of 181
  Tokens 180–2
child commercial sexual exploitation (CSEC) 131
child migration 129
child slavery 138
children *see also* Afghan minors
  coercion or manipulation of 137
  displaced 81, 82
  employed as house-helpers 138
  impact of migration on 82
  involvement in prostitution 131, 138, 139, 141
  safeguarding of 89, 131, 138
  sexual abuse of 134
children's rights 131
classic trauma recovery pathway 96
coercion 68, 134, 136, 137, 139
Cohen, Marika 9, 145
collective collaboration 190
collective recovery 95
communal gatherings 120
communal healing, with refugee and asylum-seeking young people 102
community arts work 9, 145
  with asylum-seeking women 159–73
  with refugee and asylum-seeking young people 174–88
community-based participatory research (CBPR) 19, 83
community development
  asset-based (ABCD) 36, 42
  asset-focused forms of 36
  and resistance 36–7
community leaders, acting as researchers 19
community storytelling 95
cosmopolitanism 69
cost of living crisis 32
Coutin, S.B. 82
COVID-19 pandemic 32, 104, 147, 159, 169
  impact on Moving Space 170
Crawford-Browne, Sarah 9, 79, 192
creative arts practices 9, 170
creative movement and art group, with asylum-seeking women 159–73
creative processes, in social work with refugee and asylum-seeking young people 174–88
Crenshaw, Kimberle 3, 83
crisis intervention 178
critical feminist theory 2, 3
critical race theory 2, 3
Crook, Paul 179, 184
Cullinan, Finbar 9, 145, 190
cultural capital 182
cultural identity 24, 89, 91
cultural identity theory 82–4, 89
cultural literacy 182
culture programme, New Town 174–88

D

dance rituals 114
Davis, Rebecca 179
De St Croix, Tania 33, 35
Dean, Tacita 177
Deleuze, G. 120
Den Boer, R. 68
Denmark 50
depression 120
deviant social work 154
dialogical work 37
diaspora
  Afghans in the 66
  association between homeland and 65–6
diaspora cities 65
diaspora space 66
direct work 147, 150
discriminatory practices, formal challenges to 42
displaced people, camps in Pakistan for 95–100, 105
displacement 49, 81, 162
  in Afghanistan 63, 85
  conflict-induced 134
  double 72
  forced 54
  involuntary 162
  loss linked to 167
  in Malawi 132

DiStefano, A. 19
Dokter, D. 169
domestic violence 21
Dominelli, L. 155
Dóna, G. 4
Donovan, J. 148
dream space, and ritual 120
Drennan, G. 102

E

education 23, 33
  for Afghan minors 87
Ehntholt, K.A., 88
emancipatory social work 148
Emejulu, A. 36
emergency settings 94, 95
  mental health services in 99
  professional practice in 105
emic researchers 18
empowerment 7–8
engagement
  in faith-based youth and community work 33
  socio-political 38
England *see also* United Kingdom (UK)
  faith-based community workers in 31
Erdal, M.B. 65
Erel, U. 3
ethics 33, 152
etic researchers 18
Europe
  austerity in 58
  nativist movements in 192
European Parliament, far-right parties in 193
everyday ceremonies 180
extremism 41

F

Faist, T. 65
faith-based community work/workers 8, 13, 32–3, 42, 190
  development of progressive partnerships based on 'border crossings' 37
  in England and Scotland 31
  inter-faith work 40
  resistance of neoliberalism and neoexclusionism 32, 33
  spectrum of practice 37
faith-based youth work *see* faith-based community work/workers
faith communities 31–45
  challenging of division and fear by 41–2
  response to the London Grenfell Tower fire 32
far-right parties, in the European Parliament 193
Farage, Nigel 34, 193

Featherstone, D. 32, 37
financial crisis (2007–2008) 58
Finefter-Rosenbluh, I. 18
Fischer, C. 64
Flowerdew, J. 16
food
  choice of 179
  control over 179
foodbanks 32, 38
forced migration 162 *see also* migration
  management of 47
  transgenerational impact on families and communities 170
foster care 124
foster families, workshop for 179
Frankenthaler, Helen 164
fugue 127

G

gender 3, 110
gendered ideas 66
Germany 50
Gilao, M.A. 65
Gilmore, Ruth Wilson 127
Glick Schiller, N. 64
The Global Agenda for Social Work and Social Development: Extending the Influence of Social Work (Truell and Jones) 155
Global Compact on Refugees (UNHCR) 49
global financial crisis (2007–2008) 58
Global North 55, 129
  'offshoring' policies 50
  political trends in 192
  treatment of refugees and asylum seekers 46
global political movements 190, 191, 192, 193
global protection drought 47, 59, 192–3
Global South 46, 50, 55, 94, 129
Goldsmiths, University of London, Department of Social, Therapeutic and Community Studies 176
Golightley, M. 155
Goodson, L. 19
Graeber, D. 51
Graham, C. 84
group homes 124
Guattari, F. 120
Guiding Principles on International Displacement (UNHCR) 48
Guinea 100

H

Habermas, J. 58
Hamber, B. 102
Hamilton, T. 90–1
Harper, Eric 9, 79, 190, 191
Harris-Hogan, S. 88

Harris, J. 148
Hart, Peter 8, 13, 190
Hartman, S. 118, 127
hate crime 21–2
Haverig, A. 6
healing forums 117
Herman, J.L. 96, 98
Higgs, A. 148
Hirsch, M. 64
Hobfoll, S.E. 103, 104
Holloway, M. 155
home 64–5
  comfort and safety of 73
  concept of 63, 67
  as identity crisis 72–3
  importance of 190
  as a place of comfort 71
  as a site of emotions 71–2
  as spirituality and religion 67–71
homeland, links between the diaspora and 65–6
hopeful disruption 176–8, 185, 191
Horváth, Z.E. 17
housing, for Afghan minors 87
housing crisis, in London 34
Hoyt, Elizabeth 82
Hughes, Rachel 9, 145, 191
human rights 109, 149
humanitarian mental health programmes 95
Humphries, B. 148
Hungary, right-wing ruling party 193

I

IASC model *see* Inter-agency Standing Committee (IASC)
identity formation, during adolescence 82
images
  listening to 112–15
  low-frequency 117
immigrants, violent attacks on 192
immigration 129
  and politics 129
  UK policy on 34, 192
imprisonment 120
indefinite leave to remain 168–9
individual discretion 154
individualisation 34
  resisting 39–40
insider researchers 17–18, 19, 27
  engagement with reflexivity 18
  participants feeling safe with 20–2
insiders 4, 27, 28 *see also* outsiders
  in community research 5, 15
  insider-outsider positionalities 63, 67
integration 6–7, 169
  of Afghan minors in the UK 81–93

of migrant women in community and society 22–3
  as a mutual process 8
Inter-agency Standing Committee (IASC) 98–9
  intervention pyramid for mental health and psychosocial support in emergencies (model) 98f, 102, 106
  Mental Health and Psychosocial Services Working Group 98
inter-faith work 37
intergenerational mentoring 39
Intergovernmental Consultations on Asylum, Refugees and Migration 49
internally displaced persons (IDPs) 47, 48, 55
  in Afghanistan 81
International Day for Torture Survivors 116
International Federation of Social Workers 155
international migration, and need for social work across borders 155
International Protection 46
International Refugee Law 46
interpretative phenomenological analysis (IPA) 33, 88
intersectionality 3, 4, 82–4, 89, 110, 122, 190, 191–2
Iraqi refugees, in the UK 88
Islamophobia 35
Italy, right-wing ruling party 193

J

Jews 40
Jordan, B. 148
Judging, Arendt's concept of 191, 194

K

Khan, H. 88
Khanna, R. 114
Kibria, N. 65
kinaesthetic entanglement 165
Kline, R.B. 84
Konecny, P. 88
Kortmann, M. 6
Kurdi, Alan 50

L

Labour Party 192
landscapes 166
Levine, Peter 164
Li, S.S. 84, 88, 90
Liberia 100
Lipsky, M. 148, 154
Lipson, J.G. 17
local authorities 87, 152
  bureaucratic audit culture 178
  social care 174, 177, 181

localism, progressive 37
localism agendas, in the UK 32
London
  Grenfell Tower fire, responses of faith communities to 32
  housing crisis 34
  as an inclusive space 69
  migrant Muslim women in 3, 15
  second-generation Afghans in 9, 63–77
longitudinal research 16–17, 20
loss, linked to displacement 167
loudspeakers 177–8
low-frequency images 117

M

MacLeod, M.A. 36
Mahmoodi, M. 88
Make Your Own English group 183, 184, 185
Malawi 132
  black refugees and asylum seekers in 130
  Child Care, Justice, and Protection Act (2010) 138
  displacement in 132
  labour migration from 134
  lax enforcement of labour laws in 138
Manzo, L. 71
'marking' 113
Mason, Barry 185
mass disaster responses 103
mass trauma intervention model 104
Mate, Gabor 164
mavuto (chronic deprivation) 140, 141, 192
Mayo, M. 34, 35
Meleis, A.I. 17
mental health
  of Afghan minors 87, 88
  and psychosocial support in emergencies, intervention pyramid 98*f*
mental health programmes 95
mentoring, intergenerational 39
meritocracy 33
migrant families, presentation as threat by right-wing political discourses 3
migrant women
  arts-based interventions with 9, 159–73
  in London 3, 15
migrants
  definition of 6
  distrust of 17
  undocumented 6
migration *see also* forced migration
  impact on a child's life 82
  public view of 162
  as a transient state of being 163
  and transnational studies 65–6
Miller, K.E. 99
mirroring 111
mixed migration *see* mixed movements
mixed movements 49
modern culture, loss of ritual in 120
modern slavery 129, 132, 141, 192
Moran, R. 4
Moussaoui, L. 88
movement, importance of in healing from trauma 164
Moving Space group 159, 160–1
  finding new ground theme 168–70
  making into being theme 166–8
  staying afloat theme 163–6
  travelling water theme 161–3
Muslim(s) 40
  creating a community in a homeless hostel 121
  hostility towards 70, 73
  identifying as 70
  Muslim women, in London 3, 15
  Scouts group 38, 40, 41
  stigmatisation and isolation of 36

N

Narayan, K. 17
Nasimi, Rabia 5, 8, 9, 13, 25, 26, 190, 191
'nativist' exclusionary politics 58
nativist movements, in North America and Europe 192
Nawa, F. 66
Neale, B. 16
neoexclusionism 31–2, 34, 35, 40, 43
neoliberal politics 150, 151
neoliberalism 31, 32
  in relation to community and youth work 34
New Town Culture programme 174–88
Nkhoma, Pearson 9, 79, 192
North America, nativist movements in 192
'not knowing', case histories of young migrants 184–5

O

Occupied Palestinian Territory 81
Oeppen, C. 65
Office for National Statistics 66
'offshoring' policies 46, 50
oppression 3, 4, 8, 83, 110, 194
outsider researchers 19, 23–4
outsiders 4, 7, 18, 27, 28 *see also* insiders
  in community research 5, 15
  engagement with 22
  outsider-insider positionalities 191
  refugees and migrants treated as 17

P

Pakistan, emergency camp after 2005 earthquake 95–100

Papadopoulos, Renos 170
participatory action research 15, 19–20, 130, 141
participatory research 4, 5, 27
Payne, R. 139
'perfect party' workshop 179–80
Phelps, R. 84
Phillimore, J. 19
Pica, Amalia 177
Pike, K.L. 18
Polish migrants, in the UK 25
political movements 190, 191, 192, 193
political oppression 194
political trends, in the Global North 192
politics, immigration and 129
populism 35
positive disruption 177
positive implicit memory 170
post-conflict communal healing 102
post memory concept 64
post-traumatic stress disorder (PTSD) 105
Potrony, Albert 178, 185
poverty 140
power, in participatory and action research 4–5
practitioners, responsible for guiding minors through the integration process 90
progressive localism 37
prostitution 132
  children and young women's lived experiences of 130
  children trapped in 134–7
  exploitation of children beyond the age of consent 141
psychological healing 102
psychosocial, safety 104, 105
psychosocial workers 97

Q

Qualitative Longitudinal Research (QLR) 16–17
qualitative research 84

R

race 110
racial abuse 121
racial identity 24
racism 86
Rackstraw, Angela 9, 79, 190, 191
radical hospitality 178–80, 185, 191
Rasmussen, A. 99
reflexivity 18–19, 25, 27, 110
Reform UK 34, 35, 193
'refugee regime complex' 46, 49, 51
refugee status 5
Refugee Week 121

refugees
  definition of 5
  distrust of 17
  double displacement of 72
  practice-based research with 4
  witnessing unstable passages to safety 95
religion
  home as spirituality and 67–71
  importance of, for second generation Afghans 73
religious abuse 121
religious identity 67
religious practices 67, 68
right-wing nationalist movements 35
right-wing populism 31, 34, 39, 193
ritual
  dream space and 120
  migration and 120
Rodney, Walter 141
Rova, Marina 9, 145
Rushton, Malcolm 170
Rwanda, UK government attempt to send asylum seekers to 46, 129

S

Sadan, E. 8
safe spaces 20, 22, 36, 37, 40–1, 168
safe uncertainty 185
safeguarding
  of children 89, 131, 138–9
  contextual 180
safety 71, 96
  psychosocial 104, 105
Sage Handbook of Youth Work Practice 33
Sandercock, L. 69
Schlapobersky, J.R. 168
Schlenkhoff, A. 64, 66
Schneid, A.F. 102
schooling *see* education
Scotland *see also* United Kingdom (UK)
  faith-based community workers in 31
  'New Scots: Refugee Integration Strategy 2018 to 2022' 7
second-generation Afghans 9, 63–77
  experiences of 63–4
  trip to their parents' home of origin 65
self-care 168
Sen, Amartya 141
sewing in community 111
sex work 131
sexual abuse, of children 85, 134, 138
sexual exploitation
  of children *see* sexual abuse
Sharpe, C. 113, 122
Sheringham, O. 70
Sidiqi, Rohina 9, 79
Sierra Leone 94, 105
  psychosocial programme in 100–2

Sikh community
  challenge of discriminatory practices of a high-street chain 42
  safe space for Sikh young people 41
  welcome for homeless people 32
Silverman, D. 84
Skeggs, B. 69
social action projects 38
social care
  impact of art and creative processes on 174
  rules on sharing things about oneself with service users 179
social care practitioners 174
social justice 148, 155
  as a driving force for SWWB volunteers 149–50
  for social workers 148
social networks, of Afghan and Iraqi refugees in the UK 88
social spaces 185
  transnational 65
social work
  creative processes in 174–88
  emancipatory 148
  as an internationally connected profession 149
  with migrants as part of an international cause 154–5
  since the mid-2010s 180
  statutory 152
  value base of 148
social workers
  International Federation of Social Workers 155
  motivations of people to become 148
  responsible for guiding minors through the integration process 91
  volunteering with SWWB 149–55
Social Workers Without Borders (SWWB) 147
  as a collective voice for a political profession 153–4
  as a critical space for contemporary practice 152–3
  motivations to volunteer for 149–55
  provision of an opportunity for collectively challenging policies 152–3
  volunteers practising in accordance with their values 150–2
societal altruism 151
socio-political engagement 38–9
Solas, J. 148
sound mirrors 177–8
South Africa 103, 105, 132, 134
  labour laws 138
  Trauma Centre for Victims of Violence and Torture, Cape Town 116

statutory social work 152
Staub, E. 102
Steedman, Marijke 9, 145, 175, 185, 191
Stevens, M. 151
stillness 113
stitching 111, 114, 115, 127
  as a bridge to a community 116–18
  in community partnership 120–2
stitching groups 117
story cloths 111
storytelling, community 95
sub-Saharan Africa, migration within and between countries in 132
Sunak, Rishi 192
Sunday Schools, criticism of 31
Swartz, L. 102
SWWB *see* Social Workers Without Borders (SWWB)
Syria 81

T

Tambulasi, R. 132
Tanzania, asylum control practices towards Burundian refugees 50
Tate Modern, West exhibition 183
Temple, B. 4
therapeutic practice, with African refugees 109–28
therapists
  positions of, within the therapeutic frame 110, 191
therapy 119
Thompson, N. 3, 5, 8, 13, 24, 25, 83, 167, 190, 191
Tokens (ceremony) 180–2
Tol, W.A. 99
Tolia-Kelly, D. 68
Townsend, Peter 141
trafficking, intra-country 136
Transform Yourself workshop 178
transnational social spaces 65
transnational studies, migration and 65–6
transnationalism 65
trauma
  classic trauma recovery pathway 96
  encountered by Afghan minors 86
  importance played by movement in the healing from 164
  intervention principles 95–100
  mass trauma intervention model 104
  recovery pathway 96
  recovery principles 95, 98
  theory 181
  trauma-focused interventions 105
  trauma-informed approach 105
  trauma-informed creative arts practice 171
  work 170
travelling water theme 161–3

Trump, Donald 129
  on immigrants 193
Trussell Trust 32
trust 84
Tsoucalas, G. 88
Turkey 50

U

UK Independence Party (UKIP) (now Reform UK) 35
Ukraine 81, 114
unaccompanied Afghan minors, in the UK 81–93
UNICEF 81
United Kingdom (UK) *see also* England; Scotland
  Afghan minors in 9, 81–93
  austerity in 32
  counter-terrorism strategy 34, 36
  foodbanks 32
  hostility towards Islam and Muslims in 70
  localism agendas in the 32
  'offshoring' policies 50
  plans to deport illegal immigrants and asylum seekers to Rwanda 46, 129
  Polish migrants in 25
  'refugee' status 6
  unaccompanied Afghan minors in 81–93
United Nations
  Convention Relating to the Status of Refugees (1951) 5, 47, 48, 49, 51, 57
  General Assembly 49, 58
  Protocol Relating to the Status of Refugees (1967) 48
United Nations High Commissioner for Refugees (UNHCR) 6, 9, 46–62, 81, 190
  The 10-Point Plan in Action 49
  donor-oriented approach 54
  frustrations of employees 53–5
  Global Appeal 48
  'global drought of protection' 55
  global workforce 48
  humanitarian purpose of 56
  lack of resources 53
  mandate and work 48
  motivations of employees 55–7
  structural issues 53–4
  survey of employees 51–2
United Nations Human Rights Council 130
Universal Declaration of Human Rights (1948) 47, 58, 193
unlocking cultures 182–4, 185, 192

V

Valtonen, K. 7
Veroff, J. 19
violence
  in Afghanistan 63
  domestic 21
  prevention of 102
  symbolic 19
  against women of colour 83
  xenophobic 104, 112
Viruell-Fuentes, E.A. 6
Vromans, L. 167

W

wake work 110–12, 114, 115, 122
Walter, B. 72
Warner, J. 179
water, group images of 163
Wenham, A. 16
west Africa, tradition of palaver (open community conversations) 101, 102
West, Franz 183
White, Alice 179
Whittington, C. 148
Whittington, M. 148
Witness to Truth (film) 101
women
  Black women, experiences of oppression for 3
  migrant Muslim women, in London 3, 15
  in temporary accommodation, arts-based interventions with 9, 159–73
work
  dialogical 37
  direct 147, 150
working together, between different faiths and groups 40

X

xenophobic attacks, in South Africa 104, 112, 115, 129–30, 193
xenophobic civil society movements 50

Y

York, H. 88
young people 38, 39 *see also* Afghan minors
  age assessments on 152
  community arts work with 174–88
  criticism of Sunday Schools teaching reading and writing to 31
  faith-based youth and community work with 33
  inter-faith work with 37, 40
  refugee and asylum-seeking 9, 145, 174–88
  safe spaces for 40–1, 81
Your Future group 179, 182–4
youth clubs 38
Youth Justice Service 175
youth migration 81

Z

Zaki, Leila 112
Zaman, H. 88
Zulfacar, M. 17